Hot Hors-d'Oeuvre

by
THE EDITORS OF TIME-LIFE BOOKS

TIME-LIFE BOOKS
EUROPEAN EDITOR: Kit van Tulleken
Design Director: Louis Klein
Photography Director: Pamela Marke
Chief of Research: Vanessa Kramer
Special Projects Editor: Windsor Chorlton
Chief Sub-Editor: Ilse Gray

THE GOOD COOK
Series Editor: Alan Lothian
Series Co-ordinator: Liz Timothy
Head Designer: Rick Bowring

Editorial Staff for *Hot Hors-d'Oeuvre*
Text Editor: Gillian Boucher
Anthology Editor: Josephine Bacon
Staff Writers: Alexandra Carlier, Jay Ferguson,
Ellen Galford, Thom Henvey
Senior Researcher: Suad McCoy
Designers: Mary Staples, Michael Morey
Sub-Editors: Kathy Eason, Sally Rowland
Anthology Researcher: Deborah Litton
Anthology Assistant: Debra Dick
Design Assistants: Sally Curnock, Ian Midson
Proofreader: Aquila Kegan
Editorial Assistant: Molly Sutherland

EDITORIAL PRODUCTION FOR THE SERIES
Chief: Ellen Brush
Quality Control: Douglas Whitworth
Traffic Co-ordinators: Linda Mallett, Helen
Whitehorn
Picture Co-ordinators: Kate Cann, Philip Garner
Art Department: Julia West
Editorial Department: Debra Lelliott, Beverley Doe,
Lesley Kinahan

THE EPIC OF FLIGHT
THE SEAFARERS
WORLD WAR II
THE GOOD COOK
THE TIME-LIFE ENCYCLOPAEDIA OF GARDENING
HUMAN BEHAVIOUR
THE GREAT CITIES
THE ART OF SEWING
THE OLD WEST
THE WORLD'S WILD PLACES
THE EMERGENCE OF MAN
LIFE LIBRARY OF PHOTOGRAPHY
THIS FABULOUS CENTURY
FOODS OF THE WORLD
TIME-LIFE LIBRARY OF ART
GREAT AGES OF MAN
LIFE SCIENCE LIBRARY
LIFE NATURE LIBRARY
YOUNG READERS LIBRARY
LIFE WORLD LIBRARY
THE TIME-LIFE BOOK OF BOATING
TECHNIQUES OF PHOTOGRAPHY
LIFE AT WAR
LIFE GOES TO THE MOVIES
BEST OF LIFE

Cover: A delicate blend of seafood and vegetables in a
rich fish sauce is spooned into crisp vol-au-vents. The
prawns, mussels, asparagus tips, sweet red peppers and
mushrooms used to fill the vol-au-vents were pre-cooked
separately, then heated together in the sauce.

THE CHIEF CONSULTANT:
Richard Olney, an American, has lived and worked since 1951
in France, where he is a highly regarded authority on food and
wine. A regular contributor to the influential journals *Cuisine et
Vins de France* and *La Revue du Vin de France,* he has also
written numerous articles for other gastronomic magazines in
France and the United States, and is the author of *The French
Menu Cookbook* and the award-winning *Simple French
Food.* He has directed cooking courses in France and the
United States and is a member of several distinguished gas-
tronomic societies, including *La Confrérie de Chevaliers du
Tastevin, La Commanderie du Bontemps de Médoc et des
Graves* and *Les Amitiés Gastronomiques Internationales.*

THE PHOTOGRAPHER:
Tom Belshaw was born near London and started his working career in films. He now
has his own studio in London. He specializes in food and still-life photography,
undertaking both editorial and advertising assignments.

THE INTERNATIONAL CONSULTANTS:
Great Britain: *Jane Grigson* was born in Gloucester and brought up in the north of
England. She is a graduate of Cambridge University. Her first book on food, *Charcu-
terie and French Pork Cookery,* was published in 1967; since then, she has published a
number of cookery books, including *Good Things, English Food* and *Jane Grigson's
Vegetable Book.* She became cookery correspondent for the colour magazine of the
London *Observer* in 1968. *Alan Davidson* is the author of *Fish and Fish Dishes of
Laos, Mediterranean Seafood* and *North Atlantic Seafood.* He is writing *The Oxford
Companion to Food,* to be published by the Oxford University Press. *Jean Reynolds,*
who prepared some of the hors-d'oeuvre in this volume, is an American from San
Francisco. She trained as a cook in the kitchens of several of France's great restaurants.
Richard Sax, who also prepared some of the hors-d'oeuvre in this volume, was for two
years Chef-Director of the test kitchens for *The International Review of Food and Wine.*
He trained in New York and in Paris, where he served an apprenticeship at the Hotel
Plaza-Athénée. **France:** *Michel Lemonnier* was born in Normandy. He began contri-
buting to the magazine *Cuisine et Vins de France* in 1960, and also writes for several
other important French food and wine periodicals. The co-founder and vice-president
of the society *Les Amitiés Gastronomiques Internationales,* he is a frequent lecturer on
wine and vineyards, and a member of most of the vinicultural confraternities in France.
Germany: *Jochen Kuchenbecker* trained as a chef, but worked for 10 years as a food
photographer in many European countries before opening his own restaurant in
Hamburg. *Anne Brakemeier,* who also lives in Hamburg, has published articles on food
and cooking in many German periodicals. She is the co-author of three cookery books.
Italy: *Massimo Alberini* divides his time between Milan and Venice. He is a well-known
food writer and journalist, with a particular interest in culinary history. Among his 14
books are *Storia del Pranzo all'Italiana, 4000 Anni a Tavola* and *100 Ricette Storiche.*
The Netherlands: *Hugh Jans,* a resident of Amsterdam, has been translating cookery
books and articles for more than 25 years. He has also published several books of his
own, including *Bistro Koken* and *Sla, Slaatjes, Snacks,* and his recipes are published in
many Dutch magazines. **The United States:** *Carol Cutler,* who lives in Washington,
DC, is the author of three cookery books, including the award-winning *The Six-Minute
Soufflé and Other Culinary Delights. Julie Dannenbaum* has directed a cooking school
in Philadelphia, Pa., for 16 years and is the author of two cookery books and numerous
magazine articles. *Judith Olney* received her culinary training in England and France
and has written two cookery books. *Robert Shoffner* has been wine and food editor of
the *Washingtonian* magazine since 1975.

Valuable help was given in the preparation of this volume by the following members of
Time-Life Books: *Maria Vincenza Aloisi, Joséphine du Brusle* (Paris); *Janny Hovinga,*
(Amsterdam); *Elisabeth Kraemer* (Bonn); *Ann Natanson* (Rome); *Bona Schmid*
(Milan).

CONTENTS

A Beneficent Beginning

A hot hors-d'oeuvre ushers in a meal with a flourish and stimulates enthusiasm for what is to follow. Indeed, its very name is inseparable from the idea of a meal as a sequence of courses. Literally "outside the work", it leads to the work proper—a substantial main course and dessert or cheese or, in more formal meals, a calculated progression of several courses. Being the first course, it is approached with an eager and attentive palate—and hence is especially rewarding for cook and diner alike.

Hot hors-d'oeuvre do not encompass all first courses, even all hot first courses. A meal might begin instead with a salad or pâté, soup or pasta. Although the category is not all-embracing, the range of dishes within it is so varied as almost to defy generalization. Soufflés and pies, sausages and snails, deep-fried vegetables and grilled seafood all appear in the chapters that follow. All are designed to be served in small helpings that do not sate the appetite; but their most important common feature is a careful presentation that makes them doubly inviting—both in themselves and as heralds of the rest of the meal.

Choosing an hors-d'oeuvre

The most typical ingredients of hot hors-d'oeuvre are delicacies such as asparagus and mushrooms, prawns and snails, frogs' legs, brains and sweetbreads. The subtle flavours of these foods are perceived most distinctly at the start of a meal. In addition, some, such as frogs' legs, are too small to be very satisfactory as a main course, and others, such as snails and brains, are so rich that they are best enjoyed in small quantities. But hot hors-d'oeuvre are by no means always composed of these exquisite morsels. If the presentation is well chosen, small fish, such as sardines or herrings, humble vegetables such as pumpkin and carrot, and leftovers of all kinds can be put to use.

Skilful—although not necessarily elaborate—presentation is of key importance for all hot hors-d'oeuvre. However luxurious the ingredients, a handful of them surrounded by a large empty plate would look mean and dull. But the same foods presented in a vol-au-vent, on a skewer, or in individual china dishes, acquire a new charm. Pancakes or ravioli dough can provide a decorous wrapping for leftovers. In the form of a smooth purée, many vegetables animate soufflés or pies. And sauces play an important part in many of the presentations; their richness may be more welcome at the opening of a meal than later, when the appetite has lost its edge.

When deciding on a presentation, you should consider the hors-d'oeuvre in the context of the whole meal. Thus, a generously sauced hors-d'oeuvre should be followed by a plainer, more robust dish—a simple roast, perhaps. If, on the other hand, you want to serve a sauced dish as a main course, begin with something less elaborate, such as a few morsels grilled on a skewer. And if your main course is a complicated assortment of meats and vegetables, serve as a first course a dish with relatively few elements: a simple gratin, for example, or a soufflé. Each of these suggested presentations can be adapted to dozens of different ingredients. To help you experiment and invent your own dishes, this book is divided up according to presentation rather than by ingredient or cooking method.

The book begins with four pages showing common elements in stuffings and pie fillings, elements that can be combined with each other, and with additional flavourings, in many different ways. There follow six pages showing a number of basic sauces and simple variations on them. The first chapter of the book, on pies and tarts, introduces an important category of hot hors-d'oeuvre and teaches basic pastry-making techniques that are developed in later chapters. The second chapter describes the preparation and presentation of richly sauced delicacies—shellfish and asparagus, for example—in individual vol-au-vents or other containers. The next chapter introduces a range of cases, edible or otherwise, that can be filled with a stuffing; they include pancakes, snail shells, sausage casings and conveniently shaped vegetables such as the artichokes pictured opposite. Next comes a chapter of dishes in which eggs play a background but important role. The first half of the book ends by showing some other treatments suitable for the delicacies presented earlier: sautéing, deep frying, baking and grilling.

The second half of the book consists of an Anthology of the best published hot hors-d'oeuvre recipes. Even before you have run through them, you will find yourself inventing more.

Serving wine with hot hors-d'oeuvre

Just as a robustly flavoured roast is often served after a subtle hors-d'oeuvre, red wine normally follows white in the course of a formal meal. That rule coincides neatly with the requirements of hot hors-d'oeuvre, most of which are best enjoyed with a white wine. White wine complements white meat and fish, and sauces enriched with cream or egg; red wine, with its tannic edge, would seem harsh in such company. But an exception is made for an hors-d'oeuvre with a red wine sauce, which may be more agreeably accompanied by a light-bodied red wine. And many less complex hors-d'oeuvre, such as pancakes or deep-fried ravioli with a meat stuffing, would be equally well served by a white wine or a light red wine. Explore the wine possibilities with the same spirit of adventure as you contrive the hors-d'oeuvre, and many pleasant discoveries will reward you.

Devising Stuffings and Fillings

The ideal stuffing or pie filling is well flavoured, firm and fairly dry—but rich enough in fat to offset the dryness. It is rare to find all these qualities in the same material, so most stuffings are made up of several elements which between them supply the necessary features. Some of the most adaptable elements are shown here and on pages 8 and 9. By selecting combinations of them, you can create scores of different fillings for pastry (*Chapter 1*), pancakes, sausage casings or hollowed-out vegetables (*Chapter 3*).

The ingredients shown below and on the right—rice, bread, fresh cheese, egg and butter—are the mild-flavoured background components of a stuffing. Rice and bread provide bulk, egg provides firmness and fresh cheese provides both. Butter is often included for richness. These elements may be enlivened by one or more of the well-flavoured ingredients shown overleaf: spinach, *duxelles*—a combination of finely chopped mushrooms, onions and parsley—a smooth vegetable purée, pumpkin and minced meat. Other common flavourings include grated cheese,

herbs, tomatoes, garlic and onions. Thus a well-balanced stuffing might be based on bread, bound with egg, enriched with butter and flavoured with spinach or chopped meat and herbs.

One of the simplest ways to keep rice grains separate and fluffy as they cook is to coat the grains with butter, then simmer them in a measured amount of liquid (*below*). Bread for a stuffing may be either reduced to crumbs or softened by soaking in liquid, then squeezed as dry as possible (*opposite page, above, left and centre*). Fresh breadcrumbs are especially valuable in a stuffing if the other ingredients are at all moist: the crumbs will absorb the excess liquid.

Fresh cheese and egg (*opposite page, above, right*) both firm up on cooking and thus bind a stuffing; in addition, fresh cheese offers unassertive bulk. Although butter is usually a secondary element, flavoured butter alone can sometimes be enough for a filling. To make a stuffing for snails or shellfish, for example, butter is pounded with anchovy fillets and garlic

(*opposite page, below; recipe, page 126*).

Many of the vegetables shown overleaf exude liquid and must be prepared with care to keep a filling dry. Spinach is sautéed after being parboiled, squeezed and chopped, and the mushrooms and onions that make up *duxelles* are cooked briskly to evaporate their liquid. Pumpkin—which has a very high water content—is baked and then drained under weights.

Most cooked vegetables can be puréed by passing them through a food mill and sieving the resulting rough pulp. Starchy vegetables such as peas form a firm purée unaided; other vegetables often require the addition of starchy ingredients to give them body. French beans are puréed with rice on page 9; flageolet beans would be a delicious alternative to the rice.

If cooked meat is included in a stuffing, it can be left coarsely chopped. Raw meat should be minced so that it can cook through quickly. Meat grinders, however, tend to squeeze the juice out of the flesh; chopping with two knives, as demonstrated overleaf, produces less mangled results with little more effort.

Rice for Satisfying Bulk

1 **Pouring in boiling water.** Melt a little butter in a saucepan set on a fireproof mat. Add rice and cook it gently, stirring continuously, until the rice grains turn translucent—2 to 3 minutes. The fat that the grains absorb on their surfaces will help to keep them separate. Bring twice the rice's volume of water or stock to the boil and pour it over the rice (*above*).

2 **Cooking the rice.** Add salt, unless you are cooking the rice in stock that is already salted. Stir once to make sure no grains are stuck to the bottom of the saucepan. Adjust the heat so that the liquid barely simmers and cover the pan (*above*). Do not stir the rice again, or the grains may stick together. Leave the rice to cook undisturbed for about 18 minutes.

3 **Forking in butter.** As soon as all the liquid is absorbed, take the pan off the heat. To enrich the rice and help separate the grains, cut butter into small cubes and toss the rice with it; use forks rather than a spoon, to avoid damaging the grains.

Crumbs to Extend a Mixture

Using a food processor. Slice the crusts off a piece of fresh or stale bread. Tear the bread into chunks; reduce the chunks to crumbs in an electric food processor (*above*) or blender. To make crumbs without such a machine, you will have to use stale bread; rub it against a grater, and sieve the resulting fragments.

Soaked Bread for Easy Blending

Squeezing moistened bread. Cut the crust off a slice of fresh or slightly stale bread. Dip the bread in water or milk, until it is moist right through; squeeze the bread very hard to eliminate as much of the liquid as possible.

Egg and Cheese for Binding

Mixing with a fork. Use a fork (*above*) to incorporate a whole egg into a stuffing and to break down any lumps in a fresh cheese—*ricotta*, as here, cottage cheese or home-made curd cheese.

Enhancement from Butter

1 **Pounding garlic and anchovies.** Soak salt anchovies in cold water for about 15 minutes to rid them of excess salt and soften them. Peel the two fillets away from either side of the backbone, rinse them and pat them dry. Put the anchovy fillets in a mortar with whole, peeled garlic cloves and pound them to a paste.

2 **Distributing the flavourings.** Leave a chunk of butter at room temperature for an hour or so to soften. Add it to the mortar and pound with the pestle until the garlic and anchovy mixture is dispersed uniformly throughout the butter.

3 **Adding seasonings.** Season the butter with pepper and salt, taking into account the saltiness of the anchovies. If you like, add a little cayenne pepper, chopped parsley, lemon juice and a few drops of pastis—anise-flavoured spirit. Pound the butter to incorporate all the flavourings.

The Fresh Flavour of Green Leaves

1 **Boiling and draining.** Remove the stems and tough central ribs of spinach. Wash the leaves. Bring a large pan of salted water to a rolling boil and plunge the leaves into the water to cook for about 2 minutes. Drain the leaves in a colander and rinse them with cold water. Squeeze the leaves, a handful at a time, to remove as much of the water as possible.

2 **Chopping the leaves.** Steadying the leaves with one hand, slice each handful of leaves as thinly as possible with a large knife (*above*). Cut across the slices to reduce the size of the pieces.

3 **Removing moisture.** Put some butter in a frying pan and distribute the chopped greens in the pan. Cook them over a fairly high heat for a few minutes, tossing them often, so excess liquid evaporates.

A Concentrate of Mushroom and Onion

1 **Adding mushrooms.** Chop onions finely. Cook them gently in butter in a shallow pan until they soften—about 5 minutes. Finely chop mushrooms or mushroom stalks just before cooking them, so that they do not blacken. Use at least twice the weight of mushrooms to onions. Transfer the mushrooms to the pan.

2 **Sprinkling with lemon juice.** As soon as the mushrooms are in the pan, raise the heat to evaporate their abundant juices. Cook the mixture for about 10 minutes, stirring and shaking constantly, until it seems dry. Season with salt, pepper and nutmeg and add a handful of chopped parsley and lemon juice to taste.

3 **Evaporating the remaining liquid.** Stir in the flavourings. Continue to cook the *duxelles* over a high heat for about 2 minutes, stirring constantly, until the lemon juice has evaporated. If possible, use the *duxelles* immediately, before it begins to darken. Otherwise, store it covered closely with plastic film.

A Bean Purée Reinforced with Rice

1 **Adding rice to beans.** Sprinkle 1 to 2 spoonfuls of rice into boiling salted water and boil it for about 30 minutes. Drain and rinse the rice. Bring a pan of fresh, salted water to the boil and add French beans. (There is no need to trim the beans, since sieving will remove the tough parts later.) Tip the rice into the pan with the beans.

2 **Milling the mixture.** Cook the beans and rice for 5 to 10 minutes, until the beans are very tender but still bright green. Leave them to drain for 30 minutes to rid them of as much water as possible. To break down the beans and rice to a coarse purée, pass them through the medium disc of a food mill into a bowl.

3 **Sieving the coarse purée.** Use a plastic scraper to press the purée through a fine-meshed drum sieve a spoonful at a time. Scrape the resulting fine purée from the bottom of the sieve at intervals and transfer it to a bowl. Discard the fibres that accumulate on top of the sieve.

Pumpkin: Special Treatment to Remove Liquid

1 **Scooping out the flesh.** Wrap seeded sections of pumpkin in aluminium foil so that they do not burn, and bake them for about 1½ hours in a 200°C (400°F or Mark 6) oven, or until a knife stuck through the foil penetrates the flesh easily. Open the packages and scoop out the flesh with a spoon. Lay the flesh on a towel draped over a colander (*above*).

2 **Weighting the flesh.** To help draw out the liquid, intersperse the layers of pumpkin flesh with salt. Fold the corners of the towel over the pumpkin; place a plate on the towel and some heavy object, such as a tin (*above*), on the plate. Leave the pumpkin to drain for at least 4 hours, or overnight. Mash it with a fork before incorporating it into a stuffing.

Raw Meat for Savour

Chopping with two knives. Remove all fat and gristle from a chunk of raw beef, veal, lamb or pork. Cut the meat into small cubes; use two heavy knives of equal size and weight to speed the chopping. Let one knife then the other fall on to the meat in a regular rhythm; gravity rather than muscle power should provide most of the chopping force.

Bases for Velvety Sauces

The sauces used to accompany hot hors-d'oeuvre or to unify the elements of an assembly are, with a few exceptions (*page 14*), simply liquids thickened with flour. An important group of these sauces, demonstrated here, are based on stock and are collectively known as velouté—literally "velvety" (*recipes, page 167*). A sauce based on fish stock (*right*) will echo the flavour of fish dishes; one that is based on delicate veal stock (*right, below*) can be served with meat and vegetable dishes.

The stock is prepared by gently simmering meat or fish trimmings in water with herbs and aromatic vegetables. The fish trimmings could be the bones, skins and heads of the fish that you intend to serve with the sauce; veal stock is usually made with a knuckle—which provides both flavour and gelatine for body—supplemented with inexpensive chicken pieces. A veal stock takes several hours to make, but fish gives up its flavour in about 30 minutes. Wine is usually added to fish stock—but only part-way through cooking, since its acidity slows down the release of the vegetables' flavour. Because the stocks will be reduced during the preparation of a sauce, they should be salted only lightly. When all the flavour has been drawn out of the solid ingredients, they are strained from the liquid.

To transform stock into a velouté, combine it with a flour and butter paste—a roux—and simmer the mixture for about 40 minutes to cook the flour and to reduce the sauce to a creamy consistency. During simmering, fat and impurities rise to the surface and are easily skimmed off.

A velouté sauce may be coloured with vegetables or a spice (*page 13*) or enriched just before serving with cream, butter or egg yolks. If a sauce enriched with yolks is returned to the heat and cooked for a moment—gently, to prevent the yolks from curdling—the yolks will thicken smoothly and provide extra body.

Two variations based on velouté are shown here. In one, a mixture of eggs and lemon juice is added for a sauce at once rich and lively (*opposite page, below, left*). In the other, red wine—reduced and flavoured by prolonged simmering with herbs and vegetables—transforms a veal velouté (*opposite page, below, right*).

From Fish to Velouté

1 **Starting the stock.** Put some fish trimmings—here, the bones, heads and skins of sole—in a large pan; cover with water. Bring the liquid slowly to a simmer, and spoon off any scum that forms. Add herbs and sliced aromatic vegetables—in this case, fennel, parsley stems, thyme, bay leaves, garlic, celery, carrots and onions. Season the stock lightly.

2 **Cooking and straining.** Partly cover the pan. Adjust the heat to maintain a simmer for 15 minutes. Add wine—at least one quarter of the amount of water used—return the liquid to a simmer and cook for 5 more minutes; add peppercorns and simmer for a final 10 minutes. Strain the stock through a colander lined with two layers of damp muslin (*above*).

Veal Stock: a Classic Beginning

1 **Starting the stock.** To prevent meaty bones from sticking, put a wire rack in the bottom of a deep pan. Add veal shank—cut into 7.5 cm (3 inch) pieces—knuckle of veal, and a handful of chickens' necks and feet. Pour in cold water to cover the meat and bones by about 2.5 cm (1 inch). Bring the water slowly to a simmer.

2 **Removing scum.** Remove the scum that forms (*above*); add a little cold water to encourage more scum to rise. Add salt, vegetables and herbs and simmer, partially covered and undisturbed, for 5 hours. Strain and refrigerate the stock overnight. Scrape off the surface fat, and reheat to liquefy the stock before making a velouté (*Steps 3 to 5, above*).

3 **Making a velouté sauce.** To prepare a roux, melt butter in a pan over low heat; add an equal quantity of flour and stir the roux with a whisk for a minute or so until smoothly blended. Ladle in the stock (*above*), then raise the heat, and whisk continuously until the sauce boils.

4 **Cleansing the velouté.** To remove any unwanted fat and impurities that are held in suspension, set the pan half off the heat; keep the sauce at a light boil and, with a metal spoon, keep removing the skin that repeatedly forms at the side of the pan (*above*). The skin will take with it the unwanted fats that rise to the surface.

5 **Finishing the sauce.** Continue to cleanse the velouté at intervals for about 40 minutes, or until no more fat rises to the surface. During the purification process, the sauce will reduce to the consistency of cream (*above*), and the pasty taste of under-cooked flour will vanish. Before serving the sauce, adjust its seasoning.

An Enrichment of Yolks and Lemon Juice

1 **Warming yolks and lemon juice.** Heat some fish or veal velouté sauce gently in a heavy pan. In a small bowl, mix two or three egg yolks with the juice of a lemon. To help the ingredients to blend smoothly, warm the mixture by stirring into it a few spoonfuls of the hot velouté (*above*).

2 **Finishing the sauce.** Turn the heat very low. Stir the warmed egg mixture into the pan (*above*). Continue stirring for 2 to 3 minutes. As soon as the sauce thickens to the consistency of a pouring custard, remove it from the heat. The sauce must not approach the boil or the heat will coagulate the egg proteins unevenly and make the sauce grainy.

A Full-Bodied Red Wine Sauce

Straining the wine. Chop shallots and carrots finely; put them into a sauté pan. Add thyme, bay leaves, garlic cloves and at least a bottle of red wine. Simmer for 1 hour, or until the wine reduces by about two-thirds; strain it into a veal velouté (*above*). Boil the sauce rapidly, stirring constantly, for about 10 minutes—until it is reduced to the desired consistency.

White Sauce: Theme and Variation

A white sauce (*right*) is thickened with the same flour and butter combination as a velouté (*page 10*), but its base is milk instead of stock (*recipe, page 166*). Like a velouté, it can serve to unite diverse ingredients for a presentation (*Chapter 2*); its mild flavour marries well with fish, vegetables and delicate meats such as brains and chicken. A little white sauce is also valuable for binding the ingredients of a stuffing (*page 56*).

The preparation of a white sauce is simpler than that of a velouté since the first major step—the preparation of a stock—is eliminated. The other difference is that while a white sauce simmers, the butter in it remains bound to the milk and flour, and does not rise to the surface. So no skimming is needed during cooking.

One possible addition to a white sauce is a purée of baked onions (*below*); the bland, creamy sauce provides a good background for the strong, sweet taste of the onions. You could also enrich the sauce with cream, or add any of the colourings shown on the opposite page.

Preparing the Basic Sauce

1 Making a roux. Melt butter over a low heat. Add an equal quantity of flour (*above*), stir the butter and flour together with a whisk. Cook the roux gently for 2 minutes, stirring constantly.

2 Whisking in milk. Pour in cold milk—about 60 cl (1 pint) for 2 tablespoons of flour—raise the heat and whisk continuously until the sauce boils. Set the pan on a fireproof mat and simmer the sauce, uncovered, for 40 minutes. The final consistency should be like that of cream—or somewhat thicker if you plan to use the sauce in a stuffing.

Adding a Purée of Onions

1 Peeling baked onions. Wrap unpeeled onions individually in aluminium foil. Bake them in a 190°C (375°F or Mark 5) oven until a skewer inserted through the foil will penetrate the onions easily—about 1¼ hours for medium-sized onions. Unwrap the foil; when the onions are cool, pull off their skins (*above*) and place them in a sieve set over a bowl.

2 Puréeing the onions. Use a wooden pestle to push the onion flesh through the sieve into the bowl. If you prefer, you can purée the onions in a food processor instead of sieving them.

3 Combining purée and sauce. Add the onion purée to the sauce and stir until they are evenly blended. The proportions are up to you: here, the quantities of sauce and purée used are about equal.

A Touch of Colour for Velouté and White Sauces

Various spices and puréed vegetables both flavour and colour a velouté or white sauce. Spinach, saffron and red peppers are prepared here; sorrel, tomatoes and paprika are other possibilities. The coloured sauces can be served with almost any hors-d'oeuvre ingredient, although sorrel and saffron have a special affinity with seafood and white meats.

Spinach (*right*) is simply parboiled and drained well before it is reduced to a purée in a food processor. Sweet peppers (*below*) should be grilled before they are puréed; grilling softens their flesh, refines their flavour and makes their papery skins easy to peel off. Purée them through a sieve, never in a food processor or blender, which would reduce them to a pale, frothy liquid. Tomatoes should be stewed and sieved (*page 14*). Sorrel needs no puréeing; after stewing for a few minutes in butter, it will disintegrate and be ready to add to a sauce.

To ensure that saffron (*far right*) dissolves completely, it should be stirred into a spoonful of hot water before it is mixed into the sauce.

Spinach for a Vivid Green

Making the purée. Trim, clean, parboil, drain and squeeze spinach (*page 8*). Put it in a food processor and reduce it to a purée. Alternatively, chop the spinach finely and push it through a sieve with a pestle. Stir the purée into a sauce only a spoonful at a time (*above*): the spinach has a surprisingly strong colouring effect.

The Golden Tint of Saffron

Dissolving the powder. Put a pinch of powdered saffron in a tablespoon and add hot water. Stir with a teaspoon until the liquid turns red. Add it to the sauce: diluted, the saffron will make the sauce yellow. (If your saffron is in threads, dry it in a warm oven for a few minutes until it crumbles easily, and pound it with a pestle before you dissolve it.)

A Warm Red from Peppers

1 **Peeling grilled peppers.** Grill peppers, turning them regularly, until their skins are blistered on all sides. Place them under a damp towel: the towel will trap the steam they release and loosen the skins, making them easier to peel off. When the peppers are cool enough to handle, peel off the skins (*above*) and remove the stalk, seeds and the white pith.

2 **Puréeing the peppers.** Set a sturdy metal sieve over a bowl. Push the peppers through the sieve with a pestle. A pepper purée produced by sieving has more body and a more uniform consistency than one made by any other method.

3 **Embellishing the sauce.** Add the purée to either a velouté or white sauce in whatever proportions you want; neither the colour nor the flavour of the peppers is so intense as to demand caution.

Sauces That Need No Thickener

Some sauces do not need a thickening of flour; the basic ingredients provide sufficient body. Four such sauces are demonstrated here. Three use the pulpy flesh of tomatoes for both flavour and body; one derives its creamy consistency from carefully heated butter.

Depending on how they are prepared, tomatoes yield either an even or a rough-textured sauce (*recipes, page 166*). A smooth tomato purée (*right*) is made by simmering quartered, unpeeled tomatoes in their juice, with aromatic vegetables and herbs for extra flavour. When the tomatoes become a mush, the seeds and the skins are sieved out and cooking continues until the sauce is as thick as you want. You can add cream to the purée if you wish (*opposite page, above, right*), to make a similar but richer sauce.

For a sauce that retains the rough texture and fresh flavour of raw tomatoes, very gentle heat is essential (*right, below*). Chopped tomatoes, moistened with oil and flavoured with herbs and spices, are warmed up in the moderate heat of a water bath; they are neither simmered nor sieved. Since the tomatoes are not sieved, they must be peeled and seeded before they are warmed.

When butter is whisked into a small amount of liquid over a very low heat, it forms a creamy emulsion instead of melting to oil. The liquid may be any strong-flavoured essence: a reduction of stock, wine or vinegar for example. The *beurre blanc* shown here (*opposite page, below; recipe, page 164*) is made with a reduction of shallots, wine and vinegar, into which butter is whisked.

Because prolonged or fierce heat would ruin it, *beurre blanc* is always served as an accompanying sauce and never as an integral part of a cooked dish. Its sharp flavour makes it most successful with fish dishes (*pages 38 and 60*). Tomato sauces, on the other hand, are very versatile. They can be served with many meat, fish and vegetable dishes, whether as an accompaniment (*page 84*), as a moist topping for a baked dish (*page 48*), or as an element in a stuffing (*page 44*).

A Purée of Tomatoes

1 **Seasoning tomatoes.** Finely chop onions and sauté them in a little oil until they are soft. Quarter tomatoes and add them to the onions. Add salt, a bay leaf, thyme and crushed garlic cloves (*above*). Cook the ingredients over a gentle heat, stirring occasionally, until the tomatoes totally disintegrate—about 30 minutes.

2 **Sieving the tomatoes.** Set a sieve over a large bowl. Use a broad wooden pestle to push the tomatoes through the sieve. Discard the seeds and skins, and the herbs that remain in the sieve. Pour the resulting purée back into the pan.

An Uncooked Blend of Tomatoes and Spices

1 **Preparing tomatoes.** Immerse tomatoes in boiling water for about 10 seconds. Peel off the softened skin and cut the tomatoes in half crosswise. Squeeze out the seed clusters. Cut the flesh into small pieces and place it in a cooking pot. Add the flavourings—here, chopped parsley, garlic, chervil, chives, coriander, tarragon—and olive oil.

2 **Heating the sauce.** Season the tomatoes with salt and pepper. Place a trivet in a large pan. Set the pot of tomatoes on the trivet. Fill the pan with enough warm water to reach just above the level of the tomatoes. Warm the tomatoes over a low heat for about 30 minutes, stirring the sauce occasionally.

3 **Reducing the purée.** Cook the tomato purée over a low heat for 20 to 30 minutes, until it reduces to the required consistency. Stir it frequently to prevent it sticking, especially towards the end of cooking. Season the sauce with pepper and, if you wish, add chopped fresh herbs, such as basil or parsley.

A Tomato Sauce with Cream

1 **Adding cream.** Prepare a tomato purée (*left*). Leave the sauce on the heat and pour double cream into it. Here, the proportion of cream to purée is about one quarter. You can add more cream to make the sauce still more delicate.

2 **Blending the sauce.** Stir the cream into the tomato purée until they are thoroughly blended. If the sauce is too thin, simmer it for a few minutes, stirring constantly, until it reaches the consistency you desire.

Beurre Blanc: a Tingling Transformation of Butter

1 **Preparing the base.** Pour equal amounts of white wine and white wine vinegar into a saucepan. Set the pan over a low heat. Finely chop shallots and add them to the combined liquids. Add a little salt. Leave the mixture to simmer until the liquid has almost disappeared—15 minutes or more.

2 **Adding butter.** Remove the pan from the heat and allow the contents to cool for a few seconds. Place a fireproof mat over a low heat and set the pan on it. Grind in some pepper. Add a few cubes of butter and whisk vigorously. Add more butter when the first batch begins to soften, leaving more space for whisking.

3 **Whisking the sauce.** Continue adding butter, a handful at a time, whisking constantly, until the sauce has the right balance of sharpness and richness for your palate. Take the pan off the heat just as the last butter cubes are melting, but whisk for a few seconds more.
Serve the sauce as soon as it is ready: reheating will turn the butter oily.

1
Pies and Tarts
Techniques for Perfect Pastry

Whether used as a frame to display its contents or as a sealed container to keep them from view, a carefully sculpted pastry shell supplies the graceful finish expected of any hot hors-d'oeuvre. The pastry can enclose almost anything: a combination of the stuffing bases on pages 6 to 9, luxurious morsels such as wild mushrooms or oysters, or humbler delights such as sliced sausages, mussels or sardines.

Pastry varies in both construction and ingredients, but all types contain flour for body and fat for tenderness. In addition, a little water is necessary to bind the dough; sometimes egg is included for firmness, and ingredients such as wine or even anchovies (*recipes, page 103*) may be incorporated for extra flavour. In a plain shortcrust pastry (*page 18*) small pieces of butter dispersed throughout the dough give the finished pastry a crisp, somewhat flaky texture. Rough-puff pastry (*page 20*) begins with the same flour and butter combination as shortcrust, but the dough is folded and rolled out repeatedly so that the butter is pressed into leaves. The result is a light pastry composed of scores of tissue-thin sheets. By replacing the butter with olive oil, you can make versions of both plain and puff pastry, each with its own distinctive texture in addition to the flavour of the olive oil (*pages 22-25*).

Every type of pastry shown in this chapter can be fashioned into both open tarts and enclosed pies. These are often made in dishes or tins that determine their shape. But by cooking dough on a flat sheet, you can prepare other forms—turnovers, tarts rimmed with two or three thicknesses of pastry, and deep pies with lid and base firmly sealed together.

Because raw pastry will never become light and crisp if it is allowed to get wet, it is sometimes pre-baked to accommodate a moist filling—as is the case with the pepper and tomato tart on page 20. In this chapter, however, most of the pies and tarts are assembled with raw pastry—a procedure that allows the filling and casing to become a unified dish and one obligatory for any shape that requires sealing of the dough's edges. Any filling ingredients that require moist cooking (rice, for example) or that give out liquid when they start to cook (mushrooms or vegetable fruits) are cooked in advance—and so, of course, are any ingredients that require longer cooking time than the pastry.

A circular lid of shortcrust dough, draped over a rolling pin for easy transport, is laid in place on a "stargazey" pie of sardines and *duxelles* (*page 18*). The lid, cut to size with a plate as a guide, is intentionally smaller than the base; the silvery heads of the fresh sardines are left uncovered as decoration round the rim of the pie.

An Unusual Fish Pie with Shortcrust

Simple to make and equally suitable for tarts, turnovers and pies, crisp shortcrust (*recipe, page 165*) is the most widely used of all pastries. To prepare the dough, cubed butter is tossed into about twice its weight of flour and cut into smaller pieces with two knives (*Step 2, below*). Be careful not to overdo the cutting: if the butter were reduced to tiny pieces, the pastry would be crumbly instead of crisp. To ensure that the butter remains in distinct pieces, start with very cold butter, use cold water to bind the dough, and handle the dough as little as possible.

Minimal handling is important for an-other reason. When flour is moistened and kneaded, an elastic substance called gluten develops in it. Although gluten is valuable in some foods—in bread, for example—its elasticity could easily make a shortcrust pastry tough. To restrict the formation of gluten, add just enough li-quid to bind the dough, and knead it only until it coheres.

In this demonstration, shortcrust is used to make an unusual fish pie, with a lid cut smaller than its base. Small fish—sardines, pilchards or herrings—bake with their bodies protected by the lid from the drying heat of the oven. Their heads, however, need no such protection; peep-ing out from beneath the lid, they form part of the dish's decoration and earn the pie its traditional name of "stargazey" (*recipe, page 92*). To flavour the fish, you can stuff them with herbs and onions and surround them with bacon; or substitute one of the stuffing bases on pages 8 and 9, such as the *duxelles*—a mixture of mush-rooms and onions—used here.

The dough for the stargazey pie should be divided into two—a larger section for the base, a smaller for the lid. The base can be trimmed when in place on the pie dish; the lid should be trimmed—using an inverted plate as a guide—before it is transferred to the pie for baking.

1 **Preparing the dough ingredients.** In a large bowl, mix flour and salt. Cut chilled butter into 1 cm (½ inch) cubes. Scatter the butter pieces over the flour.

2 **Coating the butter with flour.** Holding a table knife in each hand, cut the butter into the flour with a rapid, criss-cross action. Continue until about half the butter has been reduced to smaller pieces.

3 **Adding water.** Add a little cold water and stir it in with a fork. If the dough is still crumbly, add a few drops more. Blend the water evenly into the pastry dough.

4 **Making the dough cohere.** Work the dough lightly with your fingertips until you can squeeze it into a ball. Wrap it in plastic film, waxed paper or foil and leave it to chill in the refrigerator for about 1 hour to make it firm and easier to roll out.

5 **Rolling out the dough.** Lightly flour the work surface and flatten the dough with a smack from the rolling pin. Turn the dough over and divide it into two unequal parts. Reserve the smaller piece and roll out the larger one into a circular shape.

6 **Moulding the pie base.** Drape the dough loosely round the rolling pin and transfer it to a shallow pie plate with sloping walls. To make a patterned rim, tuck under the excess dough and press all round the edge of the dough with your thumb.

7 **Boning the sardines.** Scale each fish by rubbing it gently with your thumb. Slit the belly from the vent to just below the head; gut the fish. Cut the backbone free at the head end. Insert a fingertip between the flesh and rib bones, and ease the bones free. When you reach the tail end, cut the backbone from the flesh (*above*) and remove the bones with the tail.

8 **Stuffing the fish.** Season the inside of each fish with salt and pepper, then stuff it with *duxelles*. Press the sardine into shape once more. Symmetrically arrange the sardines on the pie base, with their heads on the rim of the pie and their tail ends pointing towards the centre.

9 **Glazing the pie rim.** Pack more *duxelles* between the fish and in the centre of the pie. Sprinkle chopped parsley over the fish. For a glaze, brush the rim of the dough with milk (*above*) or beaten egg Roll out the reserved dough and cut it into a round large enough to cover the fish bodies, leaving their heads exposed.

10 **Baking and serving.** Drape the dough lid over a rolling pin and transfer it to the pie. Press it down between each pair of fish (*above*). Brush the lid with milk. Bake the pie at 200°C (400°F or Mark 6) for 30 minutes, then at 180°C (350°F or Mark 4) for a further 15 minutes. Slice the pie to give each person one or two fish (*right*).☐

Colourful Vegetables Framed in Feather-Light Pastry

Puff pastry is wonderfully light and flaky—but only if it can rise unimpeded. Because fillings weigh it down, it is used to best advantage as a pie lid or in a wide-bordered tart, such as the one shown here. The rectangular tart's broad rims are from a double thickness of puff pastry; its filling could be virtually anything. Here it is a stew of peppers and tomatoes, pre-cooked to a fairly dry consistency and topped with anchovies (*recipe, page 103*). You could vary the vegetable stew by adding aubergines, courgettes or olives, and herbs such as basil or oregano.

There are a number of possible starting points for puff pastry. Classic puff begins by enclosing a sheet of softened butter within a folded sheet of flour and water dough. The less time-consuming rough-puff pastry demonstrated here (*recipe, page 165*) starts from the same combination of flour and cubed butter as the short-crust pastry on page 18. It is only the proportions that differ: rough-puff pastry generally contains a larger quantity of butter than shortcrust.

Once water has been added to bind the flour and butter, the dough is repeatedly rolled into a strip and folded in four. Each rolling flattens the knobs of butter, and each folding creates more layers of flat-tened butter interspersed with dough. Baking turns the dough's moisture into steam, which raises and separates the layers into fragile buttery flakes.

To guard against the butter melting and destroying the layered structure, the dough must be put in the refrigerator or freezer to cool after every two repetitions of the rolling and folding. The chilling periods also allow time for the dough to relax, so that repeated rollings-out do not make the dough elastic and tough.

To help protect the dough from the moisture of the vegetable stew, the pastry shell in this demonstration is brushed with diluted egg yolks and baked, empty, just long enough for the yolks to set to a glaze. Only then is the filling spooned into place. After the final baking, the pastry beneath the filling remains crisp.

1 **Rolling and folding the dough.** Prepare and chill a dough (*page 18, Steps 1 to 4*); use a weight of butter between half and equal to that of the flour. (The larger proportion of butter will give a better-flavoured, lighter pastry but more care will be needed to keep the butter from melting.) Flour a work surface: marble is best because it helps to keep the dough cool. Roll the dough into a strip about 5 mm (¼ inch) thick and four times as long as it is wide (*above, left*). Fold the ends to meet in the centre, then fold in half (*above, right*).

4 **Glazing the dough.** Dilute an egg yolk with water and use it to stick the dough strips along the edge of the rectangle. Prick the bottom of the case with a fork to keep it from blistering. Paint the case with the egg mixture (*above*). Draw the back of a fork over the border to pattern the glaze. Put the case in a 220°C (425°F or Mark 7) oven for 10 minutes.

5 **Preparing vegetables.** Dip tomatoes in boiling water for a few seconds; peel, halve and seed them, then chop them coarsely. Roast or grill several sweet peppers until they blister (*page 13*). Cover them with a damp towel until they are cool. Peel, halve and seed them; cut them into strips (*above*). Peel and chop finely two or three garlic cloves.

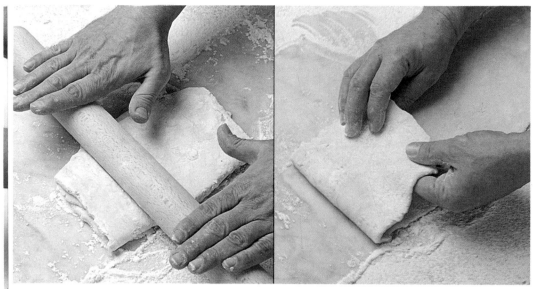

2 **Repeating the rolling and folding.** Give the dough a quarter turn, so that one of its open sides is facing you. Roll it out again (*above, left*). Fold the dough in four as before (*above, right*), then wrap it in plastic film and chill it until it is quite firm—1 to 2 hours in the refrigerator or 15 to 20 minutes in the freezer. Repeat Steps 1 and 2; for an even lighter pastry, repeat the sequence a third time.

3 **Cutting the dough.** Roll out the chilled dough to a thickness of about 3 mm ($\frac{1}{8}$ inch). Using a dough scraper, trim the dough into a rectangle. Cut a 2 cm ($\frac{3}{4}$ inch) strip from all four sides (*above*). Then place the remaining rectangle on a baking sheet.

6 **Stewing the vegetables.** Heat a little oil in a pan and add the chopped tomatoes, the garlic and salt. Cook the tomatoes, uncovered, for about 20 minutes over a fairly high heat, stirring occasionally, until they have reduced to a thick pulp. Add the pepper strips and stew the mixture for 10 more minutes. Correct the seasoning; if you like, add a few drops of vinegar.

7 **Filling and baking the tart.** Soak and then bone several salted anchovies; moisten them with a little olive oil. Spoon the vegetable stew on to the dough.(*inset*). Arrange the anchovies in a criss-cross pattern on top. Bake the tart at 190°C (375°F or Mark 5) for 20 to 30 minutes, until the pastry is well coloured. Transfer the tart to a dish, sprinkle the tart with chopped parsley and serve it in sections.□

2
Little Stews
Richly Sauced Compositions

A velouté sauce, enriched with egg yolks and coloured with saffron, is spooned over a crisp bread case that encloses a stew. The stew's ingredients—diced roast chicken and ham, cubes of parboiled and sautéed cucumber, and slivers of truffle—have been prepared separately and warmed up in the sauce.

Imaginatively selected delicacies, separately cooked and brought together in a luxurious sauce, make marvellous hors-d'oeuvre. Such preparations—presented as individual servings—may include those foods too rich, too rare or too subtle in flavour to appear often in a main course except as a garnish: truffles, for example, asparagus or scallops. But exotic ingredients are not the rule—tiny onions, perfectly fresh peas, strips of ham or bacon also find a place. Modern cookery has no single term to describe combinations of these delights, but old French cookery books call them *petits ragoûts de béatilles*, or "little stews of titbits".

Whatever the ingredients for a little stew, the sauce that fuses them will help determine the character of the dish. A rich fish velouté mirrors the delicacy of the seafood it accompanies, while a piquant tomato sauce gives a colourful, informal air to a mélange of French beans, peppers, chicken and ham (*page 39*). All the sauces demonstrated on pages 12 to 15 are suitable for the seductive presentations on the following pages.

All little stews are assembled in much the same way; the differences among them lie in the choice of ingredients and the manner of pre-cooking them. This chapter begins by showing how you can prepare and pre-cook vegetables, seafood and meat (including offal) in ways that retain their flavour and colour (*pages 28-33*). Subsequent demonstrations describe how to make edible cases for little stews—shells of puff pastry, containers carved from bread and cooked rice moulded into rings (*page 34*)—and how to combine the cases and their contents. Ingredients may be either warmed in sauce on the top of the stove or baked with their sauce in small gratin dishes, until the mixture bubbles under a light crust or "gratin" of breadcrumbs or grated cheese (*page 36*). With either technique, you can prepare all the elements of the stew well in advance of the meal, leaving only the heating in sauce to the last minute.

The chapter concludes with suggestions for eight different presentations, ranging from a sole and mushroom stew bathed in *beurre blanc* (*page 38*) to a creamy blend of morels, asparagus and other delicacies in a pastry case (*page 40*). These presentations are delicious in themselves, but the real purpose of showing them is to spur your imagination, and encourage you to devise many memorable stews of your own.

Scrupulous Treatment for Vegetables

So that their flavours remain undistorted, the delicate vegetables used in little stews need brief and simple cooking—and immaculate preparation. The vegetables shown here are good choices for little stews—but do not exhaust the options.

Initial treatment varies from rinsing or skinning to the salting and lengthy draining needed to dry out tomatoes (*below*). Artichokes (*bottom*) are rid of their outer leaves and central choke. (To avoid discoloration, use a stainless steel knife, rub the cut vegetables with lemon juice, and keep them in water acidulated with lemon juice.) Cucumbers are peeled and seeded and asparagus stalks simply peeled (*opposite page, above left and centre left*). Dried morels are rehydrated by soaking

in water (*opposite page, centre right*).

Brief sautéing in butter is sufficient to cook tomatoes, morels and very young artichokes. But sautéing is too slow a cooking method for older artichokes, asparagus, mange-tout and salsify: it would make them greasy and their flavours muddy. Instead, parboil them in plenty of salted water until almost tender—half a minute from the time the water returns to the boil for sliced asparagus and mange-tout, 10 minutes or more for artichokes and salsify—then sauté them briefly to dry them out and flavour them. Cucumbers should be parboiled in heavily salted water, then sautéed; the salt helps to draw out their abundant liquid. French beans

are also parboiled, but they drain easily and do not need sautéing to dry them.

Small onions could be either sautéed in butter (with the pan lid on so they remain white) or parboiled and then sautéed. But they gain an especially pleasing flavour if simmered in veal stock (*opposite page, above right*). Mushrooms can be sautéed, too, but boiling them briefly with lemon juice and butter (*opposite page, below left*) will keep them white and plump. The liquid from the mushrooms and onions can be included in a sauce or used to poach another stew ingredient.

Fresh truffles should be cooked very briefly, in butter or a few drops of brandy. But preserved truffles (*opposite page, below right*) only need slicing or chopping.

Extracting Excess Moisture from Tomatoes

1 Salting tomatoes. Peel and halve the tomatoes; remove their seeds. Cut them into large pieces. Put the tomatoes on a piece of muslin; sprinkle them lightly with some salt to draw out their moisture.

2 Draining the tomatoes. Gather up the muslin to make a bag (*above*). Tie it round the neck with string; hang the bag from the kitchen tap to drain for several hours, or until the dripping has stopped.

3 Stewing the tomatoes. Melt butter in a shallow pan. Add the tomatoes and stew them over a gentle heat for 1 to 2 minutes, tossing rather than stirring them in order to keep the tender pieces intact.

Uncovering an Artichoke's Tender Interior

1 Paring. Break off the stem. Bend back each outer leaf to break it; pull down to remove the tough upper part. Stop at the pale inner leaves. Slice off the artichoke's top two-thirds. Pare the base (*above*).

2 Removing the chokes. Rub lemon over the cut surfaces. Cut each artichoke into six or eight pieces. With a stainless steel knife, remove the fibrous chokes (*above*). Put the pieces in acidulated water.

3 Sautéing artichokes. Boil the artichokes in salted water for 10 minutes or until tender; drain them. Add the artichokes to melting butter in a sauté pan; toss the artichokes in the butter for 1 to 2 minutes.

Drawing the Water from a Cucumber

1 **Cubing a cucumber.** Peel a cucumber with a vegetable peeler. Cut it in half lengthwise; remove the seeds by running your finger down each piece. Halve the pieces lengthwise again; cut into chunks.

2 **Sautéing the pieces.** Parboil cucumber pieces in heavily salted water for about 2 minutes; drain them well. Melt butter in a pan; add the cucumber pieces (*above*); sauté them gently for 1 to 2 minutes.

Peeling Asparagus Stalks

1 **Peeling asparagus.** Trim the dry white base from each stalk. With a small knife, peel the asparagus, starting at the bottom and peeling more thinly towards the top (*above*). Slice the peeled stalks.

2 **Sautéing the pieces.** Cook the pieces in boiling, salted water for half a minute. Melt butter in a shallow pan; add the asparagus pieces (*above*); sauté for 2 to 3 minutes, tossing rather than stirring.

Keeping Fresh Mushrooms White

1 **Adding liquid to mushrooms.** Trim mushroom stems so they are flush with the caps; save the stems for *duxelles (page 8)*. Put the caps in a pan with salt, pepper, a knob of butter and lemon juice.

2 **Simmering the mushrooms.** Add a splash of water, cover, and bring to the boil. The mushrooms will release copious liquid (*above*). Remove the mushrooms from the heat. Drain them just before serving.

Bathing Onions in Flavour

Simmering onions. Drop small onions in boiling water for 1 minute to loosen their skins; top, tail and peel them. Put them in a pan; add enough veal stock to cover them; simmer for 10 minutes, until tender.

Softening Dried Mushrooms

Preparing morels. Soak dried morels for 30 to 40 minutes in cold water, until they soften. Trim the stem bases if they are earthy; halve the morels and rinse them. Stew them in butter for 10 minutes.

Exploiting the Truffle

Chopping and slicing. Slice truffles thinly. Cut slices into strips. For small cubes, cut the strips crosswise. Finely chop any trimmings. Stir large pieces into a stew; scatter smaller pieces over the top.

Accenting the Flavours of Fish and Shellfish

With their subtle flavours and compact flesh, all kinds of shellfish—and many kinds of fish—are welcome in little stews. Scallops, prawns and mussels are prepared in these demonstrations; shrimps and crayfish can be treated like prawns, and clams like the mussels. Among fish, choose those whose flesh is firm and well flavoured: soft fish such as whiting would disintegrate when cut into the requisite small pieces and cooked. Good fish for small stews are the sole shown here, angler fish, turbot and John Dory.

Fish and shellfish require only brief cooking, and their delicate flavours are enhanced if they are poached or steamed in a liquid already fragrant with the essences of complementary ingredients. Wine, fish stock (*page 10*) and the liquid in which mushrooms have cooked (*page 29*) are all suitable. Another possibility is a court-bouillon—a mixture of water and wine in which aromatic vegetables and herbs have simmered (*recipe, page 164*).

A court-bouillon is used here to poach scallops (*right*) and prawns (*right, below*). Sole strips (*opposite page, above*) are poached in mushroom liquid. But the various liquids can be used interchangeably for cooking the fish and shellfish.

Bivalves such as mussels (*opposite page, below*) require a different approach, since the shellfish and their abundant liquid are trapped between the tightly clamped shells. Steaming is the method used both to open the shells and to cook the shellfish. A little wine provides the initial steam; after a minute or two, it is augmented by the mussels' own liquid. Herbs and aromatics perfume the liquid—which, like the poaching liquid for the other fish and shellfish, make an admirable addition to a sauce.

Poaching Scallops in a Wine-Flavoured Broth

1 **Straining a court-bouillon.** Slice onions and carrots and crush garlic cloves. Put them in a pan with celery and herbs. Add cold water and bring it to the boil. Simmer for 30 minutes, adding a glass of white wine after 15 minutes and peppercorns after 20 minutes. Place prepared raw scallops in a pan. Pour the liquid, through a sieve, on to the scallops (*above*).

2 **Slicing the scallops.** Put the pan on the heat and simmer for about 4 minutes. Do not allow the liquid to boil. When the flesh is firm, remove the pan from the heat. Allow the scallops to cool in the liquid. Remove them from the pan and, with a knife, separate the coral from the white flesh and slice the white flesh into rounds.

Poaching and Peeling Prawns

1 **Peeling prawns.** Simmer raw prawns in a court-bouillon (*Step 1, above*) for about 7 minutes until deep pink. Allow them to cool in the liquor. Peel away the soft shell and little claws from each prawn and pull away the tail. If you want to extract the flavour from the shells, pound and sieve them; add the resulting purée to a sauce.

2 **Slicing the prawns.** With a small, sharp knife, slice each prawn lengthwise into two (*above*). With your fingers, pull away and discard the fine black strand that runs down the back of the prawn. Dice the prawns if you wish. Reserve the poaching liquor in the pan to add to a sauce.

Cooking Sole Strips in Mushroom Juices

1 **Draining the fillets.** Ask the fishmonger to skin and fillet a sole. Keep the trimmings for a fish stock (*page 10*). Half-fill a long, shallow dish with cold water. Put in the fillets for a minute so that any blood soaks out of them. When the fillets are white, lay them on paper towels to dry (*above*).

2 **Cutting the fillets into strips.** On a wooden board, cut each fillet diagonally into strips 1.5 cm (½ inch) wide (*above*). Generously butter a heavy sauté pan and lay the strips of sole in the pan.

3 **Poaching the fillets.** Ladle the hot juice from cooked mushrooms (*page 29*) on to the sole pieces. Add some white wine. Transfer the pan to the heat and bring the liquid just to the boil. Immediately remove the pan from the heat and cover it, so that the strips cool slowly and complete their cooking. Remove the strips from the liquid only just before using them in a stew.

Steaming Mussels Open

1 **Scraping mussels clean.** Soak mussels in a bowl of cold, salted water for an hour or so until they have discharged all sand and dirt. With a short knife, scrape all the barnacles from each shell (*above*). Pull out the "beard"—the fibrous strands that emerge between the halves—grasping it between the knife and your fingers. Discard any mussels that are open.

2 **Steaming.** Put the mussels into a deep pan. Add chopped onions, garlic, a bay leaf, dried and fresh herbs and a splash of white wine (*above*). Cover the pan. Place it on a high heat for 3 to 5 minutes until all the shells have opened, shaking the pan occasionally to redistribute the mussels. Remove the pan from the heat. Let the mussels and their cooking liquid cool.

3 **Shelling the mussels.** Take the mussels one by one from the pan. Pull the flesh free of the shells. Strain the liquid into a bowl through a sieve lined with several layers of muslin. Moisten the mussels with a little of the liquid. Reserve the rest for a sauce.

Techniques for Delicate Meats

Meat used in little stews is chosen with a bias towards richness and delicacy. Offal plays a prime role: brains, sweetbreads and chicken liver have a subtlety of flavour and a melting tenderness that suit them perfectly to small-scale, abundantly sauced creations. Bone marrow shares these characteristics, and earns itself a valued place. More everyday meats are also important. Bacon provides a fine foil for other flavours; ham, poultry or game will combine well with almost any sauce.

Most of these meats need special treatment to prepare them for a little stew, but none of the preliminaries is complex. Chicken livers (*right, above*) must be rid of tough membranes and any bitter tasting bile stains. They need only brief sautéing—enough to colour their surface but leave their interiors pink. Longer cooking would make them dry and bitter.

Bacon for a little stew should be bought in a chunk rather than slices, so that you can dice it (*opposite page, above*). Choose unsmoked streaky bacon—smoked would be too strong. To reduce its saltiness, parboil it in unsalted water; then sauté it to draw out fat and complete the cooking.

To extract the marrow from a beef leg bone in a neat cylinder, boil the bone briefly in salted water (*right, centre*). The heat-softened marrow is easily shaken out of the bone. The marrow is then sliced and simmered in water—but only just before the stew is ready to serve; if it were left standing in the liquid, it would disintegrate. Because of its fragility, bone marrow is not warmed up in sauce but placed on and round the stew as a garnish.

Brains (*opposite page, centre*) and sweetbreads (*right, below*) must both be soaked to remove any blood. The surface membrane of brains can be removed after soaking alone. The brains can then be poached in the wine-flavoured court-bouillon used for fish (*page 30*), but vinegar-flavoured court-bouillon suits their rich flavour even better. The membrane covering sweetbreads can only be removed after parboiling. After a period under a weight to compress their loose structure, the sweetbreads can be simmered in a court-bouillon or in veal stock; or simply sautéed gently in butter.

Sautéing Chicken Livers in Butter

1 **Preparing chicken livers.** With a small paring knife, trim off any sections of chicken liver that are stained green from proximity to the gall bladder. Excise the white membranes and halve each liver.

2 **Sautéing the livers.** Melt some butter in a shallow pan. Add the livers in a single layer. Season them and sauté them for 2 to 3 minutes over a medium heat, tossing them so that they cook and colour evenly.

Extracting Bone Marrow in One Piece

1 **Boiling bones.** Lower sections of beef leg bone into a pan of lightly salted boiling water. Bring the water back to the boil, reduce the heat and simmer, uncovered, for 10 minutes. Lift out the bones.

2 **Shaking out the marrow.** Protecting your hand with a towel, sharply shake the bone so the marrow slides out. When the stew is ready, slice the marrow and poach it in salted water for 2 minutes.

Cleaning and Pressing Sweetbreads

1 **Soaking sweetbreads.** Immerse the sweetbreads in cold water for 1 hour. To firm them, put them in a pan of cold water, bring to the boil and simmer for 2 minutes. Drain and refresh them in cold water.

2 **Removing the membrane.** Peel off the surface membrane and attached fat and gristle. Do not delve too deeply or you will separate the lobes. Put the sweetbreads on a towel spread over a board.

Relieving Bacon of Excess Salt

1 Removing the bacon rind. Place a slab of unsmoked streaky bacon on a board, rind side down. Insert a knife in the layer of fat between the rind and flesh, and slice parallel to the board to remove the rind.

2 Cutting into pieces. Slice the bacon lengthwise into thin strips. Cut across the strips at 1 cm (½ inch) intervals. Place the bacon pieces in a pan and cover with cold water. Bring the water to the boil.

3 Sautéing in butter. When the water boils, remove the pan from the heat. Drain the bacon pieces and rinse them. Sauté them in butter for 5 minutes, shaking the pan to cook the pieces of bacon evenly.

Poaching Brains in Court-Bouillon

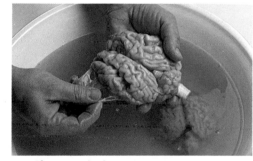

1 Cleaning the brains. Soak calf's brains in cold water for at least 30 minutes. Pull off the surface membrane (*above*). Soak the brains in fresh cold water for another 30 minutes to remove all blood.

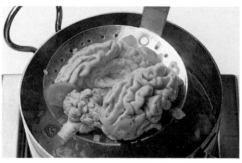

2 Poaching in a court-bouillon. Prepare a vinegar court-bouillon (*recipe, page 164*). Poach the brains, partially covered, for 20 minutes. Lift them out of the court-bouillon with a large slotted spoon.

3 Slicing the brains. If you do not use the brains at once, cover them with a towel soaked in the court-bouillon, so that they remain moist and white. Cut the brains crosswise into 1 cm (½ inch) slices.

3 Weighting the sweetbreads. Cover the sweetbreads with a towel. Put another board on top. Put a heavy weight on top of the board. Leave the sweetbreads to compact; it will take at least 2 hours.

4 Cooking in stock. Put the sweetbreads in a pan and ladle in some liquid— here, veal stock. If you like, surround them with diced onions and carrots. Cover and braise for 30 to 40 minutes.

5 Separating the lobes. Remove the pan from the heat and leave the sweetbreads to cool in their cooking liquid. Gently pull the lobes apart with your fingers (*above*), or cut the sweetbreads into cubes.

Fashioning Edible Containers

An edible case of rice, puff pastry or bread offers a striking, three-dimensional setting for a little stew—and in addition provides a pleasant contrast of texture. Rice cases (*right*) are the simplest to prepare. Freshly cooked and buttered rice (*page 6*) is spooned into a small ring mould and packed down firmly so that the rice will cohere when turned out. Since reheating would dry the rice, the cases should be prepared at the last moment and used at once.

Pastry and bread cases take more time to fashion. Although at their best when freshly made, they can be prepared in advance and reheated. Both may be made in rounds, squares or rectangles.

The round vol-au-vents shown opposite, above, and the rectangular pastry cases on the right, below, may be made from either butter rough-puff pastry (*page 20*) or olive oil puff (*page 24*). Each shape is built up from several thin layers of dough—which puff up more than just a single thick layer—and becomes a hollow form only after cooking.

Vol-au-vents are made out of three rounds of dough, stamped with a fluted pastry cutter, stacked and glued together with water. To mark a lid, lightly press into the top round of dough with a small cutter before you set the round in place. When cooking has crisped and coloured the outside of the vol-au-vent, cut out the lid. The exposed inside of the vol-au-vent is still soft. Scoop out and discard the partially cooked dough and return the shell to the oven until its inside surface dries.

Rectangular cases are made in essentially the same way, but the shapes are cut with a fluted pastry wheel or a dough scraper. Like the vol-au-vents, rectangular cases are built up from three layers of dough, but the whole of the top layer forms the lid. To help the lid come away from the base, do not stick the top rectangle of dough to the middle rectangle.

For bread cases (*opposite page, below*), use a firm, slightly stale white tin loaf. After carving the bread into a hollow shape, paint it generously with melted butter and bake it until it crisps.

Moulding a Ring of Rice

1 **Packing a mould.** Cook some rice and fork some small cubes of butter into it (*page 6*). While the rice is still hot, spoon it into a small ring mould. Pack the rice down firmly with the back of the spoon. When the mould is full, smooth the exposed surface of the rice to give the ring a level base when it is unmoulded.

2 **Unmoulding the rice.** Invert a heated serving plate on top of the ring mould. Holding the mould against the plate, turn them over so the mould sits on the plate. Lift away the mould (*above*). Fill the centre of the ring with a stew and serve.

Building Rectangular Pastry Cases

1 **Cutting out the dough.** With a pastry wheel, cut a thin sheet of dough into rectangles; here, a piece of paper serves as a guide. Use three pieces of dough for each case. Assemble, glaze and bake as for vol-au-vents (*Steps 1 and 2; opposite page, above*); do not brush the middle layer with water or indent the top layer.

2 **Finishing the cases.** As soon as the cases are out of the oven, slice off the top layer from each one to make the lids. Remove raw pastry from the underside of each lid and the inside of each base. Place the lids upside down on the baking sheet next to the bases. Return the cases to the oven for 5 to 10 minutes to dry them out.

3 **Adding butter.** Take the pan off [...] and stir in the egg mixture. Retur[...] to a very low heat and stir the ste[...] the sauce thickens. Remove the [...] the heat and add chunks of butte[...] were added while the pan was s[...] heat, the butter would rapidly me[...] turn oily. Stir with a wooden spo[...] the butter is incorporated into the [...]

Constructing a Vol-au-Vent

1 **Assembling the layers.** Dampen a baking sheet so that the cases do not slip about when the butter melts. Lay a round of dough on the sheet. Prick the dough's centre to stop it puffing up; brush its edge with water. Lay a second round on top (*above*); brush its edge with water. Score a lid in a third round: place it on top.

2 **Baking the cases.** Glaze the top of each case with a mixture of egg yolk and water. Do not glaze the sides, or the cases will not rise. Chill for 20 minutes. Bake them in a preheated 200°C (400°F or Mark 6) oven for 30 minutes, turning the baking sheet at intervals so that the cases brown and rise evenly.

3 **Completing the shells.** Let the cases cool, then use a knife to prise out the lid from each case. Peel off and discard the raw pastry from the underside of each lid. Scoop out the raw pastry from the insides of the bases (*above*). Return the bases to a cool, 150°C (300°F or Mark 2) oven for 5 to 10 minutes to dry out.

3 **Saucing the brains and tomatoe[...]** mushroom-flavoured sauce ove[...] each gratin dish. Grate some ch[...] Gruyère—and sprinkle it over the[...] sauté breadcrumbs in butter and [...] gratins along with, or instead of, [...]

Cutting and Colouring Bread Cases

1 **Cutting the cases.** Trim the crusts from a slightly stale loaf. If the bread seems soft, put it in the freezer for a few minutes. Cut it into 5 cm (2 inch) slices. Score one side 1 cm (½ inch) in from each edge and to within 1 cm of the base. Insert the knife horizontally 1 cm above the base of one corner and swivel it (*above*).

2 **Hollowing out the centre.** Withdraw the knife and insert it in the diagonally opposite bottom corner. Swivel the knife again to loosen the centre section. With the tip of the knife, lever out the centre section (*above*). Shake out any loose crumbs of bread remaining in the case.

3 **Baking the cases.** Place the cases on a buttered baking sheet. With a pastry brush, liberally coat the inner and outer surfaces of each case with melted butter. Place the cases in an oven preheated to 170°C (325°F or Mark 3) for about 1 hour, until crisp and golden; turn them occasionally so that they colour evenly.

Two Ways to Assen

The various elements of a l
brought together only just b
The ingredients may be pr
last minute and combined v
But it is often convenient t
gredients in advance and re
gether in a sauce. Just how
done helps to determine the
the finished dish.

For a fairly liquid stew
cooked ingredients and sa
over direct heat; in this case,
ham and truffles are warn
ach-flavoured velouté. On
is heated through, the sauce
with butter, for example.
meat and vegetables are pu
container—vol-au-vents, h
hot sauce is spooned over.

As a crisp-surfaced alter
below), the cold ingredient
ranged in a dish, covered wi
heated in the oven. Alwa
dishes for this type of prese
oven and prolonged contac
would ruin edible cases su
vents. Here, brains and sau
lie under a mushroom-fla
sauce. A sprinkling of grat
breadcrumbs—on the surfa
gratin finish.

The only stews that can
bled by these methods a
sauces based on butter or
beurre blanc (*page 15*) or ho
ipe, page 166). These sau
come oily or granular if re
that include such sauces m
bled from ingredients tha
cooked and still hot, as show

Bearing in mind this li
can use the techniques shov
pare any stew (*recipes, po
Pages 38 to 41 suggest some
nations of ingredients, witl
ing a serving of each finish
devising your own stews,
than six or seven differen
with too many elements, fla
confused. And choose a sau
with the ingredients: a ro
sauce for chicken livers, f
more delicate sauce for sea

Taking Apart Layered Vegetables

Onions and fennel bulbs, although unrelated, are both made up of concentric layers. If these vegetables are carefully pulled apart, each layer can be used to enfold a stuffing (*pages 6-9*); a single vegetable can provide six to eight cases.

Onions (*right*) must be parboiled before the layers can be separated into hollow spheres. To ensure even cooking, make an incision to the centre of each onion; the cut widens as the onions boil and the layers part easily. Softened by the cooking, they will wrap themselves round a stuffing and hold it securely.

Unlike onions, fennel bulbs (*right, below*) are easily pulled apart when raw and crisp. By trimming the base of the bulb, you can loosen the curved, interlocking stalks sufficiently to remove them one by one, then parboil them until they are flexible enough to contain a stuffing.

Here, onion layers are filled with a combination of fresh cheese, ham and parsley (*recipe, page 117*) and fennel layers enclose a simple bread-based mixture. The central layers of both vegetables, too small to be stuffed, may be chopped and included in the filling.

Both the onions and the fennel in this demonstration complete their cooking in the oven. To keep them from drying out in the direct heat, the onions are masked with cream and the fennel with tomato sauce; the two coatings are interchangeable. To form a gratin surface, the tomato sauce is sprinkled with grated cheese. The cream will brown without a topping.

Onion Wrapped Round a Fresh Cheese Mixture

1 **Slitting the onions.** Top and tail some large onions and remove their skins. Make one vertical cut from the outside to the centre of each onion (*above*). Then put the slit onions in a deep pan of boiling, lightly salted water.

2 **Boiling the onions.** Boil the onions for about 15 minutes, until they start to look transparent. The cut in the onions will open out further. Using a spider or a slotted spoon, transfer the onions to a bowl of cold water to cool them quickly.

Fennel Stalks Topped with Tomato

1 **Separating fennel stalks.** Cut the green stems and feathery leaves from fennel bulbs. Cut a thin slice off the bottom of the bulb to release the curved stalks. Pull off the stalks, one at a time. If any stalk will not come away easily, shave another slice off the base. Rinse the stalks in cold water to wash away any grit. Reserve the hearts of the fennel to add to the stuffing.

2 **Removing the strings.** The three or four largest stalks of each bulb have coarse fibres embedded in their outer surfaces. To remove the fibres, cut into the top of the stalk with a small knife. Grasp a few fibres firmly between the blade and your thumb, and pull them towards the base of the stalk (*above*). Work round each stalk to remove the rest of the strings.

3 **Stuffing the onions.** Make a stuffing—here, fresh *ricotta* cheese, chopped ham, parsley, eggs and seasonings. To separate the onions into layers, slide your thumb beneath each layer in turn and ease it away from the rest of the onion. When all that remains is a heart about 2.5 cm (1 inch) in diameter, chop it up and mix into the stuffing. Holding an onion layer in the palm of one hand, hollow side uppermost, place a spoonful of stuffing near one side (*above*) and roll the rest of the layer round it. Thickly butter a large gratin dish. Pack in the onions in a single layer with their slit sides down.

4 **Serving the stuffed onions.** Moisten the onions with cream and set the gratin dish in a preheated 180°C (350°F or Mark 4) oven. Bake the stuffed onions for about 45 minutes so that the onions become very tender. If the cream seems to be drying out before the cooking time is up, add a little extra cream. When the surface is fairly evenly coloured, serve the onions directly from the baking dish. □

3 **Stuffing the fennel.** Boil the fennel stalks in salted water for 5 to 10 minutes to soften them slightly. Remove them from the water and drain them on a towel. Make a stuffing—in this case, fresh breadcrumbs and softened butter, bound with egg and flavoured with herbs, garlic and the fennel hearts. When the fennel stalks are cool enough to handle, place a spoonful of filling inside each one (*above*). Press the edges of the container close together. Rub the bottom and sides of a large gratin dish generously with softened butter. Arrange the stuffed fennel stalks closely together in the dish.

4 **Serving the fennel.** Coat the fennel with tomato sauce (*page 14*). Sprinkle the top with grated hard cheese—Parmesan, Cheddar or Gruyère, for example—or with breadcrumbs sautéed in plenty of butter. Cook in a 190°C (375°F or Mark 5) oven for 50 minutes to 1 hour, until the sauce has reduced and the top is brown. □

Scooping Out Space for a Filling

Many vegetables that have no natural cavity can house a stuffing if hollowed or halved and scooped out. An apple corer (*right*) tunnels through courgettes while leaving them outwardly unmarked; the narrow space is then filled with the aid of a piping bag. Aubergines, halved and scooped out (*below*) become ample boat-shaped containers. Roundish vegetables such as beetroot (*recipe, page 125*) can be scooped out to make cup-like vessels.

Because the apple corer works best in a firm material, the courgettes are hollowed out raw, then stuffed and baked. The filling used here (*recipe, page 123*) is based on bread, raw meat—which cooks by the time the courgettes are done—and the courgettes' own scooped-out flesh.

Halved aubergines are easier to scoop out if first sautéed to soften their flesh. Since they are pre-cooked, their stuffing is generally pre-cooked too. The stuffing used here is a mixture of poached brains, tomatoes and the aubergines' own flesh (*recipe, page 120*), topped with beaten egg which becomes a puffy golden crust.

Courgette Sections Packed with Meat

1 **Hollowing out the courgettes.** Choose fairly straight courgettes; top and tail them and cut them into 5 cm (2 inch) lengths. Push an apple corer through the centre of each section and pull out the fleshy core (*above*). Chop the cores finely, sauté them briefly in a little butter and set them aside for the stuffing.

2 **Stuffing the courgette sections.** Prepare the stuffing—in this case, softened bread (*page 7*) with chopped beef (*page 9*), eggs, herbs, garlic and the sautéed courgette centres. Spoon the stuffing into a piping bag fitted with a wide nozzle and pipe it into the courgettes. Spread any leftover stuffing in a gratin dish.

Aubergine Halves with Chopped Brains

1 **Frying aubergines.** Trim the stems from aubergines and halve them lengthwise. With a knife, score the cut side deeply in a criss-cross pattern so that the heat can penetrate easily. In a large sauté pan, heat 5 mm ($\frac{1}{4}$ inch) of oil and add the aubergines, cut side down. Fry them for about 20 minutes over a gentle heat, turning the aubergines after 15 minutes.

2 **Scooping out the flesh.** Lift the aubergine halves out of the pan and place them on paper towels to drain. When they are cool, scoop out almost all the flesh with a spoon, taking care not to tear the skin. Arrange the shells in a baking dish and chop the scooped out flesh.

3 **Cooking the flesh.** Heat a little oil in a frying pan. Add skinned, seeded and chopped tomatoes, one or two whole garlic cloves, parsley, seasonings and the chopped aubergine flesh. Stir the mixture and cook it for about 10 to 15 minutes over a high heat, to create a thick pulp. Stir frequently to prevent the mixture from sticking to the pan.

3 **Softening the courgettes.** Heat a little oil in a sauté pan and lay the courgettes on their sides in it. Cover the pan; cook the courgettes over medium heat for up to 20 minutes, turning them from time to time. Transfer the courgettes to the gratin dish, standing them in the bed of stuffing.

4 **Cooking and serving the courgettes.** Spoon the oil from the pan over the courgettes to keep them moist. Place the dish, uncovered, in a preheated 180°C (350°F or Mark 4) oven and bake for 20 to 30 minutes or until the exposed stuffing is lightly coloured. Serve immediately, garnished with the loose stuffing from the dish.□

4 **Assembling the stuffing.** Skin and poach brains (*page 33*) and leave them to cool. Chop the brains coarsely and place them in a bowl. Remove the garlic cloves from the tomato and aubergine mixture and pour the mixture over the brains (*above*). Stir the stuffing ingredients together.

5 **Filling the aubergines.** Spoon the stuffing into the prepared aubergine shells. Place them in a preheated 190°C (375°F or Mark 5) oven. After 20 minutes, lightly beat eggs, season them with salt and pepper, and ladle them over the stuffed aubergines. Return the dish to the oven.

6 **Serving the aubergines.** Bake the stuffed aubergines for a further 10 minutes or until the eggs have barely set. Before serving the aubergines, loosen the eggs from the side of the dish with a spatula. Slide the spatula under each aubergine and lift it carefully on to a plate.□

Snails: Hunting and Cooking Your Own

Snails served in their shells, immersed in bubbling garlic-flavoured butter, are an archetypal hot hors-d'oeuvre—but one more often encountered in restaurants than at home. Admittedly, not all cooks have the opportunity to buy fresh snails; but if you have a garden you can hunt your own. The striped common snail used in this demonstration is found in most gardens. The larger, paler Roman or Bourgogne snail—the type usually served in restaurants—has a more limited habitat. All other varieties that you may find in your garden are edible, but most are too small to be worth preparing.

You can gather snails only in the summer months—from April or May to October. In winter, snails hibernate; any you find under stones or in crevices will be thin, and their shells will be sealed with a plaster-like substance.

Snails live on a variety of plants, some of which are poisonous to humans. To allow time for the snails to rid their systems of any poison, you must keep them alive in captivity for a few days. Some cooks starve the snails during this period. But, to keep them plump, it is better to supply them with wholesome leaves.

Before cooking, the snails must be cleansed with vinegar and salt. They are then immersed in a boiling court-bouillon, which kills them instantly, and simmered until tender. The cooked snails are detached from the shells to lessen the diner's task, then replaced. Some recipes recommend that, before replacing the snails, you discard the black intestine at the tip of their body. In fact, the intestine is edible and its removal is optional.

When the snails are back in their shells, a little stuffing is pressed over them. If you want a container that holds more than a single animal—and more stuffing—you can pack the snails into mushroom caps (*box, opposite page*). Here, both the snails in their own shells and those in mushroom caps are covered with a mixture of butter, garlic, parsley and other flavourings (*page 7; recipe, page 126*), then briefly heated. The snails in their shells are eaten with the help of a small fork and a clamp; the snails in mushroom caps require no special equipment.

1 **Feeding the snails.** Place live snails in a deep bucket with any non-poisonous leaves—herbs or lettuce, for example. Cover the bucket with wire mesh—in this case, a coarse mason's sieve is used—to prevent the snails from escaping. Leave the bucket for three to four days so that the snails' systems are cleansed.

2 **Soaking in salt and vinegar.** Put the snails in a clean bowl. Add some coarse salt crystals and pour over a good splash of wine vinegar. Let the snails soak for about 5 minutes, stirring occasionally with your hands. The salt and vinegar will cause them to release some of their slime.

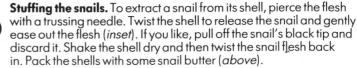

6 **Stuffing the snails.** To extract a snail from its shell, pierce the flesh with a trussing needle. Twist the shell to release the snail and gently ease out the flesh (*inset*). If you like, pull off the snail's black tip and discard it. Shake the shell dry and then twist the snail flesh back in. Pack the shells with some snail butter (*above*).

3 **Rinsing the snails.** Transfer the snails by the handful to a bowl containing plenty of clean cold water. Swirl them round to loosen the slime. If you have just a few snails, clean them by holding them, one at a time, under a running cold water tap.

4 **Pouring over the court-bouillon.** Place the snails in a saucepan. Prepare a court-bouillon from finely sliced vegetables, herbs, water and wine (*page 30*). Strain the boiling court-bouillon through a sieve into the pan of snails (*above*).

5 **Skimming the liquid.** Heat the court-bouillon until it comes to the boil again. With a ladle, remove the scum that forms on its surface (*above*). Lower the heat and simmer, partially covered, for about 2 hours or until the snails are tender. Remove the pan from the heat, leave the snails to cool in their liquid, then drain.

7 **Serving the snails.** To prevent the shells from toppling over, place them—buttered side upwards—in metal snail plates. Put them in a 200°C (400°F or Mark 6) oven for 5 minutes or until the butter bubbles. Serve with a snail clamp to hold the shell, a small fork to extract the flesh, and plenty of bread to mop up the buttery juices. □

Packing Snails into Mushroom Caps

Remove the stems of medium-sized mushrooms and toss the caps in oil (*page 46*). Place them under a hot grill for a few minutes or until their rims start to curl. Arrange four or five snails in each mushroom and mound flavoured butter over the snails (*above*). Pack the mushrooms into an ovenproof dish. Place them under a hot grill or in a preheated 200°C (400°F or Mark 6) oven until the butter starts to bubble.

Pancakes: a Flexible Wrapping

Thin pancakes make pliable yet strong wrappings for fillings, and are also light enough to be welcome at the start of a meal. An added advantage is that the pancakes can be prepared in advance, then wrapped in plastic film and stored in the refrigerator for a day or two.

The pancakes prepared here are made from a batter of flour, milk and egg, enriched with melted butter (*recipe, page 164*). To yield thin pancakes, the batter should be fairly runny—the consistency of single cream. You can enliven the basic mixture with brandy or fresh herbs.

The batter ingredients must be combined thoroughly but gently. If the batter were whisked too vigorously, it would become elastic—and uneven pancakes riddled with holes would result. Provided it is not over-beaten, the batter is ready to use as soon as it is mixed. If you do have to beat the batter vigorously to eliminate lumps, let it rest for 30 minutes before you make the pancakes to allow the gluten in the flour to relax.

To ensure that the pancakes cook evenly, use a fairly heavy iron or steel pan. Pans designed for pancake-making have perfectly flat bottoms, for good transfer of heat, and sloping sides which facilitate turning the pancake. The butter in the batter helps to prevent sticking; the pan requires only light greasing before the first pancake is made, and subsequently none at all. The pan should be preheated so that the batter sets instantly—but not too hot or the batter will burn.

Cooked pancakes can be rolled round any well-seasoned filling, whether made specially or prepared from leftovers. In this demonstration, the stuffing is a mixture of cheeses and spinach; in the box opposite, pancake stuffings are prepared from leftover beef stew and roast chicken.

Once the pancakes are stuffed, they need only be heated through in the oven. To prevent them from drying out, cover them with melted butter, as shown here, or a sauce. For the beef-stuffed pancakes, the sauce is the liquid from the beef stew combined with tomato purée; the chicken pancakes are topped with a white sauce. In each case, the pancakes are sprinkled with grated cheese for a gratin finish.

1 Mixing the batter. Mix flour and salt in a large bowl. Make a well in the centre of the flour and break in whole eggs. Slowly pour milk into the centre of the bowl; at the same time, working from the centre of the bowl outwards, whisk the eggs and the milk into the flour. Stir in melted butter as soon as the batter is smooth.

2 Starting to cook a pancake. Warm a very little butter in a heavy pan over a low to medium heat; wipe off any excess with a paper towel. Allow 2 to 3 minutes for the pan to heat up, then lift it and ladle in just enough batter to thinly coat the base. The batter should sizzle as it touches the hot metal. As you pour, tilt and roll the pan to spread the batter evenly.

6 Reheating the pancakes. Arrange the pancakes flap side down in a buttered gratin dish. Spoon enough melted butter over the surface of the pancakes to lightly coat them, and sprinkle with grated hard cheese. Cook the pancakes in an oven preheated to 190°C (375°F or Mark 5) for 20 to 25 minutes until lightly browned.

7 Garnishing the pancakes. While the pancakes reheat, prepare the garnish. Halve small skinned tomatoes and seed them, or drain whole canned tomatoes thoroughly. Stew the tomatoes in butter until softened but not pulpy. Remove the reheated pancakes from the oven and top each one with a hot tomato.□

3 **Turning the pancake.** Cook the pancake until its underside is evenly coloured and its edges curling—about 30 seconds. Slip a palette knife under the pancake. With a quick movement, lift up the pancake and flip it over. Cook the underside until it is dry and lightly speckled—about 20 seconds.

4 **Stacking the pancakes.** Slide the cooked pancake out of the pan on to a plate. Before making a fresh pancake, stir the batter in case it has settled and take the pan off the heat for a few seconds so that it does not become too hot. To keep the cooked pancakes moist, stack them one on top of the other.

5 **Stuffing the pancakes.** Cradle each pancake in turn—evenly coloured side down—in one hand. Spoon a stuffing—here, a mixture of *ricotta* and grated Parmesan, egg and chopped, cooked spinach (*page 8*)—down the centre of the pancake to within 1 cm (½ inch) of the ends. Fold both sides of the pancake over the stuffing, leaving the ends open.

Two Ways to Use Leftovers

Pancakes stuffed with a stew and sauced with its juices. Heat leftover meat stew to melt the jellied juices. Strain off and reserve the juices. Chop the meat and vegetables from the stew and mix them with an egg and fresh breadcrumbs (*above, left*). Use this mixture to stuff herbed pancakes (*recipe, page 164*). Arrange the stuffed pancakes in a buttered gratin dish. Add a little puréed tomato (*page 14*) to the reserved juices. Spoon the sauce over the pancakes (*above, right*) and sprinkle with grated cheese. Reheat in the oven until a light gratin is formed.

Chicken-stuffed pancakes coated with a creamy sauce. Dice skinned and boned cooked chicken and mix it with *duxelles* (*page 8*). Make a fairly thick white sauce (*page 12*); add just enough sauce to bind the mixture (*above, left*). Season to taste. Stuff herbed pancakes with the mixture and arrange them, flap side down, in a buttered dish. Dilute the rest of the sauce with a little cream. Coat the pancakes with the sauce (*above, right*) and sprinkle it with grated Parmesan. Place them in a preheated oven until they are hot and the sauce's surface is golden-brown.

5
Baking, Frying and Grilling
Simple Methods for Savoury Results

A first course need not be an elaborate affair: the straightforward techniques of baking and grilling, deep frying and sautéing can produce hot hors-d'oeuvre of real distinction—baked sardines with erect tails neatly aligned, for example, or mussels grouped with bacon chunks on skewers and grilled to make individual servings (*opposite and page 88*).

The fragile nature of many of the foods involved requires that the hors-d'oeuvre be cooked with special care. The enveloping heat of an oven, for instance, will dry out meats and vegetables unless provisions are made to keep them moist. If you use the oven to fuse the flavours of disparate ingredients—layers of vegetables, grains and meats or seafood, for example—you must include some liquid element such as a sauce in the assemblies. Simpler bakes, consisting of a predominant element plus herbs and aromatics, can also be beguiling, particularly if the main ingredient is as rare a treat as frogs' legs; dishes of this sort require generous basting with butter or oil to ensure a juicy finish.

A grill's heat is as dry as an oven's—and much more intense—so that careful timing is particularly important. Grilled foods may be given a protective coating of breadcrumbs, which will provide an appealingly crisp surface. You can also wrap dry ingredients such as liver in pork caul—a fatty membrane from the stomach that melts during the cooking process—to keep the food succulent (*recipe, page 161*).

Deep frying subjects delicate foods to the fierce temperatures of hot oil, and most benefit from some protection to keep them from drying. Coatings such as flour, egg and breadcrumbs or batter will not only shield the food but will also cook to a fragile golden envelope round it. More elaborate coatings also help to package the hors-d'oeuvre ingredients into individual servings: you can string different morsels on a skewer and coat them with a thick sauce before deep frying, for instance, or enclose a soft mixture in a wrapping of dough or pancake.

Sautéing—frying food in shallow oil or butter at a relatively gentle temperature—requires fewer precautions than any of the techniques demonstrated in this chapter. Frogs' legs need a dusting of flour to keep them from sticking, but many other ingredients—such as brains, sweetbreads, liver and artichokes—can be sautéed without any protection.

Skewers of mussels, alternated with chunks of bacon, are brushed with butter before the start of cooking. The coating of butter will not only nourish the food under the searing heat but will also hold a layer of fine breadcrumbs.

Colourful Baked Dishes

Gratins are among the most adaptable of hot hors-d'oeuvre—and among the most appealing. Combinations of raw or pre-cooked foods are baked together until a crust forms and the dish is ready to serve. If the ingredients are topped with bread-crumbs or grated cheese, the gratin will acquire an especially crisp surface. In any case, use a cooking vessel that is shallow and wide: it will give room for a good expanse of topping and allow the food to heat through quickly.

Although sauces are often among the ingredients, they are not obligatory. But each dish should include some moist ele-ment—sautéed onions, for example—to prevent dryness. The gratins shown here are only two of many possible variations. On the right, boned raw sardines are rolled round a spinach and onion stuffing, embedded in some of the same mixture and topped with breadcrumbs (*recipe, page 156*). In the gratin below, pre-cooked sweet red peppers, rice and prawns are layered with onion sauce, then covered with breadcrumbs sautéed in butter.

Sardines Arrayed Dramatically

1 Boning sardines. Scale the sardines by rubbing your thumb over the fish. Cut the head off each sardine, slit open its belly and gut it. Ease the rib bones free, pull the backbone and rib bones away from the flesh (*above*) and cut or pinch off the backbone at the tail end. Rinse the fish.

2 Stuffing sardines. Spread the sardines on a towel to drain. Sauté chopped onions in oil. Mix parboiled, chopped spinach (*page 8*) with the onion, and sauté the mixture briefly. Put half of it in a gratin dish; spoon some on to the head end of each fish and roll it up towards the tail (*above*). Put the rolls into the gratin dish.

Prawns and Peppers Layered with Rice

1 Preparing a gratin. Grill and peel sweet red peppers (*page 13*); halve the peppers and seed them. Cook rice and prepare fresh breadcrumbs (*page 7*); sauté the crumbs in butter. Cook prawns, shell and halve them (*page 30*). Make an onion sauce (*page 12*), and pour one-third of the sauce into a buttered gratin dish. Arrange the red pepper halves in a layer over the onion sauce (*above*).

2 Adding a layer of prawns. Put a layer of the prepared rice on top of the red peppers, making sure you cover them completely; using a spoon, spread the rice into an even layer with a smooth surface. Place the halved prawns on top of the rice; some of the sauce that forms the next layer will seep between them and moisten the rice.

3 **Assembling the gratin.** Pack the rolls snugly together so that they hold their shape. Push them well down into the bed of spinach mixture, arranging them all with their tails sticking up.

4 **Moistening with oil.** Prepare either fresh or dry breadcrumbs (*page 7*). Sprinkle the breadcrumbs evenly over the sardine rolls. Dribble some olive oil over the fish; to control the flow of oil, almost cover the mouth of the oil bottle with your thumb.

5 **Serving the fish.** Put the gratin dish into a preheated 220°C (425°F or Mark 7) oven for 15 to 20 minutes. When the top has browned, remove it from the oven. Serve some spinach mixture with each fish.□

3 **Topping the gratin with sauce and breadcrumbs.** Spoon a thick layer of onion sauce over the prawns (*above*); smooth the surface of the sauce with the back of a spoon. Sprinkle the breadcrumbs over the sauce in an even layer, completely covering the sauce.

4 **Baking the gratin.** Put the filled gratin dish into an oven preheated to about 190° to 200°C (375° to 400°F or Mark 5 to 6). Leave the gratin in the oven for 15 to 20 minutes to heat it through and allow all the different flavours to mingle. When the top of the gratin is brown and crusty, remove it from the oven and serve at once.□

Alternative Treatments for Frogs' Legs

The small size and delicate white flesh of frogs' legs make them a natural choice for hors-d'oeuvre. (The legs are the only part of a frog which have enough flesh on them to be worth eating.) If you cannot obtain fresh legs, individually wrapped frozen ones are also good. Both fresh and frozen frogs' legs have had their tough skins removed before being sold. The tender flesh that remains on the legs requires only very brief cooking.

The legs' mild but distinctive flavour is usually heightened by the addition of a sharp, clear-tasting element such as lemon or garlic. In the demonstration on the right (*recipe, page 160*), frogs' legs are baked with a mixture of breadcrumbs, shallots, garlic and parsley. Because the legs are not protected by skin, you must take special care not to let them dry out as they cook. Each leg is coated with melted butter; more butter is spooned over the breadcrumb topping to ensure that it colours evenly as it bakes.

Another way of giving frogs' legs a crisp, golden surface is to sauté them (*below*). For extra flavour, you could marinate them before cooking, in the same way as the meats and vegetables on page 82. To prevent them from sticking to the pan, the legs are dredged with flour; they are then coated with beaten egg to help them crisp and colour.

You can sauté the frogs' legs in either oil or butter, or a mixture of the two; butter burns at a much lower temperature than oil or a mixture of oil and butter, however, and you must reduce the heat accordingly. A last-minute addition of lemon juice and a combination of finely chopped parsley and garlic—a *persillade*—adds zest to the finished dish.

Depending on size, from three to six pairs of frogs' legs for each guest is a normal helping for an hors-d'oeuvre. No knives and forks are necessary—these crisp little morsels are best enjoyed eaten with your fingers.

A Gratin with Buttery Breadcrumbs

1 **Mixing breadcrumbs with herbs.** Finely chop shallots and parsley. Make some breadcrumbs with slightly dry, day-old bread (*page 7*) and sieve the crumbs. Chop a peeled garlic clove. Mix together all the ingredients in a shallow dish.

Sautéed Legs with a Parsley Finish

1 **Sautéing frogs' legs.** Season frogs' legs with salt and pepper. Dredge the legs with flour, and then dip the legs in lightly beaten egg. Cover the bottom of a large sauté pan with oil. Heat the oil over medium heat and add the frogs' legs.

2 **Turning the frogs' legs.** To ensure that the frogs' legs cook evenly, arrange them in a single layer in the pan. Do not crowd them, or they will stick to each other. Sauté them until their undersides are coloured—about 5 minutes—then turn each one over carefully with a fork.

3 **Garnishing with persillade.** Finely chop parsley and garlic to make a *persillade*. Sauté the frogs' legs for another 2 to 3 minutes, until they are cooked through and golden-brown all over. Scatter the *persillade* over the frogs' legs, add a little lemon juice and serve immediately. □

2 **Buttering frogs' legs.** Melt butter in a small, heavy saucepan; pour it into a shallow dish and let it cool. Rinse the frogs' legs and dry them thoroughly. Salt and pepper the legs, and turn them over in the butter to coat them on all sides.

3 **Coating with breadcrumbs.** One at a time, lift the frogs' legs out of the butter and put them in the dish of breadcrumbs. Sprinkle the breadcrumb mixture on to the frogs' legs and then transfer them to a buttered gratin dish.

4 **Moistening with melted butter.** Fill up any space between the frogs' legs with the breadcrumb mixture, and sprinkle the remaining breadcrumbs over the legs. Spoon melted butter over the surface.

5 **Serving the frogs' legs.** Put the frogs' legs in a preheated 200°C (400°F or Mark 6) oven. Bake them for about 15 to 20 minutes. When the breadcrumb topping is crisp and brown, take the dish out of the oven and serve the frogs' legs.□

Crisp Coatings for Moist Delicacies

If protected against drying by some form of coating—batter, perhaps, or the egg and flour mixture used here—most vegetables, meats or seafood can be deep fried to yield a simple but appetizing hors-d'oeuvre. You can make fritters from a single ingredient—artichokes or prawns, for example—but several foods deep fried at once make a more intriguing offering. In this demonstration, courgettes, young artichoke hearts, chicken livers and calf's brains are cooked together. Sweetbreads (*page 32*) and tiny lamb chops could be included and any number of other vegetables, from mushrooms to cauliflower.

Some vegetables—mature artichokes, cauliflower and French beans, for example—will need a preliminary parboiling so that they cook through in the same time as the other foods. Here, the vegetables and liver are used raw, but the brains, which require longer cooking, are first poached. For extra flavour, you can marinate any ingredient before deep frying it. The meats and vegetables in this demonstration are steeped in lemon juice, olive oil and finely chopped onion and herbs.

After they are marinated, the meats and vegetables are dusted with flour and dipped in beaten egg—which will cook to a deliciously crisp surface. In the case of a garnish such as the parsley shown opposite, no protective coating is needed; the aim is to crisp the parsley rather than to retain its moisture.

For the deep-frying medium, you can choose either a neutrally flavoured vegetable oil—or olive oil, which will impart its own unmistakable flavour to the fritters. You must use at least enough oil to immerse the ingredients completely. So that the oil seals the surface coatings of the foods instantly, instead of penetrating them and making them greasy, it should be preheated to 190°C (375°F). Check the temperature with a deep-frying thermometer, or drop a small cube of bread into the oil: if the bread sizzles instantly on contact with the oil and browns within 45 seconds, the oil has reached the right temperature. Cook only a few morsels at a time, or the temperature of the oil will drop dramatically.

1 **Marinating the ingredients.** Slice courgettes lengthwise into thin strips and prepare artichoke hearts (*page 28*). Poach brains (*page 33*) and then cut them into large cubes. Remove any bile stains from chicken livers (*page 32*). Place all the prepared ingredients in a large dish and sprinkle over them finely chopped onion, parsley, chives, tarragon and chervil. Squeeze a lemon through slightly opened fingers to collect any pips (*above, left*). Dribble olive oil over the ingredients, barely moistening them (*above, right*). Season the meats and vegetables according to taste with salt and pepper.

4 **Deep frying the morsels.** Pour oil into a large pan to a depth of at least 7.5 cm (3 inches); for safety the pan should be no more than two-thirds full. Heat the oil to 190°C (375°F). Beat one or two eggs in a shallow bowl. Dip each floured piece of meat and vegetable into the beaten egg and lower a few pieces, one at a time, into the hot oil (*above*).

5 **Completing cooking.** After about 2 to 3 minutes—when the lower surfaces of the fritters are golden—turn the pieces over with a fork. The other sides will take less time to cook: about 1 minute. When the fritters are uniformly golden, lift them out with a wire spider. Remove any floating particles of coating before adding a new batch to the hot oil.

2 **Tossing the ingredients.** Use your hands to toss the ingredients with the marinade (*above*) until each piece of meat and vegetable is well coated. Cover with a cloth and leave it at room temperature for at least 30 minutes to let the pieces absorb the marinade flavours.

3 **Adding flour.** Sieve a thin layer of flour on to a large, shallow tray. Place each piece of meat and vegetable individually on the tray and sieve more flour over them (*above*) to coat all their surfaces lightly.

1 **Drying parsley.** Wash parsley sprigs under running water and shake them vigorously. Place the sprigs on a towel. Fold the towel over the sprigs (*above*) and pat completely dry.

6 **Serving the fritters.** To drain the fritters of excess oil, transfer them to a dish lined with absorbent paper. Keep the fritters warm in a low 100°C (200°F or Mark ¼) oven until all the batches are cooked. Transfer the fritters to a napkin-lined plate and serve them with lemon wedges and, if you like, some fried parsley (*box, right*).□

2 **Frying and draining.** Drop the dried parsley sprigs all at once into deep oil heated to 190°C (375°F). Step back from the pan: the oil will splutter. Cook for about 30 seconds, until the parsley is crisp. With a wire spider, lift the sprigs from the oil and place them on a paper towel to dry.

A Protective Coating for Brochettes

A particularly appealing way to deep fry a mixture of meats and vegetables is to thread the ingredients together on to skewers, thus producing ready-made individual servings. The French name for skewers—brochettes—is often used to describe the whole presentation. Any of the ingredients mentioned on page 82 may be treated in this way. In the demonstration on the right, the brochettes are composed of pre-cooked sweetbreads, morels and ham (*recipe, page 150*).

A simple coating of egg or egg white with breadcrumbs would serve to seal the juices in with a crisp outer layer. Or, for a richer effect, you can cover the ingredients with a thick, smooth coating before adding a final layer of egg and breadcrumbs. The inner coating in this case is made from the same ingredients as a white sauce (*page 12*): flour, butter and milk. The proportion of flour is very high, even greater than in a soufflé base (*page 70*), so that the coating—once cooked and cooled—is stiff enough to cling readily to the ingredients. A rich, gelatinous stock can be substituted for the milk; the coating can be flavoured by the addition of puréed spinach or any grated hard cheese, and enriched with egg yolks.

Wooden skewers are traditionally used for deep frying, then replaced with silver skewers before serving; the intense heat of the oil could damage silver skewers. Here, wooden skewers are used for both cooking and serving. Once the ingredients are threaded on to a skewer and smeared with the inner coating, the brochettes are chilled in the refrigerator for several hours so that the inner coating sets firmly enough to hold the outer coating securely. The outer coating, too, must be given time to set: in the hot oil, the inner coating softens to a sauce and the firm outer shell of egg and breadcrumbs is all that keeps the brochettes intact.

1 Preparing a coating. Melt butter in a saucepan over a low heat. Blend flour into the butter and cook, stirring, for 2 minutes. Pour in milk and whisk for a further 5 minutes. Remove the pan from the stove. Stir grated cheese—Parmesan cheese is used here—into the hot mixture; its heat will melt the cheese. Let the mixture cool a little, then incorporate egg yolks.

2 Threading skewers. Prepare and press sweetbreads (*page 32*) and cut them into cubes. Soak, trim and halve morels (*page 29*). Sauté the morels and sweetbreads together in butter for about 10 minutes. Cube mild-flavoured cooked ham. Then thread the sweetbreads, morels and ham on to wooden skewers about 15 cm (6 inches) long to form brochettes.

6 Frying brochettes. Pour oil into a frying pan until it is at least 2.5 cm (1 inch) deep. Heat the oil to a temperature of about 190°C (375°F). Lower three or four brochettes at a time into the hot oil (*above, left*)—any more would reduce the temperature significantly. Cook the brochettes for about 3 minutes until they turn golden on one side. With a fork, turn them over and cook them on the other side for about 2 minutes. Then carefully lift the cooked brochettes from the frying pan with a wire spider (*above, right*) or fish slice.

3 **Coating brochettes.** With a spatula or spoon (*above*), paste the coating over the brochettes so that the ingredients are covered thickly. Place each brochette on a shallow tray. Place the tray of coated brochettes in the refrigerator for at least 3 hours, until the coating hardens.

4 **Dipping brochettes in egg.** Beat whole eggs in a shallow dish and spread a thick layer of dry breadcrumbs in a shallow tray. Dip each brochette in the egg so that it is covered completely, then transfer the brochette to the tray of breadcrumbs.

5 **Adding breadcrumbs.** Sprinkle some of the breadcrumbs over the brochette so that it is thickly and completely covered (*above*). Place the brochettes on a tray sprinkled with some of the breadcrumbs and leave them for about an hour in the refrigerator so that the breadcrumbs set in the egg coating.

7 **Serving brochettes.** Place the cooked brochettes on a plate covered with an absorbent towel, which will soak up any excess oil. Keep them warm in the oven until all are ready to serve. Transfer them to a napkin-lined plate. Serve each diner a brochette accompanied with tomato purée or, as shown here, a chunky, spicy tomato sauce (*page 14*). □

Wrappings for Deep-Fried Stuffings

Securely wrapped in pastry dough or a pancake, any lightly bound stuffing mixture (*pages 6-9*) can be deep fried. The wrapping both holds the stuffing together and protects it from the oil's intense heat.

On the right, spoonfuls of stuffing are sandwiched between two thin layers of dough, which are divided into squares to make outsize ravioli. Any plain or puff pastry dough (*Chapter 1*) is suitable for the ravioli. The dough used here is a mixture of flour, egg, water and olive oil—identical to the olive oil pastry dough on page 22 except that, to create a firmer wrapper in the deep-fried version, the proportion of oil is halved.

Pancakes for deep frying (*below*) are made from the same batter as those for a gratin (*page 56*). But, so that the pancakes do not overcook when immersed in hot oil, they are initially cooked on one side only. Raw side outwards, the pancakes are neatly parcelled round the stuffing and sealed with egg. Deep frying cooks the raw surface to a crisp brown exterior.

Cutting Squares for Ravioli

1 **Arranging the stuffing.** Prepare a stuffing: here, spring onions, herbs, soft white cheese, grated Parmesan and chopped roast lamb. If your stuffing contains hot foods, let it cool completely. Roll olive oil dough out into two large rectangles, each about 2 mm ($\frac{1}{16}$ inch) thick. Spoon portions of stuffing on to one rectangle, 5 cm (2 inches) apart.

2 **Covering the stuffing.** With a pastry brush, dampen the dough between the mounds of stuffing, so that it will stick easily to the second layer of dough. Spread the second rectangle of dough loosely over the first layer.

Sealing Pancakes Round a Filling

1 **Stuffing pancakes.** Prepare a batter from flour, milk, egg and melted butter. Cook pancakes on one side only; stack them on a plate. Prepare a stuffing—here, egg, *ricotta* cheese, spring onions, herbs and seasonings. Place a heaped spoonful of the stuffing mixture near one edge of the cooked side of each pancake (*above*).

2 **Shaping the pancakes.** Beat an egg in a small bowl. Fold the edge of the pancake to cover the filling. With a pastry brush, moisten the uncovered area of each pancake with the beaten egg (*above, left*). Fold the sides into the centre of each pancake. Brush the newly exposed raw side of the pancake with egg (*above, right*). Roll up each pancake and seal the flap with more of the beaten egg.

3 **Shaping ravioli.** With your fingertips, firmly press the border of the dough so that the two layers stick together. Press across and down between the mounds of stuffing (*above*) so that each heap of stuffing is sealed in on all four sides.

4 **Cutting ravioli.** With a pastry wheel, trim the border of the dough. Cut across and down between the heaped stuffing to make squares of ravioli (*above*). Heat sufficient oil to completely immerse the ravioli to about 190°C (375°F). Deep fry the ravioli a few at a time (*page 82*).

5 **Serving the ravioli.** Lift the ravioli from the pan and place them on a warm plate covered with an absorbent towel. Keep them in a warm oven while you cook the rest. Serve them as soon as the last batch is cooked. Accompany the ravioli with a sauce, if you like—a creamed tomato sauce (*page 15*), as here, or a chunky tomato sauce (*page 14*).□

3 **Cooking the shaped pancakes.** For ease of handling, fry the pancakes in a wire basket (*above*) or a fairly shallow pan (*page 84*). Heat oil to 190°C (375°F). Place two or three pancakes in a basket, flap sides down, and lower them into the oil. Cook the pancakes on one side for about 2 minutes until golden-brown. Turn them over and cook the other side.

4 **Serving the pancakes.** When the pancakes are uniformly coloured, lift the basket out of the oil and tip the pancakes on to absorbent paper. Keep them warm in the oven. When all are cooked, transfer them to a large plate covered with a folded napkin (*above*). If you like, serve with a tomato sauce (*page 14*) or lemon wedges.□

Grilling on Skewers

The aim of grilling is to sear a piece of food on all its surfaces but to keep it succulent within. The easiest way to grill morsels is to thread them on skewers so that you can rotate a number of them together and keep them well basted at the same time. Here, skewers support mussels alternated with bacon: a combination typical of Provençal cookery (*recipe, page 162*).

Before grilling, the morsels are first steamed—the most practical way of extracting them from their shells. To equalize the grilling times, the bacon is also pre-cooked. But you could, instead, grill a selection of raw ingredients on skewers—chicken, liver, mushrooms, and pieces of onion and peppers, for example.

In this demonstration, the skewered ingredients are coated with melted butter to help keep them from becoming dry; the butter also holds fine, dried breadcrumbs that give the brochettes a crisp texture. Instead of butter, you could use beaten egg to hold the crumbs and baste the brochettes with oil during grilling. The egg will seal in the mussels' juices.

1 **Assembling skewers.** Parboil pieces of bacon and sauté them in butter (*page 33*). Clean mussels and steam them until they open (*page 31*). Shell the mussels, place them in a bowl, and keep them moist with a spoonful or two of their cooking liquid. Alternate the pieces of bacon and the mussels on long metal skewers (*above*).

2 **Coating with breadcrumbs.** Brush melted butter—as here—or beaten egg on to the mussels and bacon. Grate dry bread to fine crumbs and put in a shallow tray. Roll each brochette in the breadcrumbs and sprinkle more breadcrumbs over the top so that all the surfaces are covered (*above*). Rest the skewers on the sides of a baking tray so that the ingredients are suspended.

3 **Cooking brochettes.** Place the tray under a hot grill. Allow the brochettes to cook for 2 minutes until one side has browned. Turn the brochettes to cook for 2 minutes more on the other side. Diners can slide the cooked mussels and bacon from the skewers on to warmed plates. Garnish with watercress, as here, or with shredded lettuce.▢

Anthology of Recipes

The hot hors-d'oeuvre recipes that follow have been selected by the Editors and consultants for this volume from among the best ever published. The Anthology spans 2,000 years and includes recipes by more than 125 writers, from the Roman gastronome Apicius, writing in the first century B.C., to such modern authorities as Michel Guérard, Roger Vergé and Jane Grigson. Most of the recipes in this volume are from France and Italy, but there are also dishes from more than 20 other countries, including recipes from the Far East, Central Asia and Eastern Europe. A number of the recipes—some of them from rare and out-of-print books in private collections—have never before been published in English. The recipes cover a spectrum of dishes from simple liver kebabs and the traditional garlic-flavoured snails from Provence to elaborate combinations such as stuffed fillets of sole in pastry cases and an exotic assembly of anchovies with oranges. Whatever the sources, the emphasis is on authentic dishes meticulously prepared with fresh, natural ingredients

Since many early recipe writers did not specify amounts of ingredients, these have been judiciously added, and introductory notes printed in italics have been supplied by the Editors where appropriate. Modern terms have been substituted for archaic language, but to preserve the character of the original and to create a true anthology, the authors' texts have been changed as little as possible. In cases where the cooking directions may seem somewhat abrupt, the reader should refer to the appropriate demonstration in the front of the book to find the method in question explained more fully. Cooking terms and ingredients that may be unfamiliar are explained in the combined General Index and Glossary at the end of the book.

The Anthology is organized according to the chapters in the techniques section of the book. However, the "Little Stews" section has been expanded to include main course stews that may be served in smaller portions as a first course. Recipes for standard preparations—basic doughs, stocks and sauces, pancakes and a mousseline forcemeat—appear at the end.

All recipe ingredients are listed in order of use, with the main or title ingredients first. Metric and imperial measures for each ingredient are listed in separate columns. The two sets of figures are not exact equivalents, but are consistent for each recipe. Working from either metric or imperial weights and measures will produce equally good results, but the two systems should not be mixed for the same recipe. All spoon measures are level.

Pies and Tarts

Shabra Chipple and Bacon Flan

Shabra is an old Cornish farmhouse name. The *chipples* (spring onions) are sliced lengthwise and used like leeks.

To make one 23 cm (9 inch) flan

6	spring onions, sliced lengthwise	6
4	rashers streaky bacon	4
250 g	shortcrust dough *(page 165)*	8 oz
15 g	dripping or lard	½ oz
4	eggs	4
90 g	cream cheese	3 oz
2 tbsp	finely chopped parsley	2 tbsp
	salt	
	freshly ground black pepper	

Roll out the shortcrust dough and use it to line a 23 cm (9 inch) buttered flan case. Press foil over the dough and bake it in a preheated 200°C (400°F or Mark 6) oven for 10 minutes or until the pastry is firm. Reduce the oven heat to 180°C (350°F or Mark 4), remove the foil and bake the flan case for a further 10 minutes so that it is crisp but not coloured. Take it out of the oven and leave it to cool.

Remove the rind from the bacon and roughly chop the rashers. Heat the dripping or lard in a frying pan, add the bacon pieces and the rinds and cook over a medium heat for 5 minutes. Discard the rinds and lift out the bacon with a slotted spoon. Arrange the bacon in the flan case.

Add the spring onions to the juices in the frying pan and cook over a low heat until they are soft and transparent. Drain off the fat and arrange the spring onions over the bacon.

Beat the eggs with the cream cheese (a rotary beater is best for this) until the mixture is smooth. Mix in the parsley and season fairly generously with salt and pepper. Pour the egg mixture over the bacon and spring onions, put the flan into the oven and bake it at 180°C (350°F or Mark 4) for 20 to 30 minutes or until the eggs are just set. Cover the flan with foil if the edges of the pastry tend to get too brown.

MARIKA HANBURY TENISON
RECIPES FROM A COUNTRY KITCHEN

Rich Tomato Tart

To make one 20 cm (8 inch) tart

6	tomatoes, skinned, seeded and halved	6
350 g	shortcrust dough *(page 165)*	12 oz
	salt	
3 tbsp	white breadcrumbs, browned in the oven	3 tbsp
1 tsp	chopped mixed herbs (chives, thyme, parsley, rosemary)	1 tsp
5 tbsp	double cream	5 tbsp
90 g	Gruyère, finely grated	3 oz
½ tsp	anchovy essence	½ tsp
	grated nutmeg	

Prepare the dough, chill it well, roll it out and use it to line a 20 cm (8 inch) flan tin. Sprinkle the halved tomatoes with salt and leave them for 30 minutes. Tip away any liquid and dry the halves well with absorbent paper.

Cover the bottom of the flan with the breadcrumbs and arrange the tomatoes on top. Dust with the herbs. Mix the cream and cheese together, season with the anchovy essence and a little nutmeg and spoon the mixture over the tomatoes.

Bake in a preheated 200°C (400°F or Mark 6) oven for 30 minutes, until the top is golden-brown. Serve hot.

DORSET FEDERATION OF WOMEN'S INSTITUTES
WHAT'S COOKING IN DORSET

Lenten Pie

Pasticcio di Magro

Scorzonera is a black-skinned variety of salsify. If it is not available, use salsify.

To make one 30 cm (12 inch) pie

600 g	shortcrust dough *(page 165)*	1¼ lb
	Rice filling	
200 g	cooked rice	7 oz
1	onion, chopped	1
30 g	butter	1 oz
	salt	
2	eggs, beaten	2
30 g	Parmesan cheese, grated	1 oz
	pepper	

	Vegetable filling	
1	onion, finely chopped	1
2	sticks celery, finely chopped	2
2	carrots, finely chopped	2
75 g	mushrooms, finely chopped	2½ oz
2 tbsp	finely chopped parsley	2 tbsp
1	scorzonera, simmered in water with the juice of a lemon for 40 minutes	1
300 g	shelled peas, parboiled for 5 minutes	10 oz
6	artichoke bottoms, quartered	6
45 g	butter	1½ oz
	salt	
1 tbsp	flour	1 tbsp
8 cl	hot water	3 fl oz
45 g	Parmesan cheese, grated	1½ oz
	pepper	

	Fish filling	
500 g	fish (for example, grey mullet, salmon-trout)	1 lb
8 cl	oil	3 fl oz
	salt	
2 tbsp	chopped parsley	2 tbsp
2	garlic cloves	2
2	tomatoes, skinned, seeded and chopped	2
50 g	pine-nuts, pounded	2 oz

To make the rice filling, sauté the onion in the butter with a pinch of salt. Add the rice and stir well. Remove the pan from the heat and leave to cool. Then add the beaten eggs, the cheese and a pinch of pepper. Mix well and reserve.

To make the vegetable filling, sauté the onion, celery, carrots, mushrooms and the finely chopped parsley in the butter with a pinch of salt. When the vegetables have begun to brown, add the scorzonera, peas, artichoke bottoms, flour and a pinch of salt and cook for a few minutes. Pour on hot water to barely cover the vegetables, reduce the heat and simmer the mixture for 15 minutes. Remove the pan from the heat, add the grated cheese and a pinch of pepper and stir well. Reserve.

Sauté the fish in the oil, with a pinch of salt, add the chopped parsley, the garlic and the tomatoes and stew for 10 to 12 minutes. Remove the fish from the pan, reserving the cooking liquid. Put the pounded pine-nuts into the cooking liquid and strain the liquid through a fine sieve. Fillet the fish and discard the bones and skin. Return the fish to the cooking liquid and pour the mixture into the pan containing the vegetable filling. Mix well.

Roll out two-thirds of the dough and use it to line a 30 cm (12 inch) deep pie dish. Put a layer of half the rice filling in the bottom of the pie dish, then pour in the combined fish and vegetable filling. Top with the rest of the rice filling. Roll out the rest of the dough to make a lid for the pie. Bake the pie in a preheated 180°C (350°F or Mark 4) oven for 1 hour or until it is golden-brown. Serve hot.

EMANUELE ROSSI (EDITOR)
LA VERA CUCINIERA GENOVESE

Poor Man's Pie

Tourte au Pauvre Homme

To make one 23 cm (9 inch) pie

350 g	shortcrust dough (*page 165*)	12 oz
3 tbsp	fat	3 tbsp
1	onion, chopped	1
2 or 3	tomatoes, skinned, seeded and chopped	2 or 3
About 3 tbsp	flour	About 3 tbsp
8	black olives, stoned	8
125 g	mushrooms, sliced	4 oz
	chopped thyme	
2 tbsp	chopped parsley	2 tbsp
	salt and freshly ground black pepper	
500 g	mixed sausage-meat and chopped lean bacon	1 lb

Divide the dough into two pieces, one twice the size of the other. Use the larger piece to line a 23 cm (9 inch) pie dish.

Melt the fat and cook the onion in it until it has softened, about 10 minutes. Add the tomatoes and sprinkle in the flour; stir constantly until the sauce thickens. Add the olives, mushrooms, a pinch of thyme, the parsley and salt and pepper. Simmer the mixture for 15 minutes. Remove it from the heat and stir in the sausage-meat and bacon.

Pour the mixture into the pie dish. Roll out the reserved dough and use it to make a lid for the pie. Trim and seal the edges. Cut a 1 cm (½ inch) hole in the centre of the pie to allow the steam to escape. Bake the pie in a preheated 190°C (375°F or Mark 5) oven for 30 minutes or until it is golden-brown.

HUGUETTE CASTIGNAC
LA CUISINE OCCITANE

Stargazey Pie

The technique of making this traditional Cornish dish is demonstrated on page 18. The pie can also be shaped into a long rectangle and baked with the fish heads and tails sticking out on either side.

There are all kinds of variations on the basic recipe. Sometimes the undercrust of the dough is omitted, and the fish laid on a bed of breadcrumbs, chopped onion and herbs, the plate being well buttered first. Sometimes cider, or a custard of egg and cream, is poured over the fish to make a moister pie.

To make one 23 cm (9 inch) pie

300 g	shortcrust dough (*page 165*)	10 oz
8	large sardines or medium-sized herrings, gutted, boned and cleaned, heads left on	8
	salt and pepper	
6 tbsp	finely chopped onion, mixed with 1 tbsp finely chopped fresh parsley and 1 tbsp finely chopped fresh chives, or 2 tbsp French mustard	6 tbsp
8	rashers streaky bacon (optional)	8
2	hard-boiled eggs, chopped (optional)	2
3 tbsp	warm milk mixed with ⅛ tsp powdered saffron, or 1 egg, beaten	3 tbsp

Roll out half the dough in a circle and use it to line a 23 cm (9 inch) buttered pie plate. Season each fish lavishly inside with salt and pepper, then *either* with the finely chopped onion and herbs *or* with the French mustard. Fold them into shape again and arrange them on the dough so that the heads lie evenly round the rim. If you like, put the bacon rashers and the hard-boiled egg between the fish. Roll out the rest of the dough and cut a round blanket to cover the fish, all but their heads, so that the dough circle is the diameter of the plate less the rim. Press the dough down firmly between each fish. Brush with saffron milk or beaten egg. Bake the pie in a preheated 200°C (400°F or Mark 6) oven for 30 minutes, then lower the heat to 180°C (350°F or Mark 4) and bake for a further 15 minutes.

JANE GRIGSON
FISH COOKERY

Small Hot Pies

Petits Pâtés Chauds

To make four 12.5 cm (5 inch) pies

500 g	shortcrust dough (*page 165*)	1 lb
2	salt anchovies, soaked, filleted, rinsed and chopped	2
2	shallots, finely chopped	2
1	garlic clove, finely chopped	1
1 tbsp	chopped parsley	1 tbsp
1 tbsp	finely cut chives	1 tbsp
2 tbsp	olive oil	2 tbsp
125 g	cooked veal, finely chopped	4 oz
125 g	ham, finely chopped	4 oz
60 g	beef marrow, finely chopped	2 oz
2	egg yolks, 1 beaten	2
	salt and pepper	
1 tbsp	brandy	1 tbsp

Roll out the dough and cut it into eight 12.5 cm (5 inch) rounds. To make the filling, mix the anchovy fillets, shallots, garlic, parsley and chives and pound them in a mortar. Add the oil and leave the mixture to marinate for 15 to 20 minutes.

Drain the anchovy mixture of excess oil and combine it with the chopped meats; mix well and bind with an egg yolk. Season with salt and pepper; take care not to oversalt. Moisten with the brandy. Spoon the filling on to four of the dough rounds. Cover with the remaining rounds. Moisten the edges of the dough with a little water and seal them carefully.

Place the pies on a buttered baking sheet. Glaze them with the beaten egg yolk and bake them in a preheated 220°C (425°F or Mark 7) oven for 20 to 25 minutes until they are golden-brown on top.

MICHEL BARBEROUSSE
CUISINE PROVENÇALE

Preserved Goose Pie

Tourtière d'Oie

To make preserved goose, take 1 kg (2½ lb) of goose breast or leg and sprinkle it with a large pinch of mixed herbs reduced to powder in a mortar. Add a pinch of salt and leave it overnight in an earthenware pot. Wipe the goose dry. Combine goose fat from inside the bird with 6 tablespoons of water and render the fat by melting it over a low heat. When nothing solid is left but the cracklings, strain off the fat. Cook the goose gently, well bathed in this fat, for 1 to 1½ hours, turning it after about 15 minutes. Reserve the fat. If the goose is put into a jar, covered with the fat and sealed, it will keep in a cool place for about two months. Preserved goose from France, known as confit d'oie, *can be bought in speciality grocer shops.*

	To make one 25 cm (10 inch) pie	
1 kg	leftover roast goose or preserved goose, boned, cut into small pieces, roasting juices or fat reserved	2½ lb
500 g	shortcrust dough (*page 165*)	1 lb
500 g	apples, peeled, cored and diced	1 lb
100 g	dry breadcrumbs	3½ oz
1 tbsp	sugar	1 tbsp
	salt and freshly ground pepper	
3 tbsp	dry red wine	3 tbsp
1	egg, lightly beaten with 2 tsp water	1

Divide the dough into two pieces, one twice as large as the other. Roll out the larger piece and use it to line a 25 cm (10 inch) pie dish. Line the pie shell with a layer of pieces of goose, cover with a layer of diced apple and sprinkle with the dry breadcrumbs. Add a sprinkling of sugar and season with salt and pepper. Continue layering in this way until all the ingredients are used up, finishing with a layer of breadcrumbs. Sprinkle the dish with the reserved goose fat or roasting juices and the red wine. Roll out the rest of the dough and use it to make a lid for the pie. Trim the edges and seal them firmly. Make a 5 mm (¼ inch) funnel or incision in the centre of the lid, to allow steam to escape during cooking. Brush the lid with the beaten egg and bake it in a preheated 190°C (375°F or Mark 5) oven for about 40 minutes or until the pastry is lightly browned on top.

HUGUETTE CASTIGNAC
LA CUISINE OCCITANE

Petit Patties

	To make 12 tartlets	
500 g	shortcrust dough (*page 165*)	1 lb
250 g	veal, minced	8 oz
250 g	bacon, minced	8 oz
250 g	beef suet, minced	8 oz
½ tsp	salt	½ tsp
	pepper	
1 tbsp	*fines herbes*	1 tbsp
125 g	mushrooms, chopped	4 oz
1	egg yolk, beaten	1

In a bowl mix the veal, bacon and suet together and season with the salt, pepper and *fines herbes* and add the mushrooms. Put the mixture in a saucepan and cook, stirring frequently, over a medium heat for 8 to 10 minutes or until the mixture is just beginning to brown.

Roll out two-thirds of the dough quite thickly and use it to line 12 tartlet tins. Fill the tins with the meat mixture. Roll out the rest of the dough and cut it out to cover the tartlets. Glaze the dough with egg yolk and bake the tartlets in a preheated 200°C (400°F or Mark 6) oven for about 30 minutes, or until they are golden-brown.

WILLIAM AUGUSTUS HENDERSON
THE HOUSEKEEPER'S INSTRUCTOR, OR, UNIVERSAL FAMILY COOK

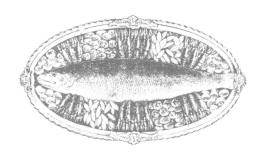

Anchovy Tart

Tarte aux Anchois

This is a Provençal dish. Down there, they call it *piscaladière*. They make it with bread dough instead of shortcrust dough.

	To make one 20 cm (8 inch) square tart	
10	salt anchovies, soaked and well drained, filleted, rinsed and dried	10
350 g	shortcrust dough (*page 165*)	12 oz
300 g	onions, chopped	10 oz
6 tbsp	olive oil	6 tbsp
7	black olives, halved and stoned	7
2	small tomatoes, sliced (optional)	2
	pepper	

Roll out the dough to a thickness of 5 mm (¼ inch) and shape it into a 20 cm (8 inch) square. Lay it on a buttered or oiled baking sheet. Roll the edges of the square inwards to make a narrow rim. Prick the dough all over with a fork.

In a frying pan, cook the onions in 4 tablespoons of the olive oil until they are golden. Spread the onions over the dough. Arrange the anchovies over the onions on a lattice pattern and place a halved olive in the centre of each square formed by the anchovies. Small slices of tomato can be added, if you like. Pepper the tart and sprinkle it with the remaining olive oil.

Bake the tart in a preheated 200°C (400°F or Mark 6) oven for about 30 minutes. Remove it from the oven when the pastry is dry and golden.

ÉDOUARD DE POMIANE
LE CARNET D'ANNA

Corn Pie

For a corn-clam pie, add 125 g (4 oz) chopped raw clams to the corn filling in this recipe.

To make one 23 cm (9 inch) pie

500 g	fresh corn kernels, cut off the cob	1 lb
250 g	shortcrust dough (*page 165*)	8 oz
4	eggs, lightly beaten	4
2 tsp	sugar	2 tsp
1 tsp	salt	1 tsp
	freshly ground pepper	
2 tbsp	flour	2 tbsp
125 g	butter, melted	4 oz

Combine the corn, eggs, sugar, salt and pepper to taste, flour and butter. Roll out half the dough to fit a 23 cm (9 inch) pie dish. Pour the mixture into the pie shell and roll out the rest of the dough to make a top crust, making a vent for the steam to escape. Bake the pie in a preheated 180°C (350°F or Mark 4) oven for 1 hour or until the pie is golden-brown.

BETTY GROFF AND JOSÉ WILSON
GOOD EARTH AND COUNTRY COOKING

Chard, Sausage and Ricotta Pie

Torta di Verdura

To make the sausage-meat, use two parts of lean pork to one part of fatty meat. Chop the meat, put it through a mincer, then season with salt, pepper, and such flavourings as dried mixed herbs, grated nutmeg or ground cloves or allspice.

To make one 25 cm (10 inch) deep-dish pie

2 kg	Swiss chard, ribs removed, parboiled for 1 minute, squeezed dry and chopped	4 lb
250 g	pork sausage-meat	8 oz
250 g	*ricotta* cheese	8 oz
500 g	shortcrust dough (*page 165*)	1 lb
1 to 2 tbsp	olive oil (optional)	1 to 2 tbsp
2	medium-sized onions, finely chopped	2
100 g	Parmesan cheese, grated	3½ oz
4	eggs, lightly beaten	4
	salt	
	freshly ground black pepper	
1	egg white, lightly beaten	1

Crumble the sausage-meat and fry it—in the olive oil if it needs more fat—until it is browned, about 8 to 10 minutes. Remove the sausage-meat with a slotted spoon and set it aside. Remove all but 2 tablespoons of the fat from the pan. Sauté the onions until they begin to colour, about 5 minutes. Remove the pan from the heat, add the chard and mix it with the onions. Then add the Parmesan cheese, *ricotta*, eggs and sausage-meat, and mix well. Add salt and pepper to taste.

Divide the shortcrust dough in half. Return one half to the refrigerator and roll out the other half to fit a 25 cm (10 inch) pie dish. Brush the bottom and sides of the dough with the beaten egg white; reserve a small amount of the white to brush the top crust. Add the filling to the pie.

Roll out the other half of the dough and cover the pie with it, working as quickly as you can, but taking time to make a decorative edge. With a small, sharp knife, make short cuts in the centre of the crust so that steam can escape during cooking. Any remaining dough can be used to make decorative shapes for the pie crust. Brush the remaining egg white on the dough. Bake the pie in a preheated 200° to 220°C (400° to 425°F or Mark 6 to 7) oven for 30 to 40 minutes. The pie will be a rich golden colour when it is done.

JOE FAMULARO AND LOUISE IMPERIALE
THE FESTIVE FAMULARO KITCHEN

Tongue and Cider Pasties

The raisins are improved if plumped out first in a little sherry.

To serve 4

250 g	shortcrust dough (*page 165*)	8 oz
4 tbsp	milk or 1 egg, beaten with 2 tsp water	4 tbsp
	Tongue and cider filling	
200 g	cooked tongue, finely chopped	7 oz
4 tbsp	cider	4 tbsp
50 g	pine-nuts or blanched, crushed almonds	2 oz
50 g	seedless raisins	2 oz
1 tsp	sugar	1 tsp
	salt	
	grated nutmeg	
	ground cloves	

Roll out the dough thinly and cut it into eight 10 cm (4 inch) rounds. Make the filling by blending all the ingredients together thoroughly. Put about 1 tablespoon of the mixture in the centre of each circle of dough, dampen the edges, fold the circle in half and press down. Make two shallow, diagonal cuts in each pasty and brush it with the milk or beaten egg. Grease a baking sheet and put the pasties on it. Bake in a preheated 190°C (375°F or Mark 5) oven for 15 to 20 minutes or until the pastry is crisp and golden.

ANNA MACMIADHACHÁIN
SPANISH REGIONAL COOKERY

Spinach or Chard Pie

Tourte aux Épinards ou aux Feuilles de Bettes

To make one 30 cm (12 inch) pie

1 kg	spinach or Swiss chard, stalks trimmed, Swiss chard ribs removed, green parts blanched in rapidly boiling salted water for 1 minute, drained, squeezed and chopped	2 to 2½ lb
350 g	shortcrust dough (*page 165*)	12 oz
6 tbsp	chopped parsley	6 tbsp
4 or 5	garlic cloves, chopped	4 or 5
100 g	butter	3½ oz
6	eggs, beaten	6
150 g	Gruyère cheese, grated	5 oz
½ litre	milk	16 fl oz
	salt and pepper	

Mix the chopped spinach or Swiss chard with the parsley and garlic. Chop the mixture together and sauté it in the butter for 7 to 8 minutes. Leave it to cool slightly, then beat in the eggs, grated cheese and the milk. Season to taste.

Divide the dough in half and use one piece to line a buttered, deep 30 cm (12 inch) pie dish. Roll out the rest of the dough and use it to cover the filling. Bake the pie in a preheated 190°C (375°F or Mark 5) oven for 45 minutes or until the pastry is golden-brown.

HENRI PHILIPPON
CUISINE DE PROVENCE

❖

Spinach, Bacon and Cheese Pie

Erbazzone Reggiano

To make one 23 cm (9 inch) pie

1 kg	spinach, trimmed, parboiled in plenty of boiling salted water for 1 minute, drained, squeezed and chopped	2 lb
150 g	green bacon, chopped	5 oz
60 g	Parmesan cheese, grated	2 oz
300 g	shortcrust dough (*page 165*)	10 oz
2 tbsp	oil	2 tbsp
4 tbsp	chopped parsley	4 tbsp
1	garlic clove, chopped	1
1	egg	1
	salt	

Sauté the spinach in the oil with 125 g (4 oz) of the bacon. Stir in the parsley and garlic. Remove the pan from the heat and mix in the egg and the Parmesan cheese and a pinch of salt.

Roll out two-thirds of the dough into a layer about 5 mm (¼ inch) thick and use it to line a 23 cm (9 inch) pie dish. Spoon in the filling. Roll out the remaining dough into a circle big enough to cover the dish. Lay the dough over the filling and seal the pie by pressing the edges together with the tines of a fork. Trim the edge of the pie and prick airholes in the top layer of dough. Sprinkle the rest of the chopped bacon over the pie crust and bake the pie in a preheated 200°C (400°F or Mark 6) for about 1 hour or until the crust is golden-brown.

WAVERLEY ROOT
THE BEST OF ITALIAN COOKING

❖

Herb Flan

Pour Faire une Tourte

This recipe comes from "a treatise on morals and domestic economy", written in about 1393 by "un bourgeois Parisien". Fennel bulb can be substituted for wild fennel; Curd, ricotta or fresh goat cheese for the soft cheese; Cheddar, Gruyère or dried goat cheese for the semi-hard cheese; Parmesan for the pressed cheese. Baking a pastry case blind is shown on page 68.

To make one 20 cm (8 inch) flan

175 g	shortcrust dough (*page 165*)	6 oz
4 tbsp	finely chopped parsley	4 tbsp
2 tbsp	finely chopped chervil	2 tbsp
1	young wild fennel heart, finely chopped	1
250 g	Swiss chard, ribs removed, finely chopped	8 oz
125 g	spinach, trimmed and finely chopped	4 oz
125 g	soft cheese, mashed	4 oz
125 g	semi-hard cheese, cut into small cubes	4 oz
4	eggs, well beaten	4
2 tsp	mixed spice or 1 cm (½ inch) of ginger root, finely chopped	2 tsp
	salt and pepper	
60 g	old pressed cheese, grated	2 oz

Butter a 20 cm (8 inch) flan tin. Roll out the dough to fit the tin and bake it blind. Mix the chopped vegetables and herbs together. In a bowl mix the soft and semi-hard cheeses with the beaten eggs; then put the vegetables into the bowl and mix all together; add the mixed spice. Alternatively, before mixing the vegetables, cheese and eggs, pound the ginger root in a mortar; then add the cheeses, eggs and vegetables to the mortar and mix them. Season to taste, pour the mixture into the pastry case, and sprinkle it with the grated cheese.

Bake the flan in a preheated 190°C (375°F or Mark 5) oven for about 20 minutes or until set. Eat it hot.

LE MÉNAGIER DE PARIS

Cabbage and Chopped Beef Pie

Coulibiac au Chou et au Boeuf Haché

Any type of puff dough is suitable for this recipe, including rough-puff and olive oil puff dough (recipes, page 165). The technique for making cabbage and chopped beef pie, using olive oil puff dough, is shown on page 24.

Coulibiac is a Russian speciality. You can substitute *kasha*—buckwheat groats—for the rice. Lightly brown 200 g (7 oz) of the groats in 50 g (2 oz) of butter, pour in ½ litre (16 fl oz) of stock or boiling water and simmer for 15 to 20 minutes, until the liquid is completely absorbed. Do not use the rice or buckwheat groats until they have completely cooled; they should be prepared on the previous day.

To make one 30 by 20 cm (12 by 8 inch) pie

4	green cabbage leaves, central ribs removed, parboiled for 3 minutes, drained and coarsely chopped	4
60g	leftover boiled beef, chopped	2 oz
500 g	rough-puff dough *(page 165)*	1 lb
1	onion, finely chopped, cooked in butter until soft	1
125 g	cold, boiled rice	4oz
	salt and pepper	
100 g	butter	3½ oz
3	eggs, hard boiled, peeled and chopped	3
1	egg white, diluted in a few drops of water	1
2	egg yolks, diluted in 1 tbsp water	2

Divide the dough into two, one piece double the size of the other. On a floured working surface, roll out the smaller piece into a rectangle about 30 by 20 cm (12 by 8 inches). Lay the dough rectangle on an oiled baking sheet.

Mix the onion with the rice and spread the mixture evenly over the dough rectangle, leaving a 2 cm (¾ inch) border. Season the chopped cabbage leaves and scatter them over the rice mixture. Cut 60 g (2 oz) of the butter into pieces and dot them over the top. Scatter the chopped, hard-boiled eggs over the cabbage leaves and season again. Add the chopped meat. Preheat the oven to 230°C (450°F or Mark 8).

Roll out the larger piece of dough into a rectangle large enough to adequately cover the lower rectangle and filling. Lay it on top of the filling and seal the top and bottom layers of dough by painting the bottom edge with the egg white and pressing the two edges firmly together. Glaze the pie generously with the egg yolks.

Make a 1 cm (½ inch) hole in the centre of the pie to allow the steam to escape during cooking. Reduce the oven temperature to 220°C (425°F or Mark 7) and bake for 35 minutes, or until the pie is golden-brown on top. Melt the rest of the butter, and when the pie is cooked, pour in the butter through the hole in the centre of the pie.

MIRIAM CENDRARS AND NINETTE LYON (EDITORS)
GRATINS, TOURTES ET TARTES

Carrot Turnovers

Petits Pâtés aux Carottes

The fillings for these little pasties can be varied infinitely. For example: cooked rice and hard-boiled eggs, chopped cabbage, chopped cooked fish, chopped cooked beef, veal or game, a stew of mushrooms, morels, lobster or crayfish tails, etc.

To make twenty 8 cm (3 inch) turnovers

500 g	carrots, cut in half lengthwise, woody cores discarded, diced and parboiled in rapidly boiling salted water for 1 minute	1 lb
350 g	rough-puff dough *(page 165)*	12 oz
40 g	butter	1½ oz
2	hard-boiled eggs, chopped	2
1 tbsp each	chopped parsley and chives	1 tbsp each
1 tbsp	thick white sauce *(page 166)*	1 tbsp
	salt and pepper	
1	egg, beaten with 2 tsp water	1

Fry the carrots in the butter with the hard-boiled eggs, parsley and chives. Stir in the thick white sauce, season with salt and pepper and leave to cool.

Roll out the rough-puff dough and cut it into about twenty 8 cm (3 inch) rounds. Put a tablespoon of the carrot mixture into the centre of each round. Moisten the edges of the rounds with a little water and fold them in half to make a turnover. Fold the edges of the pastry over each other neatly. Sprinkle a buttered baking sheet with water and lay the turnovers on the sheet, seams downwards. Brush the turnovers with the beaten egg and, with a very sharp knife, make a few parallel shallow incisions in the tops. Bake the turnovers in a preheated 200°C (400°F or Mark 6) oven for 25 minutes or until golden-brown. To serve, arrange the pasties in a pyramid on a dish and serve piping hot.

A. PETIT
LA GASTRONOMIE EN RUSSIE

Vegetable and Herb Pie

Feuilleté aux Herbes

This recipe is from the Auberge du XIIe Siècle restaurant at Saché, France.

To make one 30 by 15 cm (12 by 6 inch) pie

500 g	potatoes, peeled and very thinly sliced	1 lb
500 g	spinach, trimmed, parboiled in rapidly boiling salted water for 1 minute, drained and squeezed	1 lb
500 g	sorrel, trimmed, parboiled in rapidly boiling salted water for a few seconds, drained and squeezed	1 lb
500 g	Swiss chard, ribs removed, parboiled in rapidly boiling salted water for 1 minute, drained and squeezed	1 lb
2 tbsp	*fines herbes*	2 tbsp
500 g	rough-puff dough (*page 165*)	1 lb
60 g	butter	2 oz
2 tbsp	oil	2 tbsp
1	garlic clove, finely chopped	1
	salt and pepper	
1	egg, beaten	1
6 tbsp	*crème fraîche* or double cream	6 tbsp

Heat 30 g (1 oz) of the butter and the oil in a frying pan and sauté the potatoes. When they are lightly browned, add the *fines herbes*, garlic, salt and pepper.

Divide the rough-puff dough in half, and roll out one piece into a 30 by 15 cm (12 by 6 inch) rectangle. Lay the dough on a buttered baking sheet.

Stew the spinach, sorrel and chard separately in the rest of the butter. Mix them and spread half of the mixture over the dough. Cover with the potatoes, then add a final layer of green vegetables. Roll out the rest of the dough and use it to cover the pie. Seal the edges of the dough firmly. Brush the dough with the beaten egg. Cut three small equidistant holes in the top of the pie and put pie funnels in them.

Bake the pie in a preheated 180°C (350°F or Mark 4) oven for 1 hour or until golden-brown. Just before serving, pour a trickle of cream through each of the pie funnels.

PAUL-JACQUES LÉVÈQUE (EDITOR)
LES BONNES RECETTES DE LA CUISINE TOURANGELLE

Morel Pie

Tourte aux Morilles

To make one 25 cm (10 inch) pie

500 g	fresh morels, wiped and chopped or 60 g (2 oz) dried morels, soaked for 20 minutes and chopped	1 lb
500 g	rough-puff dough (*page 165*)	1 lb
100 g	butter, softened	3½ oz
10 cl	dry white wine or champagne	3½ fl oz
	salt and pepper	
	grated nutmeg	
15 cl	double cream	¼ pint
2	egg yolks	2
½ litre	white sauce (*page 166*)	16 fl oz
250 g	raw ham, sliced and cut into small strips	8 oz
1	egg, beaten with 2 tsp water	1

In a covered pan, stew the morels in 60 g (2 oz) of the butter, the wine and seasoning for about 15 minutes, or until cooked through. Remove the morels from the pan and set them aside. Cook the liquid, uncovered, over a high heat, until it is reduced by half, about 5 minutes, and reserve it. Mix 4 tablespoons of the cream, the egg yolks and the morel cooking liquid with the white sauce, over a low heat. Remove it from the heat and leave to cool. Stew the ham in the rest of the butter over a low heat until just cooked through. Divide the dough in half. Roll out one half to line a well-buttered or oiled 25 cm (10 inch) flan tin. Use a pastry brush to spread 1 tablespoon of the cream over the dough in the tin, leaving a 1 cm (½ inch) margin at the edge. Lay half the ham strips over the cream and top with the cooled sauce and the morels.

Sprinkle the rest of the ham over the morels. Roll out the other half of the dough to make a lid. Moisten the edges of the dough to hold the pie firmly together and lightly pinch the edges. Make a 1 cm (½ inch) pie funnel from a cardboard tube. Cut a hole in the centre of the pie and insert the funnel. Decorate the pie with trimmings from the dough, shaped into leaves. Glaze the pie with the beaten egg.

Bake the pie in a preheated 220°C (425°F or Mark 7) oven for 30 to 35 minutes, or until the top is brown and risen. Remove the pie from the oven and leave it to rest for 5 minutes. Warm 2 to 3 tablespoons of cream and pour it through the pie funnel.

DOMINIQUE WEBER
LES BONNES RECETTES DES PROVINCES DE FRANCE

Cheese and Potato Tart

Tourte de Châteaumeillant

To make one 25 cm (10 inch) tart

200 g	goat cheese	7 oz
500 g	potatoes, peeled and very thinly sliced	1 lb
400 g	rough-puff dough *(page 165)*	14 oz
	salt and pepper	
100 g	butter, cut into pieces	3½ oz

Roll out the rough-puff dough and use it to line a 25 cm (10 inch) buttered flan tin. Prick the dough with a fork all over. Slice off the rind from the goat cheese and push the cheese through a sieve over a bowl. Beat the sieved cheese until it forms a smooth paste. Season it. Put the sliced potatoes into a saucepan of cold water, bring them to the boil and cook them for 5 minutes. Then drain under cold, running water. Dry the potatoes on kitchen paper and put half of them in the pastry case. Season and dot with butter. Spread the goat cheese paste over the potatoes, and arrange the rest of the potatoes on top. Season and dot with butter. Bake the tart in a preheated 190°C (375°F or Mark 5) oven for 30 minutes, or until the top has browned. Serve piping hot.

PIERRE ANDROUET
LA CUISINE AU FROMAGE

Leek and Cream Tart

Flamiche aux Poireaux

This tart from north-eastern France is often served with ham.

To make one 25 cm (10 inch) tart

500 g	leeks, white part and small part of green finely chopped	1 lb
8 cl	double cream	3 fl oz
500 g	rough-puff dough *(page 165)*	1 lb
100 g	unsalted butter	3½ oz
3 to 4 tbsp	water	3 to 4 tbsp
	salt	
	freshly ground black pepper	
1	egg yolk, mixed with a little water	1

Gently stew the leeks in the butter, starting with half the total amount of butter and adding the rest a little at a time during the cooking. Moisten with the water, cover and cook gently until the leeks are completely soft and all the liquid has been absorbed—about 10 minutes. The leeks should not be allowed to brown. Add the cream and season well.

Divide the dough in two. On a damp baking sheet, roll out one half into a thin round about 25 cm (10 inches) in diameter.

Place the leek mixture in the middle, leaving a border of 3 cm (1 inch) all round. Brush the border with water. Roll out the rest of the dough in the same way and place it on top of the leek mixture. Press the edges firmly together so that they are well sealed. To help the dough to rise by making the puff dough layers separate during cooking, cut 3 cm (1 inch) parallel slits all round the edges with a sharp knife. Glaze the surface by brushing with the diluted egg yolk and make a trellis-work pattern on it with the point of a knife.

Put the tart into a preheated 220°C (425°F or Mark 7) oven for 10 minutes, then reduce the oven temperature to 170°C (325°F or Mark 3) for another 20 to 25 minutes. When the tart is ready, the surface of the pastry should be evenly golden with no dark spots. Serve very hot.

LOUISETTE BERTHOLLE (EDITOR)
SECRETS OF THE GREAT FRENCH RESTAURANTS

Minced Beef Pasties

Hackfleischtaschen

To make about 25 pasties

500 g	beef, minced	1 lb
750 g	rough-puff dough *(page 165)*	1½ lb
2 tbsp	vegetable oil	2 tbsp
1	large onion, finely chopped	1
2	garlic cloves, finely chopped	2
	salt	
¼ tsp	cayenne pepper	¼ tsp
1 tsp	paprika	1 tsp
	ground allspice, grated nutmeg, rosemary and thyme	
2	eggs, 1 lightly beaten, 1 yolk separated from white and both lightly beaten	2

Heat the oil and sauté the chopped onion and garlic until they are transparent. Add the minced beef and cook for a further 5 minutes. Add salt to taste and season with the cayenne pepper, paprika and a pinch each of ground allspice, grated nutmeg, rosemary and thyme. Allow the mixture to cool slightly, then stir in the beaten egg.

Roll out the dough thinly and cut it into about twenty-five 12 cm (5 inch) squares. Brush the squares with the beaten egg white. Put 2 tablespoons of the filling in the centre of each square and fold the corners to the centre, pressing the edges to seal them. Brush the pasties with the beaten egg yolk. Place them on a baking sheet sprinkled with water and bake them in a preheated 220°C (425°F or Mark 7) oven for about 25 minutes or until golden-brown.

HEDWIG MARIA STUBER
ICH HELF DIR KOCHEN

Russian Pies with Fish Filling

Rasstegai s Rȳboǐ

The pies should be served sprinkled with salt and pepper and brushed with melted butter. Hot fish or meat stock can be poured over the pies immediately before serving.

The name *rasstegai* comes from the Russian verb meaning "to unbutton", and refers to the fact that the pastry case in which the pie is baked is left, as it were, unbuttoned—that is, with a small oval aperture at the top.

To make about 25 little pies		
500 g	filleted sturgeon, salmon or salmon-trout, skinned and chopped	1 lb
500 g	rough-puff or olive oil puff dough (*page 165*)	1 lb
4 tbsp	oil	4 tbsp
60 g	onion, chopped	2 oz
125 g	boiled rice	4 oz
	salt and pepper	
2	eggs, hard boiled and finely chopped	2
3 tbsp	chopped parsley	3 tbsp
1	egg yolk, beaten	1

Fry the fish in 3 tablespoons of oil for 5 minutes or until partly cooked. In another pan, fry the onion in the remaining oil for 4 minutes or until soft and golden. Mix the onion and fish with the rice, salt and pepper, hard-boiled eggs and parsley.

Roll out the dough and cut it into about twenty-five 10 cm (4 inch) rounds. Place a generous spoonful of filling on each round. Lift the dough from the edges to the middle and press the edges together, leaving an oval aperture in the centre. Brush the pies with the beaten egg yolk and bake them in a preheated 220°C (425°F or Mark 7) oven for 10 to 15 minutes, or until the pies are golden-brown.

ALAN DAVIDSON
NORTH ATLANTIC SEAFOOD

Easter Pie

Torta Pasqualina

To make one 20 to 23 cm (8 to 9 inch) deep-dish pie

500 g	olive oil dough (*page 165*)	1 lb
2 kg	chard, ribs removed, shredded, parboiled very rapidly for 1 minute and drained	4 lb
50 g	butter	2 oz
50 g	Parmesan cheese, grated	2 oz
20 cl	double cream	7 fl oz
	marjoram	
500 g	curd cheese	1 lb
2 tbsp	flour	2 tbsp
3 tbsp	olive oil or melted butter	3 tbsp
4	eggs	4

Divide the olive oil dough into seven equal pieces. Join two of them together to make a larger piece. Leave the dough to rest for about 20 minutes before rolling out.

For the filling, sauté the chard in 30 g (1 oz) of the butter until the excess moisture has evaporated. Stir in the Parmesan cheese. Put the mixture in a bowl and combine it with the cream, a pinch of marjoram, the curd cheese and the flour.

Roll out the large piece of dough into a sheet big enough to line the pie dish and leave an overhanging flap. Roll out the remaining five pieces of dough into sheets to fit the diameter of the dish. Oil or butter the dish and line it with the large sheet of dough. Brush the surface with oil or melted butter. Cover it with a layer of filling, and lay another sheet of dough on top. Brush the dough with oil or butter, spread more filling on it, and put another sheet of dough on top. Repeat with more filling and the third small sheet of dough, buttering or oiling each sheet. Spread the third sheet with filling, make four holes in the filling and break an egg into each hollow. Dot each egg with a piece of the remaining butter. Cover with the fourth small sheet of dough, the rest of the filling, and top with the last sheet of dough. Insert a straw or pie funnel in the crust to let out steam during baking, and bake the pie in a preheated 180°C (350°F or Mark 4) oven for 45 minutes.

LUIGI VOLPICELLI AND SECONDINO FREDA (EDITORS)
L'ANTIARTUSI: 1000 RICETTE

Asparagus Pie

Torta di Asparagi

The preparation of asparagus is shown on page 29.

This pie can also be made using leeks instead of asparagus.

	To make one 20 cm (8 inch) pie	
2 kg	asparagus, trimmed, tied in bundles, parboiled for 5 to 7 minutes and drained	4 lb
500 g	olive oil dough (*page 165*)	1 lb
200 g	butter	7 oz
200 g	Parmesan cheese, grated	7 oz
6	eggs, lightly beaten	6
5 tbsp	olive oil	5 tbsp
	salt	

Make the dough and divide it into 20 to 30 small balls. Sprinkle a pastry board or work surface with flour, set the balls on it and leave them to rest for about 30 minutes.

Chop the drained, parboiled asparagus and lightly brown it in the butter. Mix it with the cheese, eggs, 2 tablespoons of the olive oil and salt to taste.

Use slightly fewer than half the dough balls—say 12 out of 30—to make the base of the pie. Roll out each ball into a thin round, slightly larger than a 20 cm (8 inch) flan tin. To make them really thin, roll as much as possible with the rolling pin, then finish with a floured fist. Brush each round, except the last, with olive oil before placing it in the baking tin. Spread the asparagus filling evenly over the dough base.

Roll out the rest of the dough in the same way. When laying the first round on top of the pie, try to ensure that some air is left between the rounds of dough, so that the pie can expand during cooking. Brush this first round very thoroughly with oil and lay the other oiled rounds on top of the first. Bake the pie in a preheated 180°C (350°F or Mark 4) oven for about 1 hour or until golden-brown.

GIUSEPPE GAVOTTI
CUCINA E VINI DI LIGURIA

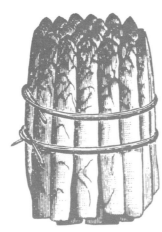

Excellent Mushroom Tart

Torta de Fongi Bona e Perfettissima

This 15th-century recipe is by Maestro Martino. He was the first Renaissance cook to have his recipes published.

	To make one 30 cm (12 inch) tart	
500 g	mushrooms, cut into large pieces	1 lb
250 g	olive oil dough (*page 165*)	8 oz
8 cl	olive oil	3 fl oz
125 g	lean green bacon, soaked in water for 30 minutes, drained and diced	4 oz
60 g	Parmesan cheese, grated	2 oz
4	eggs, beaten	4
	salt and pepper	
	grated nutmeg	
	powdered mace	

Put the oil in a pan over a gentle heat and fry the mushrooms and bacon, adding a little water if necessary to prevent them from burning. When they are cooked, remove them from the pan with a slotted spoon and put them in a bowl. Add the cheese and eggs and mix well. Season the mixture with salt and pepper and a pinch each of nutmeg and mace.

Roll out the dough thinly and use it to line a 30 cm (12 inch) tart tin. Pour in the mushroom mixture. Bake the tart in a preheated 200°C (400°F or Mark 6) oven for about 30 minutes or until the filling is set and beginning to brown.

EMILIO FACCIOLI (EDITOR)
ARTE DELLA CUCINA

Valencian Fish Pasties

Empanadillas Valencianas

	To make eight 10 cm (4 inch) pasties	
250 g	smoked haddock, poached in milk to cover for 10 minutes, skinned, boned and coarsely flaked	8 oz
250 g	olive oil dough (*page 165*), 1 tbsp of the water replaced by 1 tbsp anisette or Pernod	8 oz
250 g	tomatoes, skinned, seeded and chopped	8 oz
	salt and pepper	
	olive oil (optional)	

Put the tomatoes in a frying pan and simmer for 10 to 15 minutes, stirring frequently, to make a thick purée. Stir in the flaked fish and season with salt and pepper. Allow to cool.

On a cool, floured work surface, roll out the dough into a thin sheet and measure tablespoons of the filling on to it. Cut round them with a round pastry cutter and fold over the dough in the shape of pasties, sealing the edges with the tines of a fork. Roll out the remains of the dough again when necessary and continue until all the dough and filling have been used.

Deep fry the pasties in hot olive oil for 5 minutes on each side or bake them in an oven preheated to 200°C (400°F or Mark 6) for 15 to 20 minutes or until golden-brown.

JAN READ AND MAITE MANJÓN
FLAVOURS OF SPAIN

Pumpkin Satchels

Barba Jouan

The pumpkin can be baked instead of boiled to prevent it becoming waterlogged, in which case it should be seeded and cut into quarters and cooked in foil as shown on page 9. The technique of making pumpkin satchels is shown on page 22.

In the countryside around Nice, strong *brousse* cheese was added in small quantities to the stuffing. Pumpkin satchels can also be deep-fried in olive oil.

To make 18 to 24 satchels

2.5 kg	pumpkin, peeled, scraped and cut into pieces	5 lb
500 g	olive oil dough (page 165)	1 lb
1	garlic clove, chopped	1
1	small onion, chopped	1
1 tbsp	olive oil	1 tbsp
250 g	cooked rice	8 oz
2	eggs, beaten	2
75 g	Parmesan cheese, grated	2½ oz
	salt and pepper	

Cook the pumpkin the night before in boiling salted water to cover, until it begins to soften, about 20 minutes; drain it overnight. The pumpkin should have lost all the cooking liquid by morning. Cook the garlic and onion in the olive oil until they are transparent.

Chop the pumpkin or mash it in a bowl. Add the cooked rice, garlic, onion, eggs and grated Parmesan cheese. Season with salt and pepper and mix well.

On a floured surface, roll out the dough. Using a pastry cutter or a glass, cut out circles about 7 cm (3 inches) in diameter. Put a tablespoon of stuffing in the centre of each

circle. Press the edges of the dough together and pinch them to make the shape of a round purse. Oil baking sheets and place the satchels on them well spaced apart to permit even baking. Brush the satchels with olive oil and bake them in a preheated 220°C (425°F or Mark 7) oven for 25 to 30 minutes or until the pastry is light brown and the pinched edges dark golden.

RAYMOND ARMISEN AND ANDRÉ MARTIN
LES RECETTES DE LA TABLE NIÇOISE

Leek Tart

Porrea

This recipe was originally created by the monks of San Lorenzo, Florence, in about 1405.

To make one 20 cm (8 inch) tart

6	large leeks, white parts only, cut in four lengthwise, soaked in cold water for 5 minutes and drained	6
300 g	olive oil dough (*page 165*)	10 oz
20 cl	olive oil	7 fl oz
100 g	slice of raw ham, diced	3½ oz
200 g	fat and lean pork, minced	7 oz
200 g	veal or lamb, minced	7 oz
	salt and pepper	
	grated nutmeg	
¼ tsp	powdered saffron, dissolved in 2 tbsp water	¼ tsp
10 cl	dry red wine	3½ fl oz
30 g	Parmesan cheese, grated (optional)	1 oz

In a pan, heat half the oil and brown the ham and the minced meat. Add a little salt, pepper, nutmeg and the saffron. Cook for 2 minutes, then add the wine and cook for a further 5 minutes, until the wine evaporates.

In another saucepan, stew the leeks for a few minutes in the remainder of the oil. Take care not to let them disintegrate. Season them with salt.

Roll out three-quarters of the dough into a round and use it to line a 20 cm (8 inch) buttered pie dish about 5 cm (2 inches) deep. Pour in the stewed, minced meat mixture, adding a little more wine if it looks dry, and spread it out evenly. Arrange the leeks on top of the meat. Sprinkle with the Parmesan cheese, if you are using it. Roll out the rest of the dough, slice it into strips and arrange these over the filling in a lattice pattern. Bake the tart in a preheated 190°C (375°F or Mark 5) oven for about 40 minutes, or until it is golden-brown.

MASSIMO ALBERINI
CENTO RICETTE STORICHE

Octopus Tart

La Tièle

To make one 20 cm (8 inch) tart

400 g	baby octopus, beak and viscera removed	14 oz
250 g	olive oil dough *(page 165)*	8 oz
2 tbsp	oil	2 tbsp
1	large onion, chopped	1
5	tomatoes, skinned, seeded and coarsely chopped	5
100 g	black olives, stoned, cut into 2 or 3 pieces	3½ oz
	salt and pepper	
1 tbsp	chopped thyme	1 tbsp
1 tbsp	chopped oregano	1 tbsp

Put the octopus into a saucepan, cover with tepid water and bring to the boil. Cook for 10 minutes. Drain the octopus, skin them and remove the hard nodules on the tentacles and any other gristle. Chop the flesh and fry it in the oil for 10 minutes, until golden. Add the onion and chopped tomatoes. Stir in the olives and season well. Cover the pan and simmer the mixture for at least 1 hour, or until the octopus is tender.

Roll out the dough and use it to line a lightly oiled 20 cm (8 inch) tart tin. Pour the octopus mixture into the prepared pastry case and sprinkle it with chopped thyme and oregano. Bake the tart in a preheated 220°C (425°F or Mark 7) oven for 30 to 35 minutes, or until the edges of the pastry are browned.

SUZANNE SIMONET
LE GRAND LIVRE DE LA CUISINE OCCITANE

Cottage Cheese Flan with Fresh Dill

To make one 20 cm (8 inch) flan

1 kg	cottage cheese	2 lb
1 tbsp	finely cut fresh dill	1 tbsp
175 g	flour	6 oz
	salt	
6	eggs, 2 beaten, 4 yolks separated from whites, whites stiffly beaten	6
17.5 cl	soured cream	6 fl oz
250 g	butter, softened	8 oz

To make the dough, pour the flour and a pinch of salt on to a work surface, make a well in the centre and pour into the well the two beaten eggs and 15 cl (¼ pint) of the soured cream. Add

175 g (6 oz) of the butter and work the mixture with your fingers until it is a smooth paste, then on a floured surface knead it for 10 minutes. Cover the dough with a cloth and leave it in a cool place for 1 hour.

Roll out the dough and use it to line a buttered 20 cm (8 inch) tart tin, shaping it to fit and trimming the edges.

Mix the cottage cheese with the rest of the butter, the egg yolks, a pinch of salt and the cut dill. Fold in the egg whites. Spread the mixture on the prepared dough and brush the top with the rest of the soured cream. Bake the flan in a preheated 200°C (400°F or Mark 6) oven for 30 minutes or until the top is brown and the filling set.

JÓZSEF VENESZ
HUNGARIAN CUISINE

Prawn Dumplings

To serve 4

500 g	fresh prawns, shelled and roughly chopped	1 lb
2	spring onions, white parts only, slivered	2
4	water chestnuts, peeled and finely chopped	4
3 tsp	peanut oil	3 tsp
1 tsp	soy sauce	1 tsp
1 tsp	salt	1 tsp
	white pepper	
1	egg, beaten	1
	Egg roll or won ton wrappers	
250 g	flour	8 oz
½ tsp	salt	½ tsp
About 15 cl	cold water	About ¼ pint

Mix together the prawns, spring onions, water chestnuts, peanut oil, soy sauce, salt and a pinch of pepper and allow the mixture to stand for 20 minutes.

To make the wrappers, sift together the flour and the salt into a bowl and gradually add enough cold water to make a firm, pliable dough. Roll out the dough until it is paper thin, then cut it into 6 cm (2½ inch) rounds. On each round, place a teaspoonful of the prawn mixture. Fold the wrapper over to form a half-circle and seal the edges with the beaten egg. Place the wrappers on greaseproof paper in a steamer and steam them over boiling water for 10 minutes.

ALAN DAVIDSON
SEAFOOD OF SOUTH-EAST ASIA

Pepper and Tomato Tart

Tarte aux Poivrons et aux Tomates

Other types of dough such as rough-puff dough (recipe, page 165) can be used with this filling.

To make one 32 cm (13 inch) tart

6	sweet peppers, grilled, skinned, seeded and sliced into thin strips	6
1 kg	tomatoes, skinned, seeded and chopped	2 to 2½ lb
12.5 cl	peanut oil	4 fl oz
3	garlic cloves, chopped	3
	salt and pepper	
1	small chili pepper, crushed	1
1 tbsp	wine vinegar	1 tbsp
12	anchovy fillets	12
1	egg yolk, beaten with a little water	1
	White wine dough	
4 tbsp	white wine	4 tbsp
250 g	flour, sieved	8 oz
½ tsp	salt	½ tsp
50 g	butter, softened	2 oz
4 tbsp	olive oil	4 tbsp
2 tbsp	hot water	2 tbsp

To make the dough, put the flour into a bowl and make a well in the centre. Into the well, put the salt, butter and oil. Mix with the fingertips, so that the fat is thoroughly incorporated into the flour. Add the white wine. Work the dough for another minute and add the hot water. Knead briefly. Leave the dough to rest for at least 15 minutes.

Sauté the chopped tomatoes in the peanut oil. Add the chopped garlic. Season with salt and pepper and the crushed chili pepper. Add the strips of pepper to the tomatoes in the pan. Cook over a moderate heat for a further 10 minutes, then add the vinegar. The mixture should be fairly dry.

Roll out the dough to a thickness of about 3 mm (⅛ inch), and use about two-thirds of it to line a 32 cm (13 inch) tart tin. Reserve the remaining dough.

Pour the pepper and tomato mixture on to the dough in the tart tin. Arrange the anchovies on top. Roll out the remaining dough and cut it into strips about 5 mm (¼ inch) wide, and lay them in a lattice pattern over the filling. Glaze the latticework and borders of the dough with the egg yolk. Bake the tart in a preheated 220°C (425°F or Mark 7) oven for 30 to 40 minutes, or until the pastry is golden-brown.

SYLVIE THÉBAULT
TARTES SUCRÉES ET TARTES SALÉES

Pye (a la Oli, the Provençal Way)

The author of this recipe, Vincent La Chapelle, was head cook to Lord Chesterfield. Although he was French, his cookery book was first published in English in 1733. Two years later, La Chapelle published a French translation. He is considered to have been the leading French chef of his generation.

To make one 20 cm (8 inch) pie

350 g	olive oil puff dough (*page 165*)	12 oz
3	salt anchovies, filleted, soaked, rinsed, drained, finely chopped and pounded	3
500 g	fresh anchovies, cleaned, filleted and halved	1 lb
	salt and pepper	
1	egg, beaten with 1 tsp water	1

Make the olive oil puff dough, working in the pounded anchovies as you mix the flour with the liquid ingredients. Then roll out half of the dough to a thickness of about 5 mm (¼ inch) and use it to line a 20 cm (8 inch) pie dish. Lay the halved anchovies over the bottom of the pie shell until the surface is covered. Season them with salt and pepper. From the remaining dough, roll out a strip the breadth of a thumb and put it round the edge of the pie. Roll out the rest of the dough until it is 3 mm (⅛ inch) thick and cut it into squares the breadth of a thumb; cover the anchovies with these squares. Glaze the pie with the egg and bake in a preheated 200°C (400°F or Mark 6) oven until golden-brown but not too dry, about 35 minutes.

VINCENT LA CHAPELLE
THE MODERN COOK

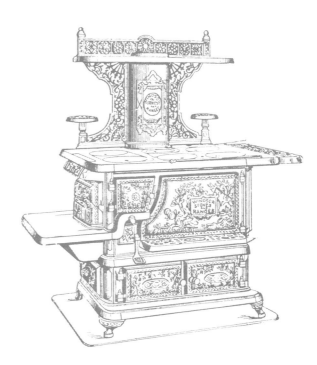

Little Stews

To Stew Green Peas the Jews' Way

This recipe is from a book published anonymously in 1747, but generally known to have been written by Hannah Glasse. A pipkin is a metal or earthenware cooking pot.

To serve 6

750 g	shelled green peas	1½ lb
6 tbsp	oil	6 tbsp
4 tbsp	water	4 tbsp
	grated nutmeg	
	powdered mace	
	powdered cloves	
	cayenne pepper	
	salt and pepper	
3 or 4	eggs, one of them beaten	3 or 4

To the peas add the oil and water, and the spices, salt and pepper; let all this stew in a broad, flat pipkin; when they are half done, about 20 minutes, with a spoon make two or three holes; into each of these holes break an egg. When the eggs are set, take the beaten egg and throw it over the whole when the mixture is cooked enough, as you will know by tasting it; and the egg being quite set send the dish to the table.

If this is not done in a very broad, open thing, it will be a great difficulty to get it out to lay in a dish. It would be better done in a silver or tin dish, and go to the table in the same dish, it is much better than putting it in another dish.

THE ART OF COOKERY, MADE PLAIN AND EASY

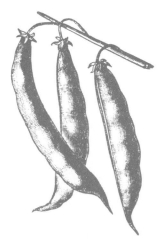

Chicory Cooked Like Aparagus

Chicons en Asperges

To serve 4

1 kg	chicory, base trimmed	2 to 2½ lb
2	lemons, juice strained	2
1 tsp	sugar	1 tsp
	salt and pepper	
60 g	flour	2 oz
4 tbsp	water	4 tbsp
150 g	butter	5 oz
4	sprigs parsley, chopped	4
4	eggs, boiled for 9 minutes, cooled in cold water and shelled	4

Put the chicory in an ovenproof dish with a tight-fitting lid. Sprinkle them with the lemon juice, sugar, salt and pepper. Cover the dish. Mix the flour with enough water to make a stiff paste. Use this paste to seal the lid. Bake the chicory in a preheated 180°C (350°F or Mark 4) oven for 1½ hours.

To serve, melt the butter—taking care not to let it brown—add the parsley and pour the liquid into a sauceboat. Let each person crush an egg on his or her plate, dilute the egg with some of the butter sauce and dip the chicory in the mixture.

CÉLINE VENCE
ENCYCLOPÉDIE HACHETTE DE LA CUISINE RÉGIONALE

Baked Ceps

Cèpes en Terrine du Ségala

To serve 6

1 kg	ceps, wiped, caps cut into 5 mm (¼ inch) slices, stems trimmed and chopped	2 to 2½ lb
10 cl	oil	3½ fl oz
50 g	butter	2 oz
2	garlic cloves, chopped	2
2	shallots, chopped	2
30 g	parsley, chopped	1 oz
2	tomatoes, skinned, seeded and chopped	2
2 tbsp	breadcrumbs	2 tbsp
1	lemon, juice strained	1
	salt and pepper	

Heat the oil in a frying pan and sauté the sliced cep caps on a high heat for 15 minutes, until they are well browned, stirring from time to time.

Melt the butter in an ovenproof casserole, and put the ceps

into it, caps downwards. Mix the chopped stems, garlic, shallots, parsley, tomatoes and the breadcrumbs; sauté them in the oil in which the ceps were cooked for 2 to 3 minutes on a high heat, stirring constantly. Spread the chopped ingredients over the mushroom caps and sprinkle with lemon juice, salt and pepper. Cover the casserole and bake it in a preheated 180°C (350°F or Mark 4) oven for 1 hour. Serve the mushrooms in the dish in which they were cooked.

LA CUISINE DU PÉRIGORD
ENCYCLOPÉDIE DE LA CUISINE RÉGIONALE

A White Fricasey of Mushrooms

This recipe is from a book published anonymously in 1747, but is generally known to have been written by Hannah Glasse.

To serve 4

500 g	button mushrooms	1 lb
3 tbsp	water	3 tbsp
3 tbsp	milk	3 tbsp
	salt	
	grated nutmeg	
	powdered mace	
30 cl	double cream	½ pint
15 g	butter, softened	½ oz
15 g	flour	½ oz

Put the mushrooms into a saucepan with the water and milk and a very little salt. Set them on a high heat and bring to the boil. Remove the pan immediately, let the contents cool for a moment, then return it to the heat and bring the contents to the boil again; repeat the process once again removing the pan from the heat immediately the mixture boils.

Off the heat, grate a little nutmeg into the mixture, put in a little powdered mace and the cream. Work the butter and flour together into a paste and add them to the mixture, while shaking the saucepan well all the time. Put the pan on a gentle heat and cook, stirring with a spoon all the time, but be careful the mixture does not curdle. When the mixture is fine and thick—about 10 minutes—dish it up.

THE ART OF COOKERY, MADE PLAIN AND EASY

Salt Cod Purée

Brandade de Morue Parmentière

This dish can be served garnished with triangles of fried bread, or it can be used to fill vol-au-vent, pastry or bread cases. The making of these cases is shown on pages 34 and 35. A variation on this typical Languedoc dish is called Salt Cod Purée in Mourning (Brandade de Morue en Deuil). For this, the garlic is omitted and a truffle poached in white wine for 15 minutes is chopped or sliced and mixed into the purée which has been left to cool.

To serve 6

750 g	salt cod, soaked for at least 24 hours in 3 or more changes of water, skinned and boned	1½ lb
¼ litre	olive oil	8 fl oz
1	small garlic clove, finely chopped and pounded in a mortar	1
500 g	potatoes, boiled, peeled and mashed to a purée	1 lb
6 tbsp	scalded milk	6 tbsp
	salt and pepper	

Put the cod into a pan of fresh, cold water to cover it. Bring the water to the boil, then reduce the heat and poach the fish for 10 to 12 minutes. Drain it and remove any remaining skin and bones. You should have about 500 g (1 lb) of cod left. Use two forks to flake the fish.

In a heavy-bottomed saucepan heat over a medium heat all but 2 tablespoons of the oil. Remove the pan from the heat and add the fish. Use a coarse-tined fork to mash the fish and oil together, beating the mixture against the sides of the pan until it forms a fibrous mass.

Return the mixture to the heat and, drop by drop as if making a mayonnaise, add the remaining oil, beating the paste constantly. Add the garlic and then alternate tablespoons of puréed potato and milk, beating hard after each addition. Add the rest of the potatoes and continue beating until all the fibres disappear and the mixture forms a soft, smooth paste. Add extra milk if necessary. Season to taste.

ALBIN MARTY
FOURMIGUETTO: SOUVENIRS, CONTES ET RECETTES DU LANGUEDOC

Frogs' Legs with Garlic

Ancas de Rana al Ajo Arriero

To serve 4

40	frogs' legs	40
8	garlic cloves, finely chopped	8
½	small onion, finely chopped	½
2	bay leaves	2
12.5 cl	wine vinegar	4 fl oz
	salt and pepper	
½	small, fresh red chili pepper, seeded and chopped	½
4 tbsp	olive oil	4 tbsp
2 tsp	paprika	2 tsp
2	hard-boiled eggs, chopped	2

Put the frogs' legs in an earthenware pan with the onion, bay leaves and vinegar. Add water to barely cover them, season with salt and pepper, and simmer the frogs' legs for 5 minutes. In another pan, fry the garlic and red pepper in the oil. When they begin to brown, add the paprika—taking care not to let it burn—and pour the mixture over the frogs' legs. Scatter the chopped hard-boiled eggs over the mixture. Cover the pan, simmer the frogs' legs for another 3 minutes, season to taste and serve very hot.

ANA MARIA CALERA
COCINA CASTELLANA

Frogs' Legs in Fish Sauce

Les Grenouilles de nos Étangs Façon Père Vacher

To serve 3

24	pairs medium-sized frogs' legs	24
10 cl	fish velouté (*page 167*)	3½ fl oz
30 g	butter	1 oz
1	onion, chopped	1
15 cl	dry white wine	¼ pint
1	bouquet garni	1
	salt and pepper	
2	egg yolks	2
4 tbsp	double cream	4 tbsp
1	lemon, juice strained	1
About 4 tbsp	chopped parsley	About 4 tbsp

In a frying pan, melt the butter. Arrange the frogs' legs in the pan side by side without overlapping. Add the chopped onion, then the white wine, the bouquet garni and a pinch of salt.

Bring the mixture to the boil over a high heat and cook for about 8 minutes, turning the frogs' legs once. Remove the frogs' legs from the pan, reserving the cooking liquid, and place them in a warmed serving dish. Strain the cooking liquid and mix it with the fish velouté. Beat the egg yolks and cream together with 3 tablespoons of the liquid. Bring the rest of the liquid to the boil, stirring gently. Remove the pan from the heat, beat in the egg yolks and cream and return the pan to the heat. Cook over a gentle heat, stirring constantly, until the sauce has begun to thicken. Season to taste. Add the lemon juice to the sauce and pour it over the frogs' legs. Sprinkle the dish liberally with chopped parsley.

FÉLIX BENOIT AND HENRY CLOS JOUVE
LA CUISINE LYONNAISE

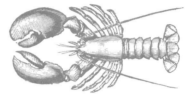

Seafood Vol-au-Vent

Vol-au-Vent de Pesce

The technique of opening clams and mussels in white wine is demonstrated on page 31.

To serve 6

300 g	sole, filleted and skinned	10 oz
300 g	live clams, opened in white wine	10 oz
¾ litre	live mussels, opened in white wine	1¼ pints
300 g	lobster, boiled for 15 minutes in salted water to cover	10 oz
200 g	sea bass, filleted and skinned	7 oz
300 g	live crayfish	10 oz
1	20 cm (8 inch) vol-au-vent case made from 500 g (1 lb) puff dough (*page 165*)	1
6 tbsp	dry white wine	6 tbsp
90 g	butter	3 oz
	bouquet garni	
30 g	flour	1 oz
4 tbsp	oil	4 tbsp
1½	salt anchovies, soaked, filleted, rinsed, drained and finely chopped	1½
1	lemon, juice strained	1
3 tbsp	chopped parsley	3 tbsp
	salt and pepper	

Cook the sole in the wine and 15 g (½ oz) of the butter over a low heat for 5 to 6 minutes. Shell the clams and mussels and reserve them with their cooking juices. Combine the lobster and the sole cooking liquid with the clam and mussel juices. Put them into a saucepan with the bouquet garni, add the bass and crayfish and poach them until they are tender, about 15 to 20 minutes. Reserve the fish stock for the sauce.

Shell the crayfish and lobster and cut all the fish and shellfish into 4 cm (1½ inch) pieces.

Measure 30 cl (½ pint) of the fish stock into a saucepan and bring it to the boil. (If there is not enough stock, add a little hot water.) Strain the stock. Combine the flour and the rest of the butter over a gentle heat until they form a smooth cream, then add the boiling stock gradually, stirring until a smooth, fairly thick sauce is obtained.

In a small pan, warm the oil. Remove it from the heat and mash the anchovies in it. Add them to the sauce and sprinkle with lemon juice to taste. Stir the fish and shellfish into the sauce, add the parsley and cook the mixture in a double saucepan, covered, for at least 10 minutes until heated through. Adjust the seasoning.

Preheat the oven to 200°C (400°F or Mark 6). Then turn off the heat and put the vol-au-vent case into the oven to warm for 5 minutes. Put the case on a serving dish, pour in the boiling hot fish in the sauce. Replace the lid and serve.

JEANNE CARÒLA FRANCESCONI
LA CUCINA NAPOLETANA

Shrimp Vol-au-Vents

Bouchées de Crevettes

The making of vol-au-vent cases is shown on page 35.

To serve 18

500 g	live shrimps, cooked for 6 to 7 minutes in fish stock (*page 167*), drained, shelled, shells and cooking liquid reserved	1 lb
18	5 cm (2 inch) vol-au-vent cases made with 350 g (12 oz) rough-puff dough (*page 165*)	18
About 125 g	butter, softened	About 4 oz
½ litre	fish velouté (*page 167*) made with shrimp cooking liquid	16 fl oz
6 tbsp	double cream	6 tbsp
	salt and pepper	

Pound the shrimp shells and a few whole shrimps. Pass them through a coarse-bladed food mill, then through a fine drum-sieve to eliminate the debris. Mix the pounded shrimps with an equal weight of butter.

Warm the vol-au-vent cases in a preheated 130°C (250°F or Mark ½) oven for 10 minutes.

Slice the reserved shrimp tails in half, and heat them in the

fish velouté. Add the cream, bring the mixture to the boil and remove it from the heat. Stir in the shrimp butter and season to taste. Spoon the mixture into the warmed vol-au-vent cases. Serve immediately.

JULES GOUFFÉ
LE LIVRE DE CUISINE

Turbot Vol-au-Vents

Steinbuttpastetchen

The method of making vol-au-vent cases is shown on page 35. Any firm-fleshed white fish, such as halibut, angler fish or bass, can be substituted for turbot.

To serve 4

250 g	turbot, filleted, skinned and cut into small pieces	8 oz
4	vol-au-vent cases with lids	4
15 g	butter	½ oz
½	lemon, juice strained	½
1 to 2 tbsp	water	1 to 2 tbsp
30 cl	hollandaise sauce (*page 166*)	½ pint
½ tsp	paprika	½ tsp

Place the turbot pieces in a saucepan with the butter, the lemon juice and water. Cook over a very low heat for about 15 minutes, or until the fish is cooked through, adding another tablespoon of water during the cooking, if necessary.

Warm the vol-au-vent cases in a preheated 130°C (250°F or Mark ½) oven. Remove any remaining bones from the fish and coarsely flake the flesh. Place the vol-au-vent cases on a serving dish or on individual plates and fill them with the flaked fish. Pour the hollandaise sauce, flavoured with a pinch of paprika, over the fish and put on the pastry lids. Any remaining sauce can be served separately.

ARNE KRÜGER AND ANNETTE WOLTER
KOCHEN HEUTE

Seafood Stew

La Timbale de Fruits de Mer

The technique of opening shellfish in white wine is demonstrated on page 31. This stew can be used to fill any of the cases shown on pages 34 and 35.

To serve 12

1 litre	live cockles or carpet shells, opened in white wine	1¾ pints
1 litre	small live mussels, opened in white white wine	1¾ pints
500 g	angler fish, cut into 2 or 3 pieces	1 lb
500 g	conger eel, cut into 2 or 3 pieces	1 lb
200 g	cooked, peeled shrimps	7 oz
200 g	cooked, peeled prawns	7 oz
6 to 8	live scallops, corals and white flesh removed from the shells	6 to 8
4 tbsp	olive oil	4 tbsp
½ tsp	whole allspice	½ tsp
4 tbsp	dry white wine (optional)	4 tbsp
3 or 4	shallots, chopped	3 or 4
15 g	butter	½ oz
15 cl	double cream	¼ pint
½ tsp	powdered oregano	½ tsp
¼ tsp	powdered saffron	¼ tsp
4 tbsp	milk (optional)	4 tbsp
	pepper	
2 tsp	flour worked into a paste with 15 g (½ oz) of softened butter	2 tsp

Shell the cockles and mussels. Pour enough of their cooking juices over them to prevent them drying out and put in a warm place until needed.

Sauté the angler fish and the conger eel in the olive oil with the allspice. Cover the pan and let the fish stew over a very low heat for 20 minutes or until they are tender. The liquid drawn from the fish during cooking is generally adequate for this slow stewing but, if necessary, add the wine to prevent the fish sticking to the pan.

Simmer the cockle and mussel cooking liquid for about 5 minutes before straining and reserving it. Poach the scallop flesh in the same liquid for 5 minutes. Leave the scallops to cool in their cooking liquid, then cut the white scallop flesh into large pieces, slices or dice, so that they are still recognizable. Leave the corals whole. Reserve the cooking juices in the pan. Cut the angler fish into large dice. Skin and bone the conger eel and cut it into large dice. Mix the fish, shellfish and crustaceans together and keep them warm.

Sauté the shallots in the butter, then add them to the pan in which the fish was cooked. Bring the liquid to the boil and bind it with the cream. Add the oregano and saffron. If the liquid is too salty, add enough milk to temper the saltiness. Season with the pepper. Return the fish, shellfish and crustaceans to the pan and reheat them for 10 minutes without boiling. Thicken the cooking juices with the flour and butter mixture and serve.

ALBIN MARTY
FOURMIGUETTO: SOUVENIRS, CONTES ET RECETTES DU LANGUEDOC

Oyster Loaves

The technique of opening oysters is shown on page 54.

When I can buy them, I use part-baked rolls for this dish; otherwise round rolls that have not been baked too brown. Once, in France, I used brioches, which were particularly delicious. The miniature cottage loaves sold by some bakers could also be used.

To serve 4

16	live oysters, shelled and liquor reserved	16
4	large rolls (or 8 small)	4
200 g	butter, melted	7 oz
	cayenne pepper or Tabasco sauce	
	salt and black pepper	
4 tbsp	soured cream	4 tbsp
4 tbsp	double cream	4 tbsp

Cut a slice from the top of each of the rolls and scoop out the crumb, being careful not to pierce the outside, and brush the rolls and the topknots, inside and out, with the melted butter. Place the rolls in a preheated 220°C (425°F or Mark 7) oven for 10 minutes until they are crisp and golden.

Meanwhile, in a 20 cm (8 inch) frying pan cook the oysters in the remaining butter until they turn opaque (about 1½ minutes). Remove the oysters from the pan with a perforated spoon, cut them in two or three pieces according to size and set them aside. To the pan juices, add the oyster liquor, seasonings and the soured and double cream. Boil the liquid down steadily to a very thick sauce, stirring constantly with a wooden spoon at first, then with a small wire whisk if the sauce shows a tendency to separate during the last stages of reduction. Correct the seasoning, reheat the oysters in the sauce, keeping it just below the boil, and pour it into the rolls. Replace the topknots and serve immediately.

JANE GRIGSON
ENGLISH FOOD

Stuffed Fillets of Sole in Pastry Cases

Mignonettes de Soles Sultane

The author recommends using tartlet shells made from short-crust dough. However, any type of pastry or bread cases can be used. The making of pastry and bread cases is shown on page 35. The technique of baking blind is shown on page 68. The mushrooms can also be boiled with water, butter and lemon juice (page 29) and added to the fish poaching liquid.

To serve 8

Two 250 g	soles, filleted, fillets sliced in two lengthwise, bones and trimmings reserved to use in stock	Two 8 oz
125 g	whiting fillet, made into a mousseline (*page 163*) with 1 egg white and 10 cl (3½ fl oz) double cream	4 oz
8	tartlet shells made from 125 g (4 oz) shortcrust dough (*page 165*) baked blind	8
15 cl	dry white wine	¼ pint
15 cl	fish stock (*page 167*)	¼ pint
50 g	pistachio nuts, peeled, pounded and sieved or puréed in a food processor, or puréed watercress or spinach	2 oz
100 g	butter, cut into pieces	3½ oz
125 g	cooked shrimp tails	4 oz
250 g	button mushrooms, sliced and sautéed in 15 g (½ oz) butter	8 oz

Lightly score the skin side of the sole fillets with parallel incisions about 2 cm (¾ inch) apart. Spread the skin side of the halved fillets with the whiting mousseline, and roll up the fillets lengthwise. Put the stuffed fillets in a buttered shallow pan just large enough to hold them, so that they do not unroll. Pour the wine and the fish stock over them. Cut a sheet of greaseproof paper large enough to fit the pan. Butter it and fit it over the pan. Put a lid on the pan and poach the fillets very gently for about 12 minutes or until they are cooked through. Drain the fillets, reserving the liquid, and keep them warm.

Put the tartlet shells into a preheated 130°C (250°F or Mark ½) oven to warm. In a saucepan, reduce the fish cooking liquid over a high heat until it is syrupy in consistency. Stir in the pistachio nuts or puréed watercress or spinach. Remove the pan from the heat and whisk in the butter.

Distribute the shrimps and mushrooms in the warmed tartlet shells. Put a rolled fillet of sole on top of each and pour the sauce over the fillets.

LE CORDON BLEU

Snails with Garlic Purée

Escargots à Notre Façon

The preparation of snails for cooking is shown on pages 52 and 53. Chanterelles are bright yellow wild mushrooms; they can be bought dried and must be soaked for 20 minutes before use.

The garlic purée is very easy to make and has the advantage of keeping for several days in the refrigerator. It can be used for all sorts of dishes such as fish, kidneys, lamb, frogs' legs, etc. The purée can be mixed with softened butter if it is to accompany a leg of lamb or similar meat as a sauce.

To serve 6

36	large live snails, cleaned, poached in white wine court-bouillon (*page 164*) for 2½ hours or until easily removed from their shells	36
100 g	streaky bacon, diced	3½ oz
200 g	button mushrooms or fresh chanterelles, diced, or 60 g (2 oz) dried chanterelles	7 oz
60 g	shallots, finely chopped	2 oz
60 g	butter	2 oz
36	croûtons	36
3 tbsp	chopped chervil	3 tbsp
	black pepper	
	Garlic purée	
200 g	garlic, cloves separated and left unpeeled, but with bases trimmed	7 oz
4 tbsp	*crème fraîche* or double cream	4 tbsp
4 tbsp	water	4 tbsp
	salt	

To make the garlic purée, put the cream into a saucepan with the same quantity of water, the garlic and a pinch of salt, cover and simmer for 30 minutes. If all the liquid dries up during the cooking, add a little more water. Pass the mixture through the fine disc of a food mill.

Fry the bacon for 5 minutes, then add the mushrooms or chanterelles. Sauté them until the mixture is golden. Discard the bacon fat and add the shallots. Mix well and stir in the garlic purée, butter and the snails. Pour into six individual baking dishes and bake in a preheated 240°C (475°F or Mark 9) oven for 5 minutes, or until well heated through.

Before serving, arrange the croûtons in the baking dishes and sprinkle the snails with the chopped chervil and freshly ground black pepper.

DANIEL BOUCHÉ
INVITATION À LA CUISINE BUISSONNIÈRE

Carmelite Scallop Shells

Coquilles à la Carmelite

To flavour the milk with anchovy, put one salt anchovy into a saucepan with the milk. Set the pan on a very low heat for 5 minutes; do not let the milk boil. Strain the milk.

	To serve 6	
125 g	fresh or salt cod, cooked and roughly chopped	4 oz
75 g	butter	2½ oz
15 g	flour	½ oz
30 cl	fish stock (*page 167*) or milk flavoured with anchovy	½ pint
1 tbsp	tomato sauce (*page 166*)	1 tbsp
2	hard-boiled eggs, peeled and chopped	2
2	anchovy fillets	2
	salt and pepper	
	ground mace	
60 g	breadcrumbs	2 oz

In a saucepan, mix 15 g (½ oz) of the butter with the flour and stir in the fish stock or anchovy-flavoured milk. Bring to the boil, stirring continuously, and add the tomato sauce. Mix well and pass the mixture through a sieve.

In a bowl, mix the cod, hard-boiled eggs and chopped anchovies and season with salt and pepper and a pinch of ground mace. Moisten the mixture with enough of the sauce to bring it to the consistency of rather fluid jam.

Butter six scallop shells, either of silver or china. Fill the shells with the mixture, smooth the surfaces, shake a canopy of finely sifted breadcrumbs over them, dot with the remaining butter, then bake in a preheated 180°C (350°F or Mark 4) oven for 10 to 15 minutes. Do not allow the mixture in the scallop shells to dry up in the process. They should come to the table moist and thoroughly hot.

A. KENNEY-HERBERT ("WYVERN")
FIFTY LUNCHES

Stuffed Scallop Shells

Conchiglie Ripiene

Chopped, boiled chicken may be used instead of fish.

	To serve 6	
130 g	white fish (turbot, sole, whiting, mullet or dogfish), poached for 20 minutes in boiling salted water, filleted, skinned and flaked	4 oz
20 g	Parmesan cheese, grated	¾ oz
¼ litre	white sauce (*page 166*)	8 fl oz
2	egg yolks	2
	salt and pepper	

Stir the Parmesan cheese into the white sauce, while the sauce is warm. Leave the sauce to cool a little, then stir in the egg yolks and the fish. Season with salt and pepper. Butter six scallop shells and fill them with the mixture. Cook in a preheated 200°C (400°F or Mark 6) oven for 10 to 12 minutes or until they are browned. Serve immediately.

PELLEGRINO ARTUSI
LA SCIENZA IN CUCINA E L'ARTE DI MANGIAR BENE

Spanish-Style Fish in Scallop Shells

Conchas de Pescado a la Española

	To serve 4	
150 g	cod fillets	5 oz
½ litre	milk	16 fl oz
60 g	butter	2 oz
1	onion, finely chopped	1
	salt and pepper	
170 g	bread, crusts removed, crumbled	6 oz
2	egg yolks	2
1	tomato, cut into 4 slices	1

Put the fish into a saucepan with the milk, half the butter, the onion, salt and pepper. Poach the fish until tender, about 8 to 10 minutes. Remove the fish from the cooking liquid, skin it, remove any remaining bones and flake it. Pour the cooking liquid over the bread and leave it for 10 minutes, or until all the liquid has been absorbed. Mash the bread well with a fork. Mix in the egg yolks and fish and season with salt and pepper.

Butter four scallop shells. Fill the shells with the fish mixture and top each shell with a slice of tomato. Melt the rest of the butter and pour it over the tomato slices. Bake in a preheated 180°C (350°F or Mark 4) oven for about 15 minutes, or until the tomato slices are lightly browned.

ANA MARIA CALERA
COCINA CASTELLANA

Stewed Crayfish
Écrevisses Champenoises

To serve 3

24	live crayfish	24
200 g	onions, very thinly sliced	7 oz
200 g	shallots, very thinly sliced	7 oz
6	garlic cloves, very thinly sliced	6
1	carrot, very thinly sliced	1
1 litre	water	1¾ pints
50 g	butter	2 oz
1 tbsp	marc	1 tbsp
	salt and pepper	

Put the onions, shallots, garlic and carrot in a saucepan with the water. Cook over a low heat until the liquid has reduced to about one quarter of its original volume, about 30 to 45 minutes. Put the mixture through a food mill and return it to the pan. Add the butter, marc and salt and pepper to taste.

When the mixture comes to the boil, add the crayfish and cook for 6 to 7 minutes over a moderate heat, shaking the pan several times during cooking.

CÉLINE VENCE
ENCYCLOPÉDIE HACHETTE DE LA CUISINE RÉGIONALE

Stewed Snails Tourangelle
Fricassée d'Escargots Tourangelle

The technique of preparing snails for cooking is demonstrated on page 52. This recipe comes from the Hotel de Bordeaux at Tours, in France.

To serve 4

100	small live snails, cleaned	100
100 g	butter	3½ oz
4	shallots, chopped	4
150 g	streaky bacon, diced	5 oz
6 tbsp	marc	6 tbsp
½ litre	dry white wine	16 fl oz
1 tbsp	tomato purée	1 tbsp
1	garlic head	1
1	bouquet garni	1
	salt and pepper	

In a saucepan, melt the butter and sauté the shallots and bacon for a few minutes. Add the snails. Warm the marc, then add it to the snails and set it alight. When the flame dies, pour in the wine and add the tomato purée, garlic, bouquet garni, salt and pepper. Cover the pan and simmer the mixture for 1½ to 2 hours or until the snails are tender. Remove the bouquet garni and serve the stew piping hot.

PAUL-JACQUES LÉVÊQUE (EDITOR)
LES BONNES RECETTES DE LA CUISINE TOURANGELLE

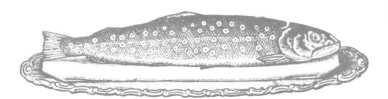

Catalan-Style Hake Balls
Albondigas de Merluza

To serve 6

750 g	hake, poached in salted water for 20 minutes, skin and bones removed and flesh flaked	1½ lb
1	egg, beaten	1
	ground cinnamon	
2 tbsp	chopped parsley	2 tbsp
2	onions, chopped	2
2	garlic cloves, chopped	2
20 cl	olive oil	7 fl oz
4	tomatoes, skinned, seeded and chopped	4
100 g	flour	3½ oz
	salt	
20 cl	water	7 fl oz
400 g	fresh peas, shelled	14 oz

Blend the flaked fish with the egg, a pinch of cinnamon and 1 tablespoon of the parsley. Mix well and form the mixture into small balls about 2.5 cm (1 inch) in diameter.

Sauté the onion, garlic and the rest of the parsley in 2 tablespoons of the oil. Add the chopped tomatoes and cook until the liquid has evaporated. Then add 1 teaspoon of the flour, salt and enough water to bring the mixture to a fluid, sauce-like consistency.

Toss the hake balls in the remaining flour, shake off the excess, and fry them in the rest of the oil, turning them frequently until browned. Drain them on absorbent paper.

Add the peas and the hake balls to the sauce. Dilute the sauce with enough water to half cover the fish. Cover the pan and simmer gently for 30 minutes.

ANA MARIA CALERA
COCINA CATALANA

Morel and Sweetbread Vol-au-Vent

La Garniture en Blanc du Vol-au-Vent

The making of vol-au-vent cases is shown on page 35. The preparation of sweetbreads for cooking is shown on page 32. Morels are wild mushrooms; they can be bought dried at continental grocers. To reconstitute dried morels, soak them in warm water for 20 minutes, rinse and drain them.

To serve 8

10	large morels, sliced in half and sautéed in 15 g (½ oz) butter, then diced	10
1	pair sweetbreads, soaked, cleaned, parboiled, diced and sautéed in 15 g (½ oz) butter	1
1	20 cm (8 inch) vol-au-vent case with lid, made with 500 g (1 lb) rough-puff dough (*page 165*)	1
250 g	veal bones, broken up	8 oz
60 g	lean green bacon, sliced into 5 cm (2 inch) strips	2 oz
1	onion, sliced	1
2	carrots, split in half lengthwise	2
	bouquet garni	
30 g	butter	1 oz
3 tbsp	flour	3 tbsp
12.5 cl	stock (*page 167*)	4 fl oz
12.5 cl	dry white wine	4 fl oz
	salt and pepper	
3	coriander seeds, ground	3
	grated nutmeg	
12.5 cl	milk	4 fl oz
¼ litre	double cream	8 fl oz
6	eggs, hard boiled and quartered	6
250 g	veal or chicken mousseline (*page 163*) shaped into small dumplings and poached for 10 minutes in boiling, salted water	8 oz

In a frying pan, cook the veal bones, bacon, onion, carrots and bouquet garni in half the butter. When they begin to brown, add the flour, stock and white wine, and stir. Cook the mixture, uncovered, for 10 minutes. Strain the mixture, return it to a low heat and season it with salt, pepper, coriander and nutmeg. Stir in the rest of the butter, the milk and cream. Taste the mixture and correct the seasoning. The sauce should be copious and smooth without being heavy. Leave the pan on a very low heat for 15 minutes without letting it come to the boil. Add the sautéed sweetbreads and simmer for a further 15 minutes. Then add the diced morels to the pan and cook for 25 minutes.

Heat the vol-au-vent case in a preheated 130°C (250°F or Mark ½) oven for 10 minutes.

Add the hard-boiled eggs and dumplings to the stew and cook for a further 5 minutes. Pour the mixture into the heated vol-au-vent case and serve.

SUZANNE ROBAGLIA
MARGARIDOU: JOURNAL ET RECETTES
D'UNE CUISINIÈRE AU
PAYS D'AUVERGNE

Chicken Vol-au-Vents

Bouchées à la Reine du "Dauphin"

These vol-au-vents were the favourite dish of Maria Leszczynska, wife of Louis XV. This recipe was created by the Dauphin restaurant in Strasbourg. The method of preparing sweetbreads for cooking is shown on page 32, and the making of vol-au-vent cases is shown on page 35.

To serve 6

1.5 kg	chicken, with giblets	3 lb
6	15 cm (6 inch) vol-au-vent cases made with 500 g (½ lb) butter puff pastry	6
1	leek, trimmed	1
1	carrot	1
1	onion	1
2	bay leaves	2
2	cloves	2
1 tbsp	salt	1 tbsp
	pepper	
300 g	sweetbreads, soaked, membranes removed	10 oz
300 g	button mushrooms	10 oz
1 tbsp	lemon juice	1 tbsp
150 g	butter	5 oz
150 g	flour	5 oz
35 cl	double cream	12 fl oz

Put the chicken into a casserole with the giblets and cover it with cold water. Tie the leek and carrot together and add them to the pot. Cut slits in the onion and stick the bay leaves through them, and stud the onion with the cloves. Put the onion in the pot and add the salt and pepper. When the water comes to the boil, reduce the heat and skim the surface to remove impurities. Cover the pan and cook the chicken for 30 minutes. Add the sweetbreads and continue cooking for a further 30 minutes, or until the chicken is completely tender.

Cook the mushrooms for 15 minutes in 15 cl (¼ pint) of salted water and the lemon juice. In a separate pan, melt the butter, add the flour and cook over a gentle heat for 10 minutes, stirring constantly with a wooden spatula. Remove the mixture from the heat and leave it to cool.

Remove the chicken and sweetbreads from their cooking liquid and leave them to cool. Return the cooking liquid to the heat and cook it, uncovered, over a high heat to reduce it to 1 litre (1¾ pints); strain it on to the butter and flour. Beat the mixture to make it smooth and simmer it for 30 minutes.

Warm the vol-au-vent cases in a preheated 180°C (350°F or Mark 4) oven for 10 minutes. Skin and bone the chicken and cut the flesh into 1 cm (½ inch) dice. Dice the cooled sweetbreads and mushrooms in the same way.

Stir the cream into the sauce and simmer it slowly, uncovered, until it is reduced and thickened. If the sauce becomes too thick it can be thinned with some of the mushroom cooking liquid. Strain the sauce through a fine sieve into a pan and add the diced chicken, sweetbreads and mushrooms; bring the mixture to the boil, taste, and adjust the seasoning. Pour the mixture into the heated vol-au-vent cases. Any remaining sauce can be served on the side.

FRANÇOIS VOEGELING
LA GASTRONOMIE ALSACIENNE

Little Chicken and Mushroom Stew

Cassolettes de Volaille à la Reine

This little stew is used to fill small porcelain dishes or pastry cases. It can also be sprinkled with breadcrumbs, dotted with butter and lightly browned in the oven.

To serve 4

500 g	cooked chicken carcass, 250 g (8 oz) of the flesh cut into 2 cm (¾ inch) rounds, bones and trimmings reserved	1 lb
250 g	button mushrooms	8 oz
60 g	butter	2 oz
2 tbsp	flour	2 tbsp
60 cl	stock (*page 167*), made with bones and trimmings from the chicken	1 pint
6 tbsp	water	6 tbsp
1	lemon, juice strained	1
	salt and pepper	
2	egg yolks, lightly beaten	2
6 tbsp	double cream	6 tbsp
30 g	truffles, sautéed in 15 g (½ oz) butter (optional)	1 oz

Melt 30 g (1 oz) of the butter in a heavy saucepan. Stir in the flour and cook over a low heat for 1 minute. Pour in the stock, whisking constantly to prevent lumps from forming. Increase the heat and continue whisking until the mixture boils. Reduce the heat, and simmer the sauce for 45 minutes, skimming occasionally. Season to taste.

Put the mushrooms in a pan with the water, lemon juice, salt and pepper and the rest of the butter. Cook them over a high heat for 5 minutes or until they are tender. Drain the mushrooms and slice them.

Remove the sauce from the heat and allow it to cool slightly. Mix the egg yolks and double cream and beat them into the sauce. Strain the sauce, return it to a gentle heat, and add the chicken pieces, mushrooms, and the truffles if you have them. Cook until the mixture is heated through.

LE CORDON BLEU

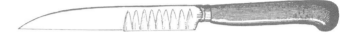

Livers in Red Wine

Les Foies de Volaille au Vin Rouge

The author recommends using this little stew to fill 12 tartlet shells baked blind and still hot from the oven. The tartlets can be made from shortcrust dough (page 165). The technique of baking blind is shown on page 68. The author suggests adding 1 tablespoon of meat glaze to the sauce. Meat glaze is a rich meat stock which has been reduced to a syrupy consistency. To produce the tablespoon of meat glaze, about ½ litre (16 fl oz) of meat stock would be needed.

To serve 6

400 g	chicken livers, trimmed and halved	14 oz
	salt and pepper	
30 g	butter	1 oz
12	green bacon lardons	12
12	tartlet shells	12
	Bordelaise sauce	
35 cl	dry red wine	12 fl oz
3	shallots, finely chopped	3
	freshly ground black pepper	
1	sprig thyme	1
15 cl	veal velouté (*page 167*)	¼ pint
60 g	beef marrow, sliced and poached in water for about 10 minutes	2 oz

To make the sauce, put the shallots into a pan and add the wine, pepper and thyme. Cook until the liquid is reduced to one quarter its original volume. Add the veal velouté and simmer for 20 minutes. Strain the sauce through a muslin cloth and add the marrow. Reserve and keep the sauce warm.

Season the livers and sauté them in half the butter. Do not overcook—they should be pink in the centre. Remove the livers from the pan and sauté the bacon. Stir the rest of the butter into the Bordelaise sauce. Fill the tartlet shells with livers, bacon and marrow and pour the sauce over them.

ÉDOUARD NIGNON
LES PLAISIRS DE LA TABLE

Stuffed Presentations

Stuffed Swiss Chard Leaves

Mahshi Silq bi Zayt

Sumac *water is sometimes substituted for the lemon juice. Sumac is a powder made from the dried berries of the sumac tree and is obtainable at Middle Eastern grocers. The powder is steeped in boiling water for about 15 minutes. Use about 1 teaspoon of powder to 12.5 cl (4 fl oz) of water. Sumac is somewhat more astringent than lemon juice.*

To serve 6

1.5 kg	Swiss chard, ribs removed, dipped in boiling salted water for 1 minute to soften	3 lb
100 g	chick peas, soaked in water overnight and drained	3½ oz
350 g	rice, rinsed and drained	12 oz
40 g	parsley, chopped	1½ oz
30 g	mint, chopped	1 oz
60 g	spring onions, finely chopped	2 oz
300 g	tomatoes, one sliced, the rest skinned, seeded and chopped	10 oz
1½ tsp	salt	1½ tsp
½ tsp	black pepper	½ tsp
¼ tsp	ground cinnamon	¼ tsp
¼ litre	olive oil	8 fl oz
12.5 cl	lemon juice	4 fl oz
6	small onions, peeled and sliced	6
3	garlic cloves	3

Crush the chick peas with a rolling pin. Discard the skins which come off during rolling. Mix the rice, chick peas, parsley, mint, spring onions, chopped tomatoes, salt, 1 teaspoon of the pepper, cinnamon, oil and 6 tablespoons of the lemon juice. Put a heaped teaspoon of this stuffing into each chard leaf. Fold the stem and tip of each leaf towards the centre, then roll the leaf up lengthwise to form a cigar shape. Lay the sliced tomato, the onions and garlic cloves in the bottom of a saucepan. Pack the leaves tightly in layers with the seams downwards. Sprinkle the leaves with the rest of the lemon juice and salt. Pour on enough water to cover. Simmer for about 1½ hours or until the stuffing is tender, adding more water as it is absorbed. Leave the pan uncovered for the last 10 minutes, to reduce the sauce.

MARIE KARAM KHAYAT AND MARGARET CLARK KEATINGE
FOOD FROM THE ARAB WORLD

Russian Stuffed Vine Leaves

Dolma

For an alternative sauce, mix 2 teaspoons of ground cinnamon with 30 g (1 oz) of icing sugar and 30 cl (½ pint) of soured milk. Buttermilk can be substituted for the soured milk.

To serve 6 to 8

400 g	fresh vine leaves, trimmed	14 oz
500 g	lamb, minced	1 lb
90 g	rice, boiled in salted water for 15 minutes and drained	3 oz
1	onion, grated	1
1 tbsp	finely cut dill	1 tbsp
	salt and pepper	
15 g	butter, melted	½ oz
¼ litre	stock (*page 167*)	8 fl oz
30 cl	soured milk, stirred	½ pint
1	garlic clove, finely chopped	1

Mix the meat with the rice, onion and dill. Season with salt and pepper. Spread the vine leaves on a table in overlapping pairs. Put a bit of stuffing on the wide end of each pair of leaves, fold the edges inwards and roll the leaves into a sausage shape. Sprinkle the leaves with salt and arrange them in rows in a shallow, buttered casserole. Pour over the butter and the stock. Cover the casserole tightly and simmer the contents over a low heat for about 1 hour or until the leaves are very tender. Pass separately the soured milk mixed with the chopped garlic and salt.

F. SIEGEL (TRANSLATOR)
RUSSIAN COOKING

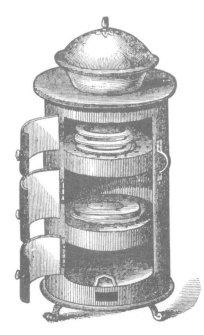

Stuffed Swiss Chard or Vine Leaves

Les Farcettes

The technique of preparing and stuffing leaves is shown on page 44. Although specific types of meat are given here, any equivalent weight of leftover meat can be used instead.

To serve 5

10	Swiss chard leaves, ribs removed, or vine leaves, steeped in boiling water for 5 minutes to soften, and well drained	10
125 g	butter	4 oz
25 g	flour	1 oz
20 cl	meat roasting juices	7 fl oz
10 cl	double cream	3½ fl oz
	salt and pepper	
90 g	roast chicken breast, skinned, flesh cut into narrow strips	3 oz
90 g	lean roast beef, cut into narrow strips	3 oz
90 g	lean roast leg of lamb, cut into narrow strips	3 oz
90 g	lean cooked ham, cut into strips	3 oz
60 g	Gruyère cheese, grated	2 oz

In a saucepan, combine about 30 g (1 oz) of the butter with the flour. Cook the mixture, stirring constantly, until it is browned, about 10 minutes. Moisten with 5 to 6 tablespoons of the meat juices and beat to make a smooth paste. Dilute the paste by gradually adding the cream, a small quantity at a time, while keeping the sauce fairly thick. Season with salt and pepper and simmer over a low heat for 5 minutes. Stir in the chicken, beef, lamb and ham.

Divide the stuffing between the 10 Swiss chard or vine leaves and fold the leaves over the stuffing to make small parcels. Transfer the parcels, seam downwards, to a gratin dish. Pour in the rest of the meat juices. Cut the remaining butter into equal-sized pieces and dot the stuffed leaves with it. Sprinkle the dish with the grated cheese and bake the stuffed leaves in a preheated 180°C (350°F or Mark 4) oven for 1 hour. Take care that the oven does not become too hot or the leaves will blacken. If they brown too quickly, reduce the heat during the cooking time.

LUCIEN TENDRET
LA TABLE AU PAYS DE BRILLAT-SAVARIN

Turkish Stuffed Vine Leaves

Yalanci Dolma

Stuffed vine leaves may also be served cold, in which case they should be well chilled before serving. The technique of stuffing vine leaves is shown on page 45. Preserved vine leaves should first be thoroughly rinsed in cold water and dried in a cloth.

To serve 4

About 40	vine leaves or cabbage leaves, parboiled, drained and rinsed in cold water	About 40
1	medium-sized onion, finely chopped	1
1 tbsp	olive oil	1 tbsp
125 g	rice, washed and drained	4 oz
60 g	currants	2 oz
60 g	pine-nuts	2 oz
1 tbsp	chopped parsley	1 tbsp
	ground allspice	
	ground cinnamon	
	salt and black pepper	
1 tbsp	tomato sauce (*page 166*) or tomato purée	1 tbsp
1	lemon, juice strained	1

Fry the onion in the olive oil until it becomes transparent. Add the rice to the onion and fry them both for a few minutes more, stirring well together; then add just enough water to cover the rice. Add the currants, pine-nuts, parsley and a pinch each of allspice, cinnamon, salt and pepper. Cook the mixture until the rice is dry. Stir in the tomato sauce or the purée to moisten the rice mixture a little.

Take 20 of the leaves. Put a teaspoon of the stuffing in the centre of each leaf, fold it up securely into a little package and pack it tightly into the bottom of a stew-pot. Between each layer of stuffed vine leaves, place some more leaves. When all are ready and wedged into the pot, press an inverted saucer on top of them and cover with water, the lemon juice and seasoning to the level of the saucer. Close the lid of the pot and simmer the vine leaves for 1 hour. Drain off the water and arrange the stuffed vine leaves on a platter.

VENICE LAMB
THE HOME BOOK OF TURKISH COOKERY

Stuffed Vine Leaves

Misov Derevapatat

If you use preserved vine leaves, there is no need to parboil them, but rinse them thoroughly with cold water and dry them with a cloth. The technique for stuffing and cooking vine leaves is demonstrated on pages 44-45.

	To serve 4 to 6	
16 to 18	fresh vine leaves, parboiled for 2 minutes	16 to 18
500 g	boneless shoulder of lamb, chopped	1 lb
250 g	onions, finely chopped	8 oz
2 tbsp	chopped parsley	2 tbsp
60 g	rice	2 oz
1 tsp	salt	1 tsp
	black pepper	
5 tbsp	puréed tomato	5 tbsp
½	lemon, juice extracted	½

Mix the lamb, onions, parsley, rice, salt and pepper, puréed tomato and lemon juice. Roll the vine leaves round teaspoons of the mixture to make small packages about 7 by 2 cm (3 by ¾ inches). Place the stuffed leaves in rows in a baking dish and cover them with water. Cover the baking dish and bake in a preheated 180°C (350°F or Mark 4) oven for 1 hour.

GEORGE MARDIKIAN
DINNER AT OMAR KHAYYAM'S

Stuffed Ceps

Les Cèpes Farcis

	To serve 4	
500 g	firm, fresh ceps, wiped clean with a damp cloth, stalks trimmed and chopped	1 lb
60 g	fresh breadcrumbs	2 oz
2	shallots, chopped	2
4 tbsp	olive oil	4 tbsp
	salt and pepper	

To make the stuffing, sauté the stalks, breadcrumbs and shallots in 2 tablespoons of the olive oil, until they are lightly browned. Lightly sauté the cep caps separately in the remaining oil. Remove them from the pan and arrange them underside upwards in an earthenware gratin dish. Garnish the ceps with the stuffing and bake them in a preheated 180°C (350°F or Mark 4) oven for about 30 minutes.

ÉDOUARD DE POMIANE
LE CODE DE LA BONNE CHÈRE

Stuffed Marrow Flowers

Fiori di Zucca Ripieni

If you have any leftover meat, use it instead of the ham. Instead of oil 60 g (2 oz) of butter may be used for frying.

	To serve 4	
12	marrow flowers, stalks trimmed	12
175 g	*mozzarella* cheese, diced	6 oz
50 g	cooked ham, chopped	2 oz
30 g	parsley, chopped	1 oz
1	garlic clove, chopped	1
	salt and pepper	
2	eggs, beaten	2
	flour	
50 g	dry breadcrumbs	2 oz
20 cl	oil	7 fl oz
30 cl	tomato sauce (*page 166*)	½ pint

Put the diced *mozzarella* and chopped ham into a small bowl with the parsley, garlic and a pinch of pepper. Mix well and season with salt if necessary. Using a teaspoon, stuff the marrow flowers with the mixture. The amount you put in each will depend on the size of the flowers, but it is best to start by putting just a little stuffing in each flower and then topping them up.

Season the beaten eggs with salt. Flour the flowers lightly, taking care to hold the petals tightly together at the top, so that none of the stuffing escapes. Shake off any excess flour. Dip the flowers in the eggs and then in the breadcrumbs, pressing the crumbs on with your palm to make sure they stick well. Heat the oil and fry the flowers over a moderate heat. As soon as they are golden-brown on one side, 3 to 4 minutes, turn them over and finish cooking. Arrange them on a serving dish and serve with the tomato sauce.

FERNANDA GOSETTI
IN CUCINA CON FERNANDA GOSETTI

Lettuce with Cheese Stuffing

Romaines Farcies au Brocciu

If brocciu *cheese is not available, use* ricotta *or curd cheese.*

	To serve 16	
16	large cos lettuce leaves, soaked in water to cover with 2 tbsp vinegar for 15 minutes, rinsed and well drained	16
1 tbsp	olive oil	1 tbsp
1	garlic clove, chopped	1
	salt	

Brocciu cheese stuffing		
500 g	*brocciu* cheese	1 lb
3	eggs, beaten	3
4 tbsp	chopped parsley	4 tbsp
	salt and freshly ground pepper	

Combine the *brocciu* cheese, eggs and parsley and season them with salt and pepper. Place about 1 tablespoon of stuffing on each lettuce leaf, and wrap each leaf round the stuffing to make a parcel. Tie the parcels securely with thread, and arrange them side by side in a shallow pan or casserole. Add water—the lettuce parcels should be three-quarters immersed—then pour in the oil, add the garlic and season with salt. Cover the pan and simmer the contents over a very low heat for 35 to 45 minutes or until the lettuce parcels are tender. Remove the parcels and drain them, reserving the cooking liquid. To serve, arrange one lettuce parcel on each plate, remove the threads and pour on a little of the cooking liquid. Exquisite!

MARIA NUNZIA FILIPPINI
LA CUISINE CORSE

Onion Layers Stuffed with Cheese

Oignons Farcis au Brocciu

If brocciu cheese is not available, ricotta or curd cheese may be substituted. An alternative method of preparing the onion layers for stuffing is shown on page 48. The onions can be moistened with cream or dotted with butter before baking; otherwise, cover the dish with foil before baking and remove it 5 minutes before the end.

To serve 10

5	large onions, trimmed and peeled	5
500 g	*brocciu* cheese, sieved	1 lb
4 tbsp	chopped parsley	4 tbsp
200 g	ham, finely diced	7 oz
1	egg, beaten	1
	salt and pepper	

Blanch the onions in plenty of boiling, salted water. Remove them from the pan after about 15 minutes; they should still be relatively firm. Cool them and slice them in half vertically. Separate the layers of halved onions and reserve them.

Mix the parsley and ham with the cheese, add the beaten egg and season with salt and pepper. Mix well and fold each onion layer around a spoonful of stuffing.

Oil a baking dish, fill it with the stuffed onion layers seam downwards and bake them in a preheated 180°C (350°F or Mark 4) oven for 45 minutes.

CHRISTIANE SCHAPIRA
LA CUISINE CORSE

Stuffed Onions and Tomatoes

Cebolada Portuensa

To serve 4

4	Spanish onions, peeled, parboiled in salted water to cover for 12 minutes and drained	4
4	tomatoes, halved crosswise, pulp removed with a teaspoon	4
125 g	lean pork, minced	4 oz
125 g	lean beef, minced	4 oz
1	egg, beaten	1
1 tbsp	capers	1 tbsp
2	salt anchovies, soaked for 15 minutes, filleted, drained and chopped	2
3 tbsp	finely chopped parsley	3 tbsp
60 g	fresh breadcrumbs	2 oz
	salt and cayenne pepper	
6 tbsp	olive oil	6 tbsp
2 tbsp	wine vinegar	2 tbsp

Scoop out the centres of the onions, leaving a shell of onion about 1 cm ($\frac{1}{2}$ inch) thick. Chop the onion centres finely and mix them with the minced meat, egg, capers, chopped anchovies, parsley and breadcrumbs. Season to taste.

Use some of this mixture to stuff the onions. Invert a tomato half over each stuffed onion and sprinkle with half the oil. Fill the four remaining tomato halves with the rest of the stuffing and sprinkle them with the vinegar, salt and cayenne pepper to taste, and the remaining oil.

Grease an ovenproof dish large enough to hold the onions and tomatoes. Arrange the stuffed vegetables in the dish and bake them in a preheated 180°C (350°F or Mark 4) oven for 20 to 30 minutes or until the onions and tomatoes are tender and the stuffing cooked through.

LILO AUREDEN
DAS SCHMECKT SO GUT

117

Baked, Stuffed Onions

Cipolle Farcite

Leftover roast meat can be used instead of ham.

To serve 6

6	large onions	6
125 g	ham, chopped	4 oz
60 g	breadcrumbs	2 oz
60 g	butter, 30 g (1 oz) of it melted	2 oz
2 tbsp	double cream	2 tbsp
	salt and pepper	
2 tbsp	chopped marjoram	2 tbsp
6 tbsp	grated Parmesan cheese	6 tbsp

Wrap each onion in foil and bake in a preheated 200°C (400°F or Mark 6) oven for 45 minutes. When the onions are soft, remove the foil and the outer skin and scoop out the centres.

Chop the centres and mix them with the ham, breadcrumbs, melted butter, double cream, salt, pepper and chopped marjoram. Fill the onions with the stuffing. Place the onions in a buttered baking dish and sprinkle them with the grated cheese and the rest of the butter, cut into little pieces. Bake the onions for a further 15 minutes in a preheated 200°C (400°F or Mark 6) oven.

JANET ROSS AND MICHAEL WATERFIELD
LEAVES FROM OUR TUSCAN KITCHEN

Stuffed Cooked Artichokes

Artichauts Farcis

The technique of preparing artichoke bottoms is shown on page 46. The technique of preparing brains for cooking is demonstrated on page 33.

When the artichokes have been cooked in advance, they should be reheated in a steamer before the hot filling is added.

To serve 12

24	artichoke bottoms, boiled in salted water for 10 minutes or until tender and drained	24
Broad bean filling		
2 kg	fresh broad beans, shelled, peeled, parboiled for 1 minute in salted water and drained	4 lb
30 g	butter	1 oz
3 to 4 tbsp	double cream	3 to 4 tbsp
1 to 2 tbsp	lemon juice	1 to 2 tbsp
2 tbsp	chopped fresh savory	2 tbsp

Spinach filling		
500 g	spinach, with a few sorrel leaves if possible, trimmed, parboiled in salted water for 1 minute, drained, squeezed and chopped	1 lb
8 cl	white sauce (*page 166*) or 40g (1½ oz) melted butter, 3 tbsp double cream and a pinch of grated nutmeg	3 fl oz
60 g	Parmesan cheese, grated	2 oz
Mushroom filling		
250 g	mushrooms, chopped	8 oz
1	small garlic clove, chopped	1
2	shallots, chopped	2
30 g	butter	1 oz
¼ litre	white sauce (*page 166*)	8 fl oz
3 tbsp	double cream	3 tbsp
60 g	Gruyère or Parmesan cheese, grated	2 oz
Brain filling		
2 to 3	pairs of brains, soaked, parboiled, membranes removed, and diced	2 to 3
2	eggs, beaten	2
100 g	Gruyère cheese, grated	3½ oz
1 tbsp each	chopped parsley and chives	1 tbsp each
2 tbsp	dry breadcrumbs	2 tbsp
40 g	butter, melted	1½ oz

To make the broad bean filling, sieve the cooked beans into a pan and reheat them with the butter, cream and lemon juice. Finally, mix in the savory.

To make the spinach filling, blend the chopped spinach or spinach and sorrel with the white sauce or with the butter and cream and a pinch of nutmeg.

To make the mushroom filling, cook the mushrooms, garlic and shallots in butter. They should not brown but the juices should be well evaporated. Add the white sauce and cream.

To make the brain filling, mix the brains with the beaten eggs, grated cheese, chopped parsley and chives.

Stuff six artichoke bottoms with each type of filling. Top the spinach and mushroom filling with the grated cheese and brown under the grill before serving. To serve the brain-stuffed artichokes, sprinkle them with the breadcrumbs and melted butter and bake them for 15 minutes in a preheated 220°C (425°F or Mark 7) oven, or until the filling is just set.

JANE GRIGSON
JANE GRIGSON'S VEGETABLE BOOK

Onions Stuffed with Tuna

Cipolle Ripiene con Tonno

To serve 4

4	large onions, peeled and trimmed, poached in boiling water for 1 minute	4
250 g	tuna, blanched in boiling salted water for 20 minutes, flaked and finely chopped	8 oz
30 g	fresh breadcrumbs, soaked in milk and squeezed	1 oz
2	eggs, beaten	2
30 g	Parmesan cheese, grated	1 oz
	salt and pepper	
10 cl	oil	3½ fl oz
4 tbsp	dry breadcrumbs	4 tbsp

Cut the onions in half crosswise and scoop out the inner layers. Chop up these layers and mix them with the chopped tuna and the soaked breadcrumbs. Chop the mixture very finely and mix it with the eggs, cheese and salt and pepper.

Pour the oil into a wide ovenproof dish and arrange the onion halves in it, hollowed-out section upwards. Pour a drop of oil into each half, then fill it with the stuffing. Sprinkle the onion halves with the dry breadcrumbs and bake them in a preheated 180°C (350°F or Mark 4) oven for 30 minutes or until the filling is firm and the crumbs are golden-brown.

EMANUELE ROSSI (EDITOR)
LA VERA CUCINIERA GENOVESE

Artichokes with Cheese Stuffing

Artichauts Farcis au Brocciu

To make the red sauce, put 125 g (4 oz) diced green bacon in a pan and melt it over a low heat. Add two finely chopped onions and sauté them. Stir in 1 tablespoon of flour. Pour in ½ litre (16 fl oz) water or stock and 2 to 3 tablespoons of tomato purée, and add a bouquet garni. Simmer for 30 minutes. If brocciu *cheese is not available, use ricotta or curd cheese.*

To serve 6

6	artichokes, leaves trimmed, stems and chokes removed and discarded	6
100 g	salt pork, diced and sautéed	3½ oz
½ litre	red sauce	16 fl oz
4 tbsp	dry breadcrumbs	4 tbsp

Brocciu cheese stuffing		
300 g	brocciu cheese	10 oz
2	eggs	2
	salt and freshly ground pepper	

Mix the stuffing ingredients together. Gently splay the leaves of each artichoke to allow more space for the stuffing; fill the centres and leaves of the artichokes generously with the stuffing mixture.

Add the sautéed salt pork to the red sauce and pour the sauce into a casserole. Lay the artichokes on top, leaves uppermost. Sprinkle them with the dry breadcrumbs. Cover the casserole tightly and simmer the artichokes gently for 1 to 1½ hours or until they are tender.

MARIA NUNZIA FILIPPINI
LA CUISINE CORSE

Stuffed Artichokes with Ceps

Carciofi Ripieni

The technique of preparing artichoke bottoms is shown on page 46. Dried ceps can be bought at continental grocers.

To serve 6

6	artichoke bottoms, tender inner leaves reserved	6
60 g	fat and lean ham, chopped	2 oz
1	small spring onion, green part discarded, white part chopped	1
1	garlic clove, finely chopped	1
1 tbsp	chopped celery leaves	1 tbsp
1 tbsp	chopped parsley	1 tbsp
1 tbsp	dried ceps, soaked for 20 minutes in warm water, drained and finely chopped	1 tbsp
60 g	fresh breadcrumbs	2 oz
	salt and pepper	

To make the stuffing, combine the chopped ham, spring onion, garlic, celery leaves, parsley, dried ceps and breadcrumbs. Chop the tender leaves removed from the centre of the artichoke and mix them with the other stuffing ingredients. Season with salt and pepper. Fill the cavities in the artichokes with the mixture and use any leftover mixture to line the bottom of a buttered baking dish. Add water to the dish so that the artichokes are partly immersed in about 2 cm (1 inch) of water. Cover the dish and bake in a preheated 180°C (350°F or Mark 4) oven for about 1 hour or until the artichokes are tender.

PELLEGRINO ARTUSI
LA SCIENZA IN CUCINA E L'ARTE DI MANGIAR BENE

Aubergine Maakoude

The maakoude *is a thick Tunisian omelette, stuffed with leftover meat, fish or vegetables.*

To serve 6 to 8

500 g	aubergines	1 lb
1 tbsp	salt	1 tbsp
6 tbsp	olive oil	6 tbsp
40 g	fresh breadcrumbs, soaked in water and squeezed dry	1½ oz
10	eggs	10
1	large garlic clove, crushed	1
4 tbsp	chopped parsley	4 tbsp
2 tsp	lemon juice	2 tsp
	ground cinnamon	
	powdered saffron	
	ground cumin seeds	
	pepper	
12.5 cl	chicken stock	4 fl oz
1	sweet red pepper, trimmed, seeded and cut into strips	1

Cut the aubergines lengthwise into 2.5 cm (1 inch) thick slices. Score the flesh of each slice with a criss-cross veneer of thin cuts and sprinkle salt over the slices. Leave them to drain for 30 minutes. Preheat a grill. Squeeze the pieces of aubergine carefully to rid them of their water, then brush each lightly on both sides with olive oil. Place the aubergines under the grill and grill them until tender, turning the slices once. Scrape the flesh from the skins and mash it with a fork until it is relatively smooth. Reserve the skins for garnish.

Mix the breadcrumbs, aubergine, eggs, garlic, parsley, lemon juice, spices and seasoning and blend well.

Heat 5 tablespoons of olive oil in a straight-sided pan, 18 to 20 cm (7 to 8 inches) in diameter (use a heavy cake tin preferably; failing that, a shallow, enamelled iron casserole). Swirl the pan to coat the sides with oil and pour in the eggs and aubergine mixture. Turn the heat to low and cover the pan tightly. In 8 to 10 minutes, the egg will set at the edges. Run a knife around the omelette to loosen the edge. Re-cover the pan and cook until the top is just firm. Uncover the pan, place an upturned plate over it and turn the pan over so that the omelette falls on to the plate. Pour a little more oil into the pan, then slide the omelette back into it to brown lightly on the other side—6 to 8 minutes.

Off the heat, pour the stock over the omelette, cover the pan and let it rest for 5 minutes. Turn it out on to a serving platter and garnish it with chopped parsley, sweet red pepper strips and the aubergine skins cut into petal shapes.

JUDITH OLNEY
COMFORTING FOOD

Egyptian-Style Aubergines

Auberginen auf Ägyptische Art

To serve 4

2	medium-sized aubergines, peeled and cut lengthwise into 1 cm (½ inch) slices	2
10 cl	oil	3½ fl oz
100 g	fresh breadcrumbs	3½ oz
1	onion, finely chopped	1
125 g	bacon, chopped	4 oz
3 tbsp	finely chopped parsley	3 tbsp
1	garlic clove, crushed	1
	salt and pepper	

Brown the aubergines on both sides in the oil and drain them on absorbent paper. Mix the breadcrumbs, onion, bacon, parsley, garlic and salt and pepper to make a stuffing. Spread the stuffing over the aubergine slices and lay the slices in a buttered gratin dish with the stuffing uppermost. Bake in a preheated 180°C (350°F or Mark 4) oven for about 20 to 30 minutes, or until the stuffing is lightly golden.

THEODOR BÖTTIGER
DAS GRILL-BUCH

Aubergine Stuffed with Brains

Another way of stuffing aubergines is to split them, score the flesh and sauté them, then scoop out the flesh, as demonstrated on page 50. The preparation of brains for cooking is shown on page 33. If you want the beaten egg topping lightly set, wait until the aubergines are half baked before adding it.

To serve 6

350 g	aubergines, trimmed	12 oz
250 g	calf's or beef brains, soaked in salted water to cover for 1 to 2 hours, membranes removed	8 oz
	salt	
4 tbsp	oil	4 tbsp
250 g	ripe tomatoes, skinned, seeded and chopped	8 oz
2	garlic cloves, peeled	2
	freshly ground black pepper	
1 tbsp	chopped parsley	1 tbsp
3	eggs, beaten to a froth	3

With a thin-bladed knife, remove 1 cm (½ inch) vertical strips from each aubergine, leaving them striped. Slice the aubergines in half lengthwise and scoop out the centre pulp, carefully leaving a 5 mm (¼ inch) thick wall of flesh in each half shell. Cube the pulp. Sprinkle each half shell and the cubed aubergine with salt and let them drain in a colander for at least 30 minutes. Squeeze them gently, then rinse well under running water. Pat them dry with paper towels.

Heat the oil in a frying pan and fry the aubergine shells on both sides over a low heat until they are soft. Remove and drain them. Reserve all but 1 tablespoon of the oil in the pan; since aubergine tends to soak up oil, you may need to add the reserved oil later.

Sauté the aubergine cubes and the chopped tomato in the oil in the pan with the garlic, salt and pepper to taste, and the parsley. Cook for a few minutes so that the flavours blend, then place the mixture in a bowl. Discard the garlic cloves.

In a saucepan, simmer the brains in salted water for about 10 minutes. Drain them and cut them into small cubes. Add them to the tomato and aubergine mixture and mix them lightly. Preheat the oven to 180°C (350°F or Mark 4).

Stuff the aubergine shells with the brain, tomato and aubergine mixture. Place the shells in a lightly oiled, oven-proof serving dish, packing them tightly so they do not fall over. Pour the beaten eggs over the stuffed aubergines. Sprinkle with salt and pepper and bake for 30 minutes. Serve directly from the dish or loosen the sides of the firmly set eggs and then invert the mixture on to a serving platter.

PAULA WOLFERT
COUSCOUS AND OTHER GOOD FOOD FROM MOROCCO

Corsican Stuffed Aubergines

Aubergines Farcies

The aubergines may be served on a large warmed serving dish covered with a spicy tomato sauce (*recipe, page 166*).

	To serve 12	
6	medium-sized aubergines, halved lengthwise	6
175 g	stale bread, crusts removed, soaked in milk and squeezed	6 oz
3	garlic cloves, chopped	3
5	large fresh basil leaves, chopped	5
	salt and freshly ground pepper	
2	eggs	2
15 g	butter, softened	½ oz
60 g	Parmesan cheese, grated	2 oz
12.5 cl	oil	4 fl oz

Parboil the aubergine halves in boiling water for 8 to 10 minutes, removing them while they are still firm. Leave them to cool to tepid, then scoop out the pulp. Strain it through an old cloth—the weave will be looser—or a sieve. Chop the strained pulp and mix it with the bread, garlic and basil; season with salt and pepper. Beat in the eggs, one at a time, then the butter and lastly the grated cheese.

Fill the 12 aubergine shells with the prepared stuffing, and fry them in the oil, on both sides, beginning with the stuffing side down, until it is golden—about 5 minutes on each side.

MARIA NUNZIA FILIPPINI
LA CUISINE CORSE

Stuffed Aubergines

Aubergines du Vallon

	To serve 4	
4	small round aubergines, trimmed, tops sliced off and reserved	4
100 g	loin of veal, chopped	3½ oz
100 g	sausage-meat	3½ oz
90 g	cooked rice	3 oz
2	eggs, beaten	2
2	garlic cloves, chopped	2
60 g	Parmesan cheese, grated	2 oz
	salt and pepper	
10 cl	oil	3½ fl oz
100 g	green streaky bacon, cut into 8 lardons	3½ oz
1	onion, coarsely chopped	1
4	tomatoes, skinned, seeded and chopped	4
10 cl	water	3½ fl oz
4	fresh basil leaves	4

Scoop out the flesh from the aubergines with a teaspoon and squeeze it to remove excess liquid. Chop it and mix it with the chopped veal, sausage-meat, rice, eggs, garlic, Parmesan cheese, salt and pepper. Mix well. Fill each aubergine shell five-sixths full with the stuffing.

Put the reserved tops back on the aubergines. In a casserole, heat the oil and bacon lardons. Add the onion and the aubergines to the pan. Cook gently, on a low heat, stirring carefully with a wooden spoon, for 10 minutes. Add the chopped tomatoes, pouring them over the aubergines. Add the water and basil, salt and pepper. Cover the pan and simmer the contents over a low heat for 1½ hours. Remove the aubergines carefully from the pan and arrange them on a serving dish. Surround them with the cooking juices.

SUZANNE SIMONET
LE GRAND LIVRE DE LA CUISINE OCCITANE

Courgettes with Veal and Prosciutto

Zucchini Ripieni

The preparation of courgettes for stuffing is shown on page 50.

When preparing stuffed courgettes, you may either slice the courgettes in half, lengthwise or crosswise, or else leave them whole. The latter method is preferred here as being more elegant and giving more attractive results.

	To serve 6	
1 kg	courgettes, ends trimmed	2 to 2½ lb
60 g	butter	2 oz
	Veal and prosciutto stuffing	
125 g	lean veal, cut into pieces	4 oz
30 g	prosciutto, finely chopped	1 oz
1	onion, finely chopped	1
2 tbsp	finely chopped parsley	2 tbsp
1	stick celery, finely chopped	1
1	carrot, finely chopped	1
2 tbsp	olive oil	2 tbsp
	salt and pepper	
About 60 cl	water	About 1 pint
100 g	bread, crusts removed	3½ oz
¼ litre	milk or stock (*page 167*)	8 fl oz
1 tsp	ground allspice	1 tsp
1	egg	1
45 g	Parmesan cheese, grated	1½ oz

Use an apple corer to scoop out the insides of the courgettes, to leave room for the stuffing. If the courgettes are large and the cavities do not seem big enough, widen them with a knife.

To make the filling, put the veal in a pan over a medium heat with the onion, parsley, celery, carrot, prosciutto, olive oil, salt and pepper. Stir the mixture frequently and when the meat has absorbed all the liquid and has begun to brown, pour in a soup ladleful of water. Continue to simmer. When the water has been absorbed, pour in another ladleful of water. Pour in two more ladlefuls of water, waiting each time for the mixture to absorb the liquid; the meat should now be tender

and there should be a little cooking liquid left with it. Strain the cooking liquid and reserve it.

Simmer the bread in the milk or stock with the ground allspice until all the liquid has been absorbed, about 15 minutes. Chop the strained meat mixture very fine in a bowl and combine it with the egg, Parmesan cheese and bread paste. Use this filling to stuff the courgettes.

Heat the butter in a frying pan until it is almost nut-brown in colour. Sauté the stuffed courgettes until they are lightly coloured. Add the reserved cooking liquid, cover and simmer until the courgettes are tender, about 20 to 25 minutes.

PELLEGRINO ARTUSI
LA SCIENZA IN CUCINA E L'ARTE DI MANGIAR BENE

French Stuffed Courgettes

Courgettes Farcies

Choose courgettes weighing about 90 g (3 oz) each. Use round ones for preference; otherwise use courgettes about 4 to 5 cm (1½ to 2 inches) in diameter, cut into 6 cm (2½ inch) lengths.

	To serve 2	
6	courgettes, stalks trimmed, 5 mm (¼ inch) round sliced from the stalk end and reserved	6
2 tbsp	coarse salt	2 tbsp
2 tbsp	chopped onion	2 tbsp
4 tbsp	olive oil	4 tbsp
3	large mushrooms, chopped	3
30 g	cooked ham, diced	1 oz
3	sage leaves, chopped	3
	salt and pepper	

In a saucepan, boil 2 litres (3½ pints) of water with the coarse salt. Plunge in the courgettes and the rounds you have cut off them and boil them for 10 minutes. Rinse them under cold running water and drain them in a colander. Hollow out the flesh with a teaspoon, taking great care not to pierce the skin. Put the shells and the rounds on one side and chop the scooped-out flesh coarsely.

Using the pan in which you have cooked the courgettes, brown the chopped onion in 2 tablespoons of the oil. Cook for 7 to 8 minutes, stirring with a wooden spoon or spatula. Then add the mushrooms, ham and sage. Stir for a further 5 minutes, then add the flesh of the courgettes. Season with salt, increase the heat and stir briskly until the liquid from the courgettes has evaporated. Take care that the mixture does not stick to the bottom of the pan and burn. Taste, season with more salt if necessary, and pepper.

Arrange the courgette shells on a buttered baking sheet or in a buttered roasting tin just large enough to hold them. They should be packed in fairly tightly. Put the stuffing into the shells with a teaspoon, pushing it well down. Cover the courgettes with their tops and sprinkle them with the remaining olive oil. Bake them in a preheated 200°C (400°F or Mark 6) oven for 35 minutes. Look at the courgettes from time to time. If their cooking liquid appears to be drying up add 1 to 2 tablespoons of warm water during the cooking.

ROGER VERGÉ
CUISINE OF THE SUN

Sweet Green Peppers Stuffed with Courgettes

Chiles Rellenos con Calabacitas

Chiles poblanos *are slightly tapered, dark green, sweet peppers. If they are not available, use any fresh sweet green peppers. To prepare the peppers for stuffing, char them evenly over a naked flame or under a very hot grill. Put them into a plastic bag or cover with a damp cloth to let them sweat for 15 to 20 minutes, then peel them. Make a slit down one side of each pepper; cut out the core holding the seeds under the base of the stem, and remove as many veins as is possible without tearing the flesh. This should leave the vegetable with the stalk base and stalk intact. Rinse the pepper under cold water to remove any remaining seeds.*

	To serve 6	
6	*chiles poblanos*, prepared for stuffing	6
750 g	courgettes, trimmed and finely diced	1½ lb
2½ tbsp	peanut or safflower oil	2½ tbsp
½	onion, finely chopped	½
2	garlic cloves, finely chopped	2
1 tsp	salt	1 tsp
¼ tsp	oregano	¼ tsp
2 tbsp	wine vinegar	2 tbsp
1	lime or lemon, juice strained	1
2 tbsp	olive oil	2 tbsp
175 g	*ricotta* or curd cheese, crumbled	6 oz
2 tbsp	unsalted butter	2 tbsp
6	lettuce leaves	6
6	radishes	6

Put 1½ tablespoons of the oil, the courgettes, all but 2 tablespoons of the onion, half the garlic and the salt into a heavy pan, then cover and cook over a medium heat for about 8 minutes, turning the mixture from time to time so that it does not stick. (The courgettes should steam in their own juices, but if they seem very dry, add a little water. Courgettes vary in moisture content, so if there appears to be too much water,

remove the lid and turn up the heat to reduce the liquid.)

Remove the pan from the heat and leave the contents to cool slightly. While the mixture is still warm, add the remaining onion and garlic, the oregano and vinegar, the lime or lemon juice, olive oil and the cheese. Adjust the seasoning. Stuff the peppers with the mixture until they are full but will still meet at the opening. There should be about 125 g (4 oz) of stuffing left over, depending on the size of the peppers. Fasten each opening with a toothpick.

Melt the butter with the remaining oil. Add the stuffed peppers and fry them over a medium heat, turning them over gently so that the stuffing does not fall out. Cook them until they are lightly browned. Arrange the peppers on a serving dish and garnish them with the lettuce leaves and radishes. Sprinkle them with the remaining stuffing.

DIANA KENNEDY
RECIPES FROM THE REGIONAL COOKS OF MEXICO

Stuffed Courgettes

The scooped-out centres of the courgettes can be used in the stuffing mixture. If you find you have made too much stuffing, use it to line the dish in which the courgettes are cooked. The technique for making stuffed courgettes is shown on page 50.

	To serve 4	
8	small courgettes, ends trimmed	8
500 g	minced beef	1 lb
1	egg	1
2	garlic cloves, finely chopped	2
2 tsp	salt	2 tsp
½ tsp	oregano	½ tsp
2	slices bread, crusts removed, soaked in water and squeezed almost dry	2
3 tbsp	olive oil	3 tbsp
	chopped parsley	

Use an apple corer to scoop out the centres of the courgettes. In a bowl, combine the minced beef, egg, chopped garlic, salt, oregano and bread. Put the meat mixture into a piping bag fitted with a plain tube and pipe the mixture into the courgettes from both ends.

Heat the olive oil in a frying pan and sauté the stuffed courgettes over a high heat until lightly browned on all sides, about 10 minutes. Arrange the courgettes in a baking dish and pour on the oil remaining in the frying pan. Bake the courgettes in an oven preheated to 180°C (350°F or Mark 4) for about 20 minutes or until they are tender. To serve, sprinkle with chopped parsley.

JULIE DANNENBAUM
MENUS FOR ALL OCCASIONS

Stuffed Tomatoes with Soured Cream Sauce

Gefüllte Tomaten

For a spicier filling, add 60 g (2 oz) finely chopped lean bacon, 1 tablespoon of chopped capers or a few drops of lemon juice and a pinch of paprika to the stuffing.

	To serve 4	
8	large tomatoes	8
¼ litre	soured cream	8 fl oz
	salt and pepper	
500 g	minced beef or pork	1 lb
90 g	butter	3 oz
2	medium-sized onions, chopped	2
100 g	cooked rice	3½ oz
1	egg	1
30 g	cheese, grated (optional)	1 oz
1 tbsp	flour	1 tbsp
2 tbsp	chopped, fresh dill or parsley	2 tbsp

Slice off a small lid from the top of each tomato and scoop out the centre pulp without damaging the flesh. Sprinkle the insides of the tomatoes with salt and pepper.

Fry the minced meat in 30 g (1 oz) of the butter until lightly browned. Add half the onions, and continue frying until the onions are transparent. Mix the meat and onions with the cooked rice, egg, salt and pepper, and use this mixture to stuff the tomatoes. Replace the tomato lids. Butter an ovenproof dish and arrange the tomatoes in it. If you like, sprinkle them with the grated cheese. Melt 30 g (1 oz) of the butter and pour it over the tomatoes. Bake them in a preheated 200°C (400°F or Mark 6) oven for about 15 minutes or until the tomatoes are cooked and the stuffing heated through.

Meanwhile, make the soured cream sauce. Cook the rest of the onions in the remaining butter until transparent. Stir in the tablespoon of flour, then the soured cream, and cook, stirring constantly, for 1 to 2 minutes.

Transfer the cooked tomatoes to a serving dish, pour over the soured cream sauce and sprinkle with dill or parsley.

KULINARISCHE GERICHTE: ZU GAST BEI FREUNDEN

Stuffed Tomatoes

Pomidoro Ripieni

	To serve 6	
12	tomatoes	12
30 g	butter	1 oz
2	onions, finely chopped	2
60 g	parsley, chopped	2 oz
125 g	fresh breadcrumbs, soaked in milk and squeezed	4 oz
60 g	Parmesan cheese, grated	2 oz
1	egg, beaten	1
	salt and pepper	
3 tbsp	chopped oregano	3 tbsp
8 cl	oil	3 fl oz
4 tbsp	dry breadcrumbs	4 tbsp

Heat the butter gently in a pan, add the onions and parsley and fry until the onions are soft. Put the contents of the pan in a large mortar, add the soaked breadcrumbs and pound the mixture into a paste. To this paste, add the grated cheese, egg, salt and pepper and oregano, and mix well.

Slice off the tops of the tomatoes and reserve them. Scoop out the seeds and juice and stuff the cavities with the onion mixture. Replace the tops. Arrange the stuffed tomatoes in a pan just large enough to hold them; sprinkle them with the oil and dry breadcrumbs. Bake in a preheated 180°C (350°F or Mark 4) oven for 40 minutes or until lightly browned.

EMANUELE ROSSI (EDITOR)
LA VERA CUCINIERA GENOVESE

Stuffed Potatoes

Gefüllte Kartoffeln

	To serve 4	
4	large, unblemished potatoes	4
	salt and pepper	
60 g	butter, half of it softened	2 oz
60 g	cheese, grated	2 oz
1	egg yolk	1
4 tbsp	soured cream	4 tbsp

Peel the potatoes and shave off a slice at one end so that they will stand level in a dish. Slice off the opposite ends and reserve them. Hollow out the centres and stand the potatoes hollow side up on a buttered baking sheet or ovenproof dish.

To make the filling, finely chop the scooped-out potato and mix it with the salt, pepper, the softened butter, half of the grated cheese, the egg yolk and soured cream.

Fill the potatoes with the mixture and replace the reserved slices. Melt the rest of the butter and brush the potatoes with it. Bake the potatoes in a preheated 180°C (350°F or Mark 4) oven for 50 minutes to 1 hour. Sprinkle them with the rest of the grated cheese before serving.

ELEK MAGYAR
KOCHBUCH FÜR FEINSCHMECKER

Stuffed Beetroot

Gefüllte Rote Rüben

To cook the beetroot, trim them carefully to avoid damaging the skin, wash them and immerse them in unsalted, rapidly boiling water to which 1 to 2 tablespoons of vinegar have been added. Simmer for about 1 hour.

To serve 6 to 8

6 to 8	medium-sized beetroot, cooked and peeled	6 to 8
1	medium-sized onion, chopped	1
60 g	butter	2 oz
500 g	minced meat, cooked	1 lb
100 g	cooked rice	3½ oz
1	egg	1
	salt and pepper	
¼ litre	soured cream	8 fl oz

Use a teaspoon to scoop out the centres of the beetroot. Fry the onion in half the butter until transparent, then mix it with the cooked meat, rice, egg, salt and pepper. Fill the beetroot with the stuffing. Butter an ovenproof dish, arrange the beetroot in it and bake them in an oven preheated to 200°C (400°F or Mark 6) for 8 to 10 minutes, to heat the stuffing.

Remove the beetroot from the oven, pour the soured cream over them and return them to the oven for a few more minutes. Transfer them to a serving dish.

KULINARISCHE GERICHTE: ZU GAST BEI FREUNDEN

Fish Balls

Polpette di Pesce

This recipe is based on one by the Roman gourmet Marcus Garius Apicius who lived in the first century B.C. The collection of his cookery writings dates from the second century A.D. The fish filling can include crustaceans such as crayfish or cuttlefish, or the fish can be replaced by chopped liver.

To serve 4

500 g	fish, cooked in boiling salted water for 20 minutes, filleted, skinned and flaked	1 lb
5 tbsp	olive oil	5 tbsp
½	onion, finely chopped	½
20	pine-nuts, chopped	20
1 tbsp	chopped rue	1 tbsp
1 tbsp	chopped marjoram	1 tbsp
	freshly ground pepper	
1	egg, beaten	1
	salt	
30 g	fresh breadcrumbs, crumbled (optional)	1 oz
300 g	pork caul	10 oz
15 g	butter	½ oz
10 cl	dry white wine	3½ fl oz
2	bay leaves	2

In a frying pan, heat the oil on a low heat and add the onion. When the onion starts to brown, in about 15 minutes, remove it from the pan and discard it. Put the fish into the pan and add the pine-nuts, rue, marjoram and a pinch of pepper. Mix well. Remove the pan from the heat and stir in the beaten egg. Season with salt. The mixture should be firm enough to hold its shape. If necessary, add a few breadcrumbs to thicken it.

On a work surface, spread out the pork caul, stretching it as much as possible without breaking it. Slice it into eight equal-sized pieces. Divide the fish mixture between the pieces of caul, placing it in the centre of each piece. Fold the sides of each piece of caul over the middle to make a little ball.

In a frying pan, melt the butter over a low heat, add the fish balls carefully and cook, turning them until the caul has given off part of its fat, about 3 minutes. Add the wine and bay leaves. Increase the heat to allow some of the liquid to evaporate. Remove the bay leaves and serve the fish balls hot.

MASSIMO ALBERINI
CENTO RICETTE STORICHE

Stuffed Sardines Catalan-Style

Popietas de Sardinas a la Catalana

To serve 4

750 g	fresh sardines, cleaned, heads removed, filleted	1½ lb
4	eggs, beaten	4
10 cl	olive oil	3½ fl oz
1 or 2	garlic cloves, finely chopped	1 or 2
2 tbsp	chopped parsley	2 tbsp
1	hard-boiled egg, chopped	1
	salt and white pepper	
1 tsp	vinegar	1 tsp
15 cl	dry white wine	¼ pint
60 g	dry breadcrumbs	2 oz
16	croûtons	16
2	tomatoes, halved and grilled	2

Take two-thirds of the sardines and open them out, cavities upwards. Brush the cavities with one of the beaten eggs and leave the sardines on a cool work surface.

Sauté the remaining sardines in 4 tablespoons of the oil, with the chopped garlic, parsley and hard-boiled egg. Break up the mixture with a fork. Add salt and pepper to taste, and the vinegar and 3 to 4 tablespoons of the wine. Beat in 1 egg to bind the mixture, stir it over a very low heat until it thickens. Leave it to cool.

Spread some of this filling on each of the open sardines. Close them, dip them in the rest of the beaten egg and the breadcrumbs and lay them side by side in a shallow ovenproof dish. Sprinkle them with the rest of the oil and the white wine, and bake them in a preheated 180°C (350°F or Mark 4) oven for 15 minutes. Serve with the croûtons and tomato halves.

GLORIA ROSSI CALLIZO
LAS MEJORES TAPAS, CENAS FRÍAS Y PLATOS COMBINADOS

Mussels with Snail Butter

Les Moules au Beurre d'Escargot

The technique of preparing mussels and opening them in white wine are shown on page 31. The quantities for the snail butter recipe were originally based on servings for 50 people and have been reduced here for home use.

To serve 8 to 10

4 litres	live mussels, cleaned and opened in white wine	7 pints
	coarse salt	

Snail butter

250 g	butter, softened	8 oz
1	salt anchovy, soaked, filleted, rinsed and drained	1
2	garlic cloves, peeled	2
2 tbsp	coarsely chopped parsley	2 tbsp
	salt and freshly ground pepper	
	cayenne pepper	
	anise liqueur	
1	lemon, juice strained	1

To make the snail butter, pound the anchovy fillets with the garlic. Beat them into the butter and gradually add the parsley, salt, pepper and a pinch of cayenne pepper, mixing well to blend thoroughly. Finally, beat in a few drops of anise liqueur and the lemon juice. When all are well blended together, taste and correct the seasoning if necessary.

Remove the mussels from their shells. Fill the bottom of each half-shell with a little snail butter. Put a mussel into each half-shell and cover it with more snail butter.

Cover with coarse salt the bottom of a gratin dish large enough to hold the mussels, or use a number of smaller dishes. Lay the mussels carefully on the bed of salt and bake them in a preheated 230°C (450°F or Mark 8) oven for 10 minutes.

ALEXANDRE DUMAINE
MA CUISINE

Stuffed Mussels

Moules à la Bordelaise

The technique of opening mussels is demonstrated on page 31.

To serve 16

4 litres	live mussels, opened in white wine	7 pints
50 g	stale bread, crusts removed	2 oz
12.5 cl	milk	4 fl oz
20 g	butter	¾ oz
2	shallots, chopped	2
1 tsp	flour	1 tsp
2 tbsp	chopped parsley	2 tbsp
1 tbsp	tomato purée	1 tbsp
	salt and pepper	

Strain the mussel cooking juices through muslin and reserve them. Twist off and discard the empty half of each mussel shell. Soak the bread in the milk.

Melt the butter in a saucepan over a low heat, add the shallots and cook for about 5 minutes or until golden. Sprinkle the flour over the shallots, moisten with the reserved mussel juices and add the parsley and tomato purée. Squeeze the bread and crumble it into the shallot mixture. Season with salt and pepper. Cook for 10 minutes, stirring constantly.

Press this stuffing into the mussels on the half-shell. Put the stuffed mussels into the pan and cook them for a further 5 minutes over a low heat until heated through.

CÉLINE VENCE
ENCYCLOPÉDIE HACHETTE DE LA CUISINE RÉGIONALE

Stuffed Oysters

Huitres Farcies

The technique of opening oysters is shown on page 54.

To serve 4

12	large live oysters	12
2 tbsp	chopped parsley	2 tbsp
2	spring onions, chopped	2
2	salt anchovies, soaked for 15 minutes, filleted, rinsed, drained and dried	2
60 g	butter	2 oz
	salt and pepper	
30 g	fresh breadcrumbs, moistened with enough cream to make a paste	1 oz
2 or 3	egg yolks	2 or 3
	grated nutmeg	
	mixed spice	
4 tbsp	dry breadcrumbs (optional)	4 tbsp
1	lemon, juice extracted (optional)	1

Shell the oysters and poach them in their own liquid for 1 minute. Drain and chop them. Mix the chopped parsley, spring onions, anchovies, half the butter and salt and pepper with the oysters. Add the bread paste, egg yolks, nutmeg and mixed spice. Pound the mixture in a mortar until it forms a smooth paste. Stuff the oyster shells with the mixture. Melt the remaining butter and pour it over the oyster shells. If you like, sprinkle them with the breadcrumbs.

Bake the oysters in a preheated 200°C (400°F or Mark 6) oven for 10 minutes, then brown them under a hot grill for 2 minutes until they are golden. Serve them as they are or sprinkled with the lemon juice.

LOUIS LIGER
LA NOUVELLE MAISON RUSTIQUE

Stuffed Sardines

Sardines Farcies

To serve 4

16	large fresh sardines, cleaned, heads removed, filleted, bones reserved	16
	salt and pepper	
1	onion, thinly sliced, separated into rings	1
3 tbsp	oil	3 tbsp
2	salt anchovies, filleted, soaked for 30 minutes, rinsed and drained	2
$\frac{1}{2}$ tsp	chopped thyme	$\frac{1}{2}$ tsp
60 g	clarified butter	2 oz
20 cl	dry white wine	7 fl oz
10 cl	oil	$3\frac{1}{2}$ fl oz

Open out the sardines. Lay them in a gratin dish insides upwards, and season them with salt and pepper. Sauté the onion rings in the oil.

Put the bones in a mortar with the anchovies, thyme and a little pepper. Pound the mixture into a smooth paste. Spread the paste into the cavities of the sardines. Smear the sardines lightly with the clarified butter, close them up and sprinkle them with the wine and 3 tablespoons of the oil.

Bake the sardines in a preheated 170°C (325°F or Mark 3) oven (the wine and oil should barely simmer) for 25 minutes or until cooked through.

To serve, lay the sardines on a dish, sprinkle them with the rest of the oil and surround them with the onion rings.

MME JEANNE SAVARIN (EDITOR)
LA CUISINE DES FAMILLES

127

Oysters Rockefeller

The spinach used in this recipe may be parboiled. If a coarser texture is preferred for the filling, do not sieve it. The technique of preparing Oysters Rockefeller is shown on page 54.

To serve 6

36	oysters, on the half-shell	36
90 g	butter	3 oz
100 g	spinach, trimmed and finely chopped	3½ oz
3 tbsp	finely chopped parsley	3 tbsp
1	heart celery, finely chopped	1
1	onion, peeled and finely chopped	1
5 tbsp	fine dry breadcrumbs	5 tbsp
	Tabasco sauce	
½ tsp	salt	½ tsp
½ tbsp	pastis or anisette	½ tbsp
	coarse salt	

In a saucepan, melt the butter and stir in all of the ingredients except the oysters and the coarse salt. Cook over a low heat, stirring constantly, for 15 minutes. Press the mixture through a sieve or food mill and set it aside.

Cover six pie dishes with a layer of coarse salt and place the oysters on the salt. Put a teaspoon of the vegetable mixture on each oyster. Grill the oysters under a preheated hot grill for 3 to 5 minutes or until the topping begins to brown. Serve immediately, in the pie dishes.

THE EDITORS OF AMERICAN HERITAGE
THE AMERICAN HERITAGE COOKBOOK

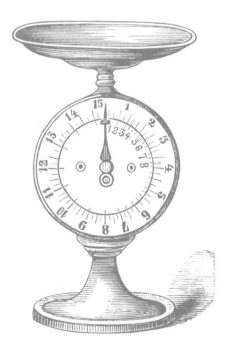

Sardines with Cheese Stuffing

Sardines Farcies au Brocciu

If brocciu *cheese is not available, use* ricotta *or* curd cheese.

To serve 3

12	fresh sardines, heads removed, cleaned and boned	12
500 g	*brocciu* cheese	1 lb
1	egg, beaten	1
	salt and freshly ground pepper	
60 g	dry breadcrumbs	2 oz
3 tbsp	olive oil	3 tbsp

To make the stuffing, mix the *brocciu* with the egg, salt and pepper. Put a tablespoon of stuffing into each sardine and arrange the sardines in an ovenproof dish. Sprinkle them with the dry breadcrumbs and the oil and bake them in a preheated 190°C (375°F or Mark 5) oven for 20 minutes or until golden-brown.

MARIA NUNZIA FILIPPINI
LA CUISINE CORSE

Montpellier-Style Stuffed Snails

Escargots à la Montpelliéraine

The preparation of snails for cooking is shown on page 52.

To serve 4

200	small live snails, cleaned	200
1 litre	white wine court-bouillon *(page 164)*	1¾ pints
5 or 6	garlic cloves, chopped	5 or 6
3 tbsp	olive oil	3 tbsp
250 g	almonds, blanched or walnuts	8 oz
2 tbsp	chopped parsley	2 tbsp
150 g	salt anchovies, soaked for 30 minutes, filleted, soaked, drained and chopped	5 oz
200 g	green streaky bacon, diced	7 oz
3 tbsp	brandy	3 tbsp
10 cl	dry white wine	3½ fl oz

Cook the snails in the court-bouillon for 2 hours. They are ready when they are easily removed from their shells. Remove them with a cocktail fork or toothpick, drain them well and reserve the snails, their shells and cooking liquid.

To make the sauce, pound the garlic in a mortar with 1 tablespoon of the oil, the almonds or walnuts, the parsley and the anchovies. In a heavy-based frying pan, heat the remaining oil and cook the bacon in it for 2 minutes. Drain off excess fat, add the purée and cook, stirring, for a further 2 minutes. Pour in the brandy, stir, then add the wine. Simmer the mixture for 15 to 20 minutes. Add $\frac{1}{4}$ litre (8 fl oz) of the court-bouillon in which the snails were cooked. Stir well and simmer until the sauce is reduced by half and thickens slightly.

Put the reserved snails into the sauce, then stuff them back into their shells. Put the filled snail shells into the sauce and simmer for 10 minutes so that the flavours of the snails and the sauce intermingle. The sauce will have thinned slightly because of the cooking liquid retained by the snails. Bring the cooking pot to the table and serve the snails piping hot.

ALBIN MARTY
FOURMIGUETTO: SOUVENIRS, CONTES ET RECETTES DU LANGUEDOC

Stuffed Snails

Limaces à la Suçarelle

Limace or limaçon is the Provençal name for the common or garden snail (helix aspersa). The French name for this recipe refers to the way in which the snails are eaten—sucer means "to suck" since the snails are sucked out of their shells. The technique of preparing snails for cooking is shown on page 52.

To serve 8

200	small live snails, cooked in a white wine court-bouillon (*page 164*) for 2 hours or until tender, and drained	200
1	onion, finely chopped	1
2 to 3	tomatoes, skinned, seeded and chopped	2 to 3
2 tbsp	olive oil	2 tbsp
1 tbsp	flour	1 tbsp
15 cl	dry white wine	$\frac{1}{4}$ pint
30 cl	water	$\frac{1}{2}$ pint
	salt and freshly ground black pepper	
1 or 2	salt anchovies, soaked in water for 30 minutes, filleted, rinsed, drained and chopped (optional)	1 or 2

Use a sharp knife to make a hole in the bulbous part of the back of the snail shells. Reserve the snails in their shells.

Sauté the onion and tomatoes in the oil. Add the flour, cook for a few more minutes, then pour in the wine. Allow the wine to evaporate, then add the water and season with salt and pepper. Cover the pan and simmer the contents for 25 minutes. Add the snails in their shells and the anchovy fillets, if you intend to use them.

Serve the snails very hot in the sauce. They are extracted from their shells through the hole in the back, either with a pin, or by being sucked out.

EUGÈNE BLANCARD
METS ET PRODUITS DE PROVENCE

Spanish Stuffed Snails

Caracoles Rellenos

The preparation of snails for cooking is shown on page 52.

To serve 4

24	large live snails, parboiled in salted boiling water for $1\frac{1}{2}$ hours, shelled, shells reserved	24
4 tbsp	olive oil	4 tbsp
1	onion, finely chopped	1
4	tomatoes, skinned, seeded and chopped	4
6	garlic cloves, chopped	6
2 tbsp	chopped parsley	2 tbsp
1 tbsp each	chopped fennel, thyme and oregano	1 tbsp
	salt and pepper	
2 tbsp	fresh breadcrumbs	2 tbsp
2 tbsp	dry white wine	2 tbsp

Chop the snail meat finely, discarding the dark bit at the very end of each snail. In a frying pan, heat 2 tablespoons of the olive oil and add the onion, tomatoes and four of the garlic cloves. Add 1 tablespoon of the parsley and all the other herbs. Season with salt and pepper and simmer gently for 20 minutes, stirring occasionally, until the mixture forms a thick sauce. Stir in the snails and cook for a few minutes, until the snails are heated through.

Spoon enough of this mixture into each shell to fill it to the top. Oil a shallow ovenproof dish and fit the stuffed shells in fairly tightly, mouth side up. If they do not fit well they will fall over and the stuffing may come out. Four small individual snail dishes may be used if preferred.

Mix the rest of the garlic with the rest of the oil, a little salt, the breadcrumbs, wine and the rest of the parsley. Sprinkle the mixture over the snails and put the dish under the grill to lightly brown the tops.

ANNA MACMIADHACHÁIN
SPANISH REGIONAL COOKERY

White Puddings

Boudin Blanc

White puddings, eaten at Christmas time in France, are made in advance, and are rolled in butter and grilled before serving. The technique of making sausages is shown on page 58.

If you cook the puddings in milk, they will be more delicate.

To make 10 sausages

250 g	pork kidney fat, cut into small dice	8 oz
1	roasted chicken breast, skinned and finely chopped	1
3	sprigs parsley	3
2	spring onions, trimmed	2
1	sprig thyme	1
1	sprig basil	1
2	shallots, peeled	2
3	cloves	3
1	bay leaf	1
10 to 12	coriander seeds	10 to 12
12	onions, peeled and quartered	12
60 cl	fatty meat stock (*page 167*)	1 pint
	salt and pepper	
125 g	white bread, crusts removed	4 oz
15 cl	milk	$\frac{1}{4}$ pint
125 g	almonds, blanched	4 oz
$\frac{1}{2}$ litre	double cream, warmed	16 fl oz
8	egg yolks	8
	salt	
	mixed spice	
2 metres	salted pork sausage casings, soaked and drained	6 feet

Tie the parsley, spring onions, thyme and basil together, and tie the shallots, cloves, bay leaf and coriander seeds in a muslin cloth. Put them in a deep saucepan with the onion quarters and stock, add salt and pepper and simmer until the onions are tender and all the liquid has been absorbed. Remove the onions from the pan and purée them.

Put the bread into a pan with the milk and cook, stirring constantly, until the bread has absorbed all the milk and is reduced to a paste. Add the bread to the puréed onion.

Pound the almonds in a mortar. Mix them with the cream, adding it gradually. Then pass the mixture through a strong tightly woven cloth to extract all the liquid. Mix the almond

cream with the bread and onion. Add the egg yolks, pork kidney fat, chicken meat, salt and spice. Mix the ingredients thoroughly and stuff them into sausage casings. Tie the casings at 7 cm (3 inch) intervals.

To cook the sausages, prick them in several places to let out the air and stop them from bursting. Start the sausages in cold or tepid milk or water and bring them to a simmer. Cook them for up to 40 minutes.

MENON
LES SOUPERS DE LA COUR

Chicken Patties

Crépinettes de Volaille Saint Germain

Crépinettes are minced meat patties wrapped in pork caul. The caul is usually bought preserved in salt and must be soaked in tepid water for at least 30 minutes, then rinsed under running water and lightly dried.

Serve the *crépinettes* on a dish with a garnish of green peas made into a purée.

To serve 8

500 g	chicken flesh, sinews removed, very finely chopped	1 lb
500 g	fresh pork belly, rind removed, very finely chopped	1 lb
	salt and pepper	
1 tbsp	double cream	1 tbsp
1 tbsp	chopped shallots, fried for 5 minutes in 15 g ($\frac{1}{2}$ oz) butter (optional)	1 tbsp
1	pork caul, soaked, rinsed and dried and cut into 7.5 by 5 (3 by 2 inch) rectangles	1
60 g	dry breadcrumbs (optional)	2 oz
45 g	butter	$1\frac{1}{2}$ oz

Put the chicken and pork into a bowl, season to taste, add the cream and the shallots, if you are using them, and beat well to make the mixture smooth. Then form the mixture into cork-shaped patties about 5 cm (2 inches) long and 2.5 cm (1 inch) thick. To wrap each patty in a piece of pork caul, put a piece of caul in the palm of one hand, lay the patty on it and press it gently flat with the other hand. Wrap the caul round the patty. Repeat until the caul and meat mixture are used up. The patties may be rolled in breadcrumbs and fried in the butter for 15 minutes on each side; or brush melted butter on the patties and grill them for 15 minutes on each side.

A. BAUTTE
MODERN FRENCH AND ENGLISH COOKERY

White Puddings with Chicken

Boudins Blancs de Volaille

The technique of making sausages is shown on page 58. These white puddings may be made well in advance and then grilled just before serving.

To make about 20 small sausages

250 g	cooked white chicken meat, finely chopped	8 oz
125 g	onions, finely chopped	4 oz
250 g	pork kidney fat, cleaned and finely diced	8 oz
200 g	white bread, crusts removed, soaked in milk and squeezed almost dry	7 oz
20 cl	thick white sauce (*page 166*)	7 fl oz
30 g	truffles, finely chopped	1 oz
125 g	mushrooms, finely chopped and sautéed in butter	4 oz
7	egg yolks	7
	salt	
2 tsp	mixed spice	2 tsp
About 2 metres	salted lamb's sausage casings, soaked and drained	About 6 feet
	butter for grilling	

Parboil the onions for a few seconds, drain them and put them in a saucepan together with the pork kidney fat. Cook over a low heat for 10 to 12 minutes.

In a mortar, pound the bread with the chicken meat. Using a drum sieve, push the purée through a little at a time into a bowl. Add the onions, pork fat and white sauce gradually to the mixture. Then add the truffles and sautéed mushrooms, and beat in the yolks. Season with salt and mixed spice.

Using a funnel or forcing bag, stuff the forcemeat mixture into the sausage casings, knotting the sausages at 7 to 8 cm (3 inch) intervals. Put the sausages in a pan of warm water and heat slowly to just below boiling point. Cover the pan and remove it from the heat; leave the sausages to cool in the liquid. When cold, drain them, wrap them in a cloth and leave them in a cool place for at least a further 5 to 6 hours before serving. To serve, prick the sausages with a larding needle, roll them in melted butter and grill them gently, turning them at frequent intervals.

URBAIN DUBOIS AND ÉMILE BERNARD
LA CUISINE CLASSIQUE

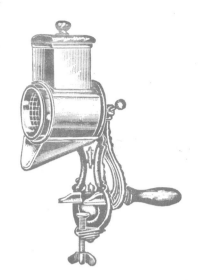

Crayfish Sausage

Boudin d'Écrevisses

These sausages are prepared in advance and may be refrigerated for several days. They are served grilled in butter. The technique of making sausages is shown on page 58. The preparation of sweetbreads for cooking is shown on page 32.

To make 12 to 16 sausages

1 kg	crayfish, cooked in white wine court-bouillon (*page 164*) for 8 to 10 minutes	2 to 2½ lb
125 g	unsalted butter, softened	4 oz
1	cooked chicken breast, skinned, sinews removed, flesh diced	1
1	pair of sweetbreads, soaked, cleaned, parboiled and diced	1
8	egg yolks	8
	salt and pepper	
10 cl	fish velouté (*page 167*) or white sauce (*page 166*)	3½ fl oz
2 metres	pork sausage casings, well cleaned	6 feet

Shell the crayfish and cut the tails into small dice. Pound the shells into a paste, pass the paste through the coarse disc of a food mill, and then through a fine drum-sieve, to eliminate all the debris. Mix the pounded crayfish with the butter. Add the mixture to a bowl with the chicken breast, diced sweetbreads and egg yolks. Season with salt and pepper, then pour in the velouté or white sauce. Stir well to blend the ingredients.

Use this mixture to stuff the sausage casings. Poach the sausages in two parts water to one part milk, seasoned with a little salt. Slash the skins very shallowly with the point of a sharp knife, and grill the sausages briefly before serving.

A. B. DE PÉRIGORD
LE TRÉSOR DE LA CUISINIÈRE ET DE LA MAÎTRESSE DE MAISON

Fish Sausages

Andouilles de Poisson

Although the author of this 18th-century recipe suggests stuffing the sausage mixture into eel skins, sausage casings of the same length can be substituted. The technique for making and poaching sausages is shown on page 58. The fish sausages are served brushed with melted butter and grilled.

To make 6 or 7 sausages

1 kg	white fish, cleaned, skinned and filleted, bones and trimmings reserved	2 to 2½ lb
¼ litre	red wine court-bouillon *(page 164)*	8 fl oz
8	egg yolks	8
	salt and freshly ground black pepper	
1 tsp	mixed spice	1 tsp
2 metres	eel skins	6 feet
30 g	butter	1 oz
90 cl	white wine court-bouillon *(page 164)*	1½ pints

Pound the bones and fish trimmings in a mortar, add them to the red wine court-bouillon and cook for 15 minutes, or until the liquid has reduced by two-thirds. Strain the liquid. Chop the fish fillets or slice them into narrow strips, and mix them with the egg yolks, salt, pepper and mixed spice. Stuff this mixture into the eel skins to make sausages about 15 cm (6 inches) long. Prick the sausages all over with a fork. Add the butter to the cold white wine court-bouillon, put the sausages into the court-bouillon and gradually heat until the liquid is just below the boil. Poach the sausages in the court-bouillon for about 20 minutes, then drain them. Serve grilled.

MENON
LES SOUPERS DE LA COUR

Cantal Pancake with Herbs

Crêpe Cantalienne

Cantal is a district in the Auvergne. The making of pancakes is shown on page 56.

To serve 4

30 g	cheese, grated	1 oz
30 cl	pancake batter *(page 164)*	½ pint
2 tbsp	*fines herbes*	2 tbsp
20 cl	white sauce *(page 166)*	7 fl oz
4	thin slices cooked ham	4
4 tbsp	dry breadcrumbs	4 tbsp
60 g	butter, melted	2 oz

Use the batter to make eight pancakes. Mix the grated cheese and *fines herbes* with the white sauce. Lay four of the pancakes in a buttered shallow baking dish or on a buttered baking sheet. Spread the four pancakes with 1 tablespoon each of the white sauce mixture, and lay a slice of ham on each. Cover with the remaining four pancakes and pour the rest of the white sauce over them. Mix the breadcrumbs with the melted butter and sprinkle them on the pancakes. Bake the pancakes in a preheated 220°C (425°F or Mark 7) oven for 10 minutes or until lightly browned.

AMICALE DES CUISINIERS ET PÂTISSIERS AUVERGNATS DE PARIS
CUISINE D'AUVERGNE

Green Spinach Crêpes

The making of pancakes is shown on page 56. The rolled pancakes should be warmed through in a preheated 230°C (450°F or Mark 8) oven for 10 minutes, before grilling.

To serve 6

750 g	spinach, parboiled in salted water for 1 minute, drained and finely chopped	1½ lb
1 litre	pancake batter *(page 164)*	1¾ pints
75 g	butter	2½ oz
250 g	mushrooms, finely chopped	8 oz
½ tsp	salt	½ tsp
	freshly ground pepper	
	cayenne pepper	
4 tbsp	double cream	4 tbsp
40 g	Parmesan cheese, grated	1½ oz

Squeeze the juice from about one-third of the spinach into the batter. Discard the squeezed spinach. Use the batter and 60 g (2 oz) of the butter to make thirty 12 cm (4½ inch) crêpes.

Sauté the mushrooms in the remaining butter for 5 minutes. Combine the mushrooms with the rest of the spinach. Season with salt and pepper and a dash of cayenne pepper. Add the cream to bind the ingredients together. Spread this mixture over one-third of the surface of each crêpe and roll the crêpe up. Place the rolled crêpes, seams downwards side by side in a buttered gratin dish. Sprinkle the crêpes lightly with the grated cheese. Brown the dish under the grill.

CHARLOTTE ADAMS
THE FOUR SEASONS COOKBOOK

Stuffed Pancake Rolls

Les Canelloni

In France, the term "cannelloni" is used to refer to pancake rolls as well as pasta rolls. The technique of making pancakes is shown on page 56.

Cannelloni can be stuffed with meat, brains, fish and mushrooms; they are an excellent way of using up leftovers.

To serve 3 or 4

12	12.5 cm (5 inch) pancakes	12
150 g	roasted or stewed meat, chopped	5 oz
30 g	ham, chopped (optional)	1 oz
1 kg	spinach, trimmed, parboiled in salted water for 1 minute, drained, squeezed and chopped	2 to 2½ lb
	salt and pepper	
	mixed spice	
2	egg yolks, beaten	2
20 cl	meat roasting juices or tomato sauce (*page 166*)	7 fl oz
60 g	Parmesan cheese, grated	2 oz

To make the stuffing, mix the chopped meat and ham, if used, with the spinach. Season with salt and pepper and mixed spice to taste. Bind the mixture with the egg yolks.

Take a pancake and put two heaped teaspoons of stuffing in the centre. Fold two opposite sides of the pancake circle to meet over the stuffing. Then roll up the pancake like a Swiss roll at right angles to the folded sides. Do the same with the other pancakes. Arrange the rolls flap side down in a buttered gratin dish just large enough to hold them. Pour over the meat juices or tomato sauce and sprinkle with the Parmesan cheese. Bake in a preheated 230°C (450°F or Mark 8) oven for 10 to 15 minutes and brown under a hot grill for 1 minute.

ÉDOUARD DE POMIANE
LE CODE DE LA BONNE CHÈRE

Pancakes Stuffed with Avocado and Crab Meat

Crêpes Farcies

The making of pancakes is shown on page 56.

To serve 6

2	avocados	2
250 g	crab meat	8 oz
½ litre	pancake batter (*page 161*)	16 fl oz
125 g	unsalted butter, softened	4 oz
	salt and white pepper	
4 tbsp	brandy	4 tbsp
12.5 cl	sherry	4 fl oz
¼ litre	double cream	8 fl oz
	cayenne pepper	
¼ litre	hollandaise sauce (*page 166*)	8 fl oz
1 tsp	Dijon mustard	1 tsp
90 g	fresh breadcrumbs	3 oz

Cut the avocados in half lengthwise; remove the stones and spread half the butter over them. Put them in an oven preheated to 200°C (400°F or Mark 6) for 5 minutes, then scoop out the avocado flesh and purée it, mixing in a pinch of salt and a pinch of white pepper. Set the purée aside.

Turn the crab meat into a saucepan, add the brandy and flambé. Add the sherry, double cream, salt and cayenne pepper. Bring the mixture to the boil. Remove the saucepan from the heat and mix the hollandaise sauce in gently, as the crab meat should be kept in lumps; then add the mustard. Adjust the seasoning for salt.

Prepare 12 pancakes. Spread them evenly with the avocado purée, topping with the crab meat. Roll them up tightly and place them in a buttered, shallow baking dish. Sprinkle with breadcrumbs and dot with the remaining butter.

When you are ready to serve the pancakes, place them in an oven preheated to 200°C (400°F or Mark 6) for 10 minutes, then under the grill for 1 minute to brown.

ANTOINE GILLY AND JACK DENTON SCOTT
ANTOINE GILLY'S FEAST OF FRANCE

Custards and Soufflés

Shellfish Quiche

Quiche Honfleuraise

The technique of baking blind is shown on page 68. Opening oysters is shown on page 54. The preparation of shellfish for cooking is shown on page 30.

To make one 30 cm (12 inch) quiche

1 litre	live mussels, soaked, shells cleaned	1¾ pints
20	live oysters, opened and shelled	20
125 g	cooked shrimps, shelled	4 oz
300 g	shortcrust dough (*page 165*)	10 oz
2	onions, chopped	2
2	shallots, chopped	2
15 cl	dry white wine	¼ pint
	salt and pepper	
3	eggs, beaten	3
¼ litre	*crème fraîche* or double cream	8 fl oz
	grated nutmeg	

Roll out the dough to fit a 30 cm (12 inch) buttered flan tin. Bake it blind until it is cooked but not coloured.

In a pan, put the onions, shallots, wine, mussels, and a pinch each of salt and pepper. Cover the pan and shake it gently while cooking, for about 10 minutes or until the mussels have opened. Remove them from the pan, strain them, reserving the cooking liquid, and shell them.

Poach the oysters in slightly salted water to cover and simmer until just firm, about 5 minutes, then drain them.

Put the cooked mussels, oysters and shrimps into the pastry case. Mix together the mussels' cooking liquid, eggs, cream, and a pinch each of salt, pepper and nutmeg and pour the mixture over the filling. Bake the tart in a preheated 220°C (425°F or Mark 7) oven for 10 minutes, then lower the temperature to 190°C (375°F or Mark 5) and bake for a further 20 minutes or until golden-brown.

MARIE BISSON
LA CUISINE NORMANDE

Cheese and Onion Tart

Tarte Paysanne

The dough in this recipe may be baked blind for 15 minutes, then the filling added and the tart baked for a further 20 minutes. The technique of baking blind is shown on page 68.

To make one 30 cm (12 inch) tart

70 g	Gruyère cheese, grated	2½ oz
750 g	onion, thinly sliced	1½ lb
350 g	shortcrust dough (*page 165*)	12 oz
100 g	butter	3½ oz
2	eggs, beaten	2

Make the shortcrust dough and roll it out to line a 30 cm (12 inch) flan tin. Cook the onions gently in the butter until transparent. In a bowl, mix together the onions, eggs and the grated cheese; season to taste, and spread the mixture in the flan tin. Bake the tart in a preheated 190°C (375°F or Mark 5) oven for 30 minutes, or until the filling has set and the pastry has turned golden-brown.

CURNONSKY
CUISINE ET VINS DE FRANCE

Onion Tart

Tarte aux Oignons

The technique of baking blind is shown on page 68.

To make one 20 cm (8 inch) tart

4	large onions, thinly sliced	4
250 g	rough-puff dough (*page 165*) made with equal quantities of butter and lard	8 oz
150 g	butter	5 oz
3	rashers streaky bacon, diced	3
3	eggs, beaten	3
4 tbsp	double cream	4 tbsp

Roll out the rough-puff dough and use it to line a buttered 20 cm (8 inch) flan tin. Bake the pastry blind for about 15 minutes, until set but not coloured.

Put the onions into cold, salted water and bring them to the boil on a high heat. When they have boiled for 3 minutes, remove them from the pan and drain them well.

Melt 30 g (1 oz) of the butter in a pan and sauté the bacon until lightly browned. In a saucepan, melt the rest of the butter, add the onions and cook them over a low heat until they are a light brown colour. Add the bacon and mix. Drain off the excess fat and reserve the onions and bacon until they are tepid. Mix the eggs and the double cream and add them to the onions and bacon. Fill the pastry case with the prepared onion mixture and bake it in a preheated 200°C (400°F or Mark 6) oven for about 15 minutes, or until the filling and pastry are lightly browned.

X. MARCEL BOULESTIN
A SECOND HELPING OR MORE DISHES FOR ENGLISH HOMES

Bacon and Cream Flan

Quiche Lorraine

The pastry case can also be baked blind before the filling is added. For the technique of baking blind, see page 68. The bacon can be lightly sautéed before being put into the case.

To make one 25 cm (10 inch) flan

60 g	streaky bacon, thinly sliced and cut into lardons 3 by 1 cm (1½ by ½ inch)	2 oz
½ litre	double cream	16 fl oz
500 g	shortcrust dough (*page 165*) made with half lard and half butter	1 lb
2	eggs	2
	salt	
30 g	unsalted butter, cut into small pieces	1 oz

Make the dough and roll it out to fit a floured 25 cm (10 inch) flan tin. Prick the dough thoroughly with a fork.

In a large bowl, mix the cream, eggs and a pinch of salt, and beat well to obtain a smooth, homogenous mixture.

Arrange the lardons of bacon in fairly compact concentric rings in the pastry case; the surface of the pastry case should be evenly and fairly closely covered with the bacon. Put pieces of the butter into a few of the empty spaces.

Pour the cream and egg mixture carefully into the pastry case. Bake the flan in a preheated 200°C (400°F or Mark 6) oven for about 25 minutes. Look at the flan occasionally; if the filling swells up, prick it gently with the point of a sharp knife, taking care not to pierce the pastry. Bake until the filling is golden-brown and the pastry has browned.

ROGER LALLEMAND
LA VRAIE CUISINE DE LA LORRAINE

Gateau of Green Vegetables

Gâteau d'Herbage à l'Ancienne

The technique of making a vegetable custard is shown on page 66. If the water in the water bath starts to simmer, turn down the oven to 180°C (350°F or Mark 4).

To make one 15 cm (6 inch) custard

4	green cabbage leaves, ribs removed, parboiled for 4 minutes, drained and pressed	4
150 g	spinach, stalks removed, rapidly parboiled, drained and pressed	5 oz
60 g	sorrel, stalks removed, parboiled for 4 minutes and well drained	2 oz
60 g	chard, stalks removed, parboiled for 4 minutes and well drained	2 oz
150 g	leeks, trimmed and thinly sliced, parboiled for 9 minutes and well drained	5 oz
1	bouquet garni	1
1	egg	1
1	egg white	1
20 cl	skimmed milk	7 fl oz
	salt and pepper	
⅓ tsp	chopped tarragon	⅓ tsp
⅓ tsp	finely cut chives	⅓ tsp
½ tsp	chopped parsley	½ tsp
½	onion, chopped	½

Parboil each vegetable separately with the bouquet garni, using the same lightly salted boiling water. Beat the egg and the egg white with a fork, just enough to mix them together. Add the skimmed milk, a pinch each of the salt and pepper, and the chopped herbs and onion.

Line a buttered 15 cm (6 inch) cake tin about 5 cm (2 inches) deep with the cabbage leaves, leaving enough hanging over the sides to cover the contents completely once the stuffing has been added. Arrange the cake in layers, first the leeks, then spinach, sorrel and chard and then spoon over some of the egg and herb mixture. Repeat with layers of vegetables and egg and herb mixture, ending with the egg and herb mixture. Fold the cabbage leaves over the top.

Cover the gateau with aluminium foil and bake it in a bain-marie in a preheated 220°C (425°F or Mark 7) oven for 1¼ hours. Take it out of the oven and allow it to rest for 15 minutes before turning it out of the cake tin, so that it can settle a bit and keep its shape when sliced.

MICHEL GUÉRARD
MICHEL GUÉRARD'S CUISINE MINCEUR

Little Fish Creams with Shrimp Sauce

Petits Crèmes à la Dieppoise

The technique of cooking cucumbers is shown on page 29.

	To serve 6	
1	whole whiting or other white fish, weighing about 500 g (1 lb)	1
30 cl	milk	½ pint
30 cl	water	½ pint
	salt and pepper	
60 g	onion, finely chopped	2 oz
15 g	celery, finely chopped	½ oz
1	sprig parsley	1
1 tsp	mixed dried herbs	1 tsp
	butter	
About 60 g	white bread, crusts removed, soaked in milk and squeezed	About 2 oz
2	eggs, beaten	2
1	egg yolk	1
2 tbsp	double cream	2 tbsp
1 tbsp	flour	1 tbsp
125 g	shrimps, finely chopped	4 oz
	cooked cucumber slices (optional)	

Take the flesh in two fillets from each side of the whiting or other white fish and put them aside. Chop up the head, bones and skin, put them into a stew-pan with the milk and water, season with salt and pepper and bring slowly to the boil over a low heat. Then add the onion, celery, parsley and dried herbs. Simmer for 45 minutes and strain into a clean saucepan.

Bring this fumet to the boil, put in the two fillets and reduce to a simmer. As soon as they are soft, take out the fillets, put them in a mortar and pound them to a paste. Weigh the paste, and for 175 g (6 oz) of whiting or other white fish, allow 60 g (2 oz) of butter and the same weight of bread soaked in milk. Mix the paste, butter and bread together and pass all through a wire sieve. Add to this purée the eggs and egg yolk. Beat well together, taste and season if required and stir in 1 tablespoon of the cream.

Butter 12 ramekins or dariole moulds and fill them with the mixture, tapping each one on a folded cloth laid on the table to ensure even filling. To poach them very gently, choose a roomy stew-pan. Lay a sheet of paper folded in four at the bottom of it, pour in hot water about 2 cm (1 inch) deep, set the pan on the heat, and when nearly boiling, slip in the ramekins or moulds; let boiling begin but at once reduce to gentle simmering, keeping the pan covered.

While this is proceeding, turn the broth in which the fillets were cooked into a sauce; mix 15 g (½ oz) of butter with the flour

in a saucepan, stir well and pour in the broth. Bring the mixture to the boil, pass it through a fine sieve, add the chopped shrimps and the rest of the cream.

When the creams are ready, after about 35 minutes, turn them out of the moulds, arrange them in a circle on a hot dish, and mask with the sauce. A pile of cooked cucumber slices may be arranged in the centre.

A. KENNEY-HERBERT ("WYVERN")
FIFTY LUNCHES

Little Hare Custards

Pains de Lièvre à la Monselet

The authors recommend serving the custards with a sauce made by cooking the hare bones and trimmings with vegetables and wine, simmering the mixture for about 2 hours, then straining it and reducing it to a syrupy consistency.

Only the hind legs of the hare are used for these custards. The front legs are used for a stew; the back or saddle may be roasted or used in a pâté. A tart apple purée, made without sugar and flavoured with lemon juice, should be served as a separate accompaniment.

	To serve 12	
2	hare hind legs, bones and sinews removed	2
	salt and freshly ground pepper	
	quatre épices	
20 cl	thick white sauce (*page 166*), cooled	7 fl oz
12.5 cl	double cream	4 fl oz
4	egg yolks	4

Put the meat into a mortar with the salt, pepper and a pinch of *quatre épices*. Stir in the thick white sauce, then the cream and lastly the egg yolks. Strain the mixture through a fine sieve. Pour the strained purée into 12 buttered individual moulds or ramekins. Place the moulds in a large pan and pour boiling water into the pan until the moulds are two-thirds immersed. Cook the custards in a preheated 180°C (350°F or Mark 4) oven for 12 minutes or until set. Unmould the custards, arranging them in a circle on a serving dish.

LE CORDON BLEU

Lyons Chicken Liver Custard

Pâté de Foie Ménagère

The preparation of livers for cooking is shown on page 32.

To serve 4

200 g	chicken livers, trimmed and finely chopped	7 oz
1	shallot, chopped	1
1	garlic clove, chopped	1
1 tbsp	chopped parsley	1 tbsp
¼ litre	milk	8 fl oz
	salt and pepper	
	grated nutmeg	
15 g	butter	½ oz
3	eggs, beaten	3
30 cl	velouté sauce (*page 167*)	½ pint

Mix together the livers, shallot, garlic and parsley. Add to the milk the salt and pepper, a pinch of nutmeg and the butter and bring the milk to the boil. Remove it from the heat and add the liver mixture and the beaten eggs. Whisk until the mixture is fairly smooth and pour it into a 1 litre (1¾ pint) buttered mould. Cook the custard in a bain-marie over a very low heat or in a preheated 170°C (325°F or Mark 3) oven for 25 minutes, or until just set. Remove the custard from the oven, and leave it to stand for 7 to 8 minutes before unmoulding it. Serve with velouté sauce or thickened meat roasting juices.

FÉLIX BENOIT AND HENRY CLOS JOUVE
LA CUISINE LYONNAISE

Oyster Patties

The method for opening oysters is demonstrated on page 54.

To make 12 patties

12	live oysters, shelled	12
350 g	shortcrust dough (*page 165*) moistened with 1 tsp lemon juice	12 oz
2	egg yolks	2
15 cl	double cream	¼ pint
½	lemon, juice strained	½
1 tbsp	finely chopped parsley	1 tbsp
	freshly ground black pepper	

Roll out the dough as thinly as possible and use it to line 12 buttered tartlet tins. Line each pastry case with foil and fill it with dried beans. Bake the shells in a preheated 220°C (425°F or Mark 7) oven for 5 minutes, then remove the foil and the beans and bake for a further 10 minutes or until the pastry is crisp and light golden in colour.

Boil the oysters in their liquid for 2 minutes. Strain the liquid through a fine sieve into a clean pan, bring it to the boil and cook over a high heat until it is reduced by about half.

Cut each oyster in half. Beat the egg yolks and cream together and cook the mixture in a pan over a very low heat until it begins to thicken. Add the lemon juice, about 3 tablespoons of the oyster liquor and the parsley. Season with pepper and mix in the oysters. Spoon the filling into the cases and serve at once.

MARIKA HANBURY TENISON
RECIPES FROM A COUNTRY KITCHEN

Onion and Crispy Pork Quiche

Quiche Tourangelle

To crisp the pork, dice 300 g (10 oz) of pork belly. Put it in a frying pan, add 6 tablespoons of milk and cook over a brisk heat. When the pieces of pork have turned golden-brown, drain them on paper towels. Season them with salt before they cool. The pastry case for this quiche can also be baked blind. The method for baking blind is shown on page 68. This recipe comes from Le Lyonnais Restaurant, Tours, France.

To make one 25 cm (10 inch) quiche

300 g	onions, thinly sliced	10 oz
200 g	crisp pork belly, chopped	7 oz
350 g	shortcrust dough (*page 165*)	12 oz
30 g	butter	1 oz
¼ litre	*crème fraîche* or double cream	8 fl oz
¼ litre	milk	8 fl oz
2	eggs, beaten	2
2	egg yolks, beaten	2
	salt and pepper	
	grated nutmeg	

Stew the onions in the butter in a covered pan until they are soft, about 20 minutes. Mix together the cream, milk, eggs, egg yolks, salt, pepper and a pinch of grated nutmeg.

Roll out the dough and use it to line a buttered 25 cm (10 inch) flan tin. Cover the dough with the onions and crispy pork. Pour on the cream and egg mixture and bake the quiche in a preheated 200°C (400°F or Mark 6) oven for 30 minutes, or until golden-brown on top.

PAUL-JACQUES LÉVÊQUE (EDITOR)
LES BONNES RECETTES DE LA CUISINE TOURANGELLE

Baked Tomato Custards

Flanes de Tomates

To serve 6

750 g	tomatoes, roughly chopped	1½ lb
40 g	butter	1½ oz
	salt	
1 tsp	sugar	1 tsp
3	eggs	3

Butter six individual moulds. Simmer the tomatoes until they are soft. Then sieve them into a saucepan containing the butter. Add a pinch of salt and the sugar and simmer gently for 10 minutes. Remove the purée from the heat and leave it to cool. Beat the eggs well and season them with salt. Add the eggs to the cooled tomatoes, and mix well. Fill the moulds with the tomato and egg mixture and cook them in a bain-marie in a preheated 190°C (375°F or Mark 5) oven for about 20 minutes, or until the custards are set.

VICTORIA SERRA
TÍA VICTORIA'S SPANISH KITCHEN

Maize Custards with Mushroom Purée

To serve 4

40 g	fine cornmeal	1½ oz
¼ tsp	salt	¼ tsp
	pepper	
2	eggs, beaten	2
About 17.5 cl	double cream	About 6 fl oz
	Mushroom purée	
125 g	mushrooms, wiped, trimmed and puréed in a blender or food processor	4 oz
30 g	butter	1 oz
	salt and pepper	
About 5 tbsp	double cream	About 5 tbsp
	lemon juice	

Mix the cornmeal, salt and pepper in a bowl. Make a well in the middle and slowly stir in the eggs and the cream. Let the mixture sit for 10 minutes, covered with a kitchen towel.

Butter eight ramekins or a deep muffin tin with eight wells. Give the batter a good stir, then divide it equally among the moulds. Place a baking tin holding 2.5 cm (1 inch) of hot water in a preheated 170°C (325°F or Mark 3) oven and put the moulds in the water. Bake for 30 minutes, checking once to make sure that the water is not boiling round the custards. Reduce the heat if necessary.

For the mushroom purée, melt the butter in a saucepan over a fairly high heat, add the puréed mushrooms and seasoning and cook briefly until the mushrooms have given off all their water and appear very soft. Pour the cream into the purée, stirring until the mixture is smooth and syrupy. Remove the pan from the heat and add a small squeeze of lemon juice. Taste again for seasoning. Reheat the sauce just before serving, if necessary.

Gently prise the maize custards from their cups and place them, two to a serving and shiny side up, on each diner's plate. Spoon mushroom purée over the custards.

JUDITH OLNEY
COMFORTING FOOD

Eggs with Apricots

Dziranov Havgit

Pilaff is made by briefly cooking rice grains in fat, then adding twice the volume of boiling water or stock to the rice and simmering until done. The technique of cooking rice in this way is demonstrated on page 6.

To serve 4

250 g	dried apricots, cooked, drained and sieved	8 oz
6	eggs, well beaten	6
60 g	butter	2 oz
250 g	rice pilaff	8 oz

Melt the butter, pour the apricot pulp into it and simmer them together for 2 minutes. Add the beaten eggs, stirring constantly so that the eggs do not form lumps. Cook for about 10 minutes or until the mixture sets. Serve it at once on hot plates with rice pilaff.

GEORGE MARDIKIAN
DINNER AT OMAR KHAYYAM'S

Chicken Liver Custard

Le Gâteau de Foies Blonds de Poulardes de la Bresse Baigné de la Sauce aux Queues d'Écrevisses

This recipe calls for pale chicken livers from chickens raised in the Bresse district of France. If pale livers are not obtainable, use livers from roasting fowl that are not less than six months old, and soak the livers in milk for several hours or overnight. The custard is traditionally served with a crayfish tail sauce. To make the sauce, cook crayfish in a court-bouillon (page

164), shell them and pound the shells with an equal quantity of butter. Push the mixture through a sieve, and whisk it, off the heat, into a white sauce (page 166) or a fish velouté sauce (page 167). Finally, add the whole crayfish tails to the sauce. Alternatively, the custard can be served with a tomato sauce (page 166). The technique of making a savoury custard is demonstrated on page 64.

	To serve 4	
3 or 4	pale chicken livers, green-stained parts removed	3 or 4
1	garlic clove	1
60 g	beef marrow	2 oz
4 tbsp	meat roasting juices, degreased	4 tbsp
30 cl	milk	½ pint
2	eggs	2
2	egg yolks	2
	salt and pepper	

Rub the bottom and sides of a mortar with the garlic clove. In the mortar, pound the chicken livers with the beef marrow. Add the meat roasting juices and milk, to make a very liquid purée; then add the eggs and egg yolks. Whisk thoroughly, add salt and pepper and pass the mixture through a sieve.

Oil a 1 litre (1¾ pint) charlotte mould, and line the bottom with a piece of oiled greaseproof paper cut to fit. Pour in the mixture. Stand the mould on a trivet in a bain-marie of warm water and cook the custard in a preheated 150°C (300°F or Mark 2) oven for 1½ hours or until it is no longer liquid in the centre. Unmould the custard before serving.

LUCIEN TENDRET
LA TABLE AU PAYS DE BRILLAT-SAVARIN

Chicken Liver Mousse
Mousse de Foies Blonds

4	chicken livers, washed and trimmed	4
4	eggs	4
20 cl	*crème fraîche* or double cream	7 fl oz
1	clove	1
1 tsp	salt	1 tsp
	freshly ground black pepper	
15 g	butter	½ oz

Break the eggs into a large electric blender; add the chicken livers, cream, clove, and salt and pepper. Blend until the mixture becomes an almost liquid purée.

Pour the purée into six well-buttered ramekins—they should be nearly full—and put the ramekins into a ovenproof baking dish. Fill the dish three-quarters full with hot water

and put the dish on a high heat. When the water comes to the boil, transfer the dish to an oven preheated to 170°C (325°F or Mark 3) and cook the mousses for 40 minutes, or until they have set. To unmould the mousses, pass the blade of a knife around the insides of the ramekins and turn the mousses out on to a warmed serving dish. Serve very hot, coated with the sauce of your choice.

MICHEL OLIVER
MES RECETTES

Spinach Pudding
Spinaziepudding

The preparation of brains for cooking is shown on page 33. The technique of unmoulding a custard is shown on page 65.

	To serve 4	
1 kg	spinach, trimmed, parboiled in plenty of salted, boiling water for 1 minute, drained, squeezed and finely chopped	2 to 2½ lb
2	eggs, yolks separated from whites, whites stiffly beaten	2
2 tbsp	fine semolina	2 tbsp
	grated nutmeg	
	salt and pepper	
4 tbsp	finely chopped onion	4 tbsp
60 g	butter	2 oz
1	calf's brain, soaked, membrane removed, parboiled and diced	1
3	salt anchovies, soaked in tepid water for 15 minutes, drained, filleted and finely chopped	3
60 g	Dutch cheese, grated	2 oz
60 cl	tomato sauce (*page 166*)	1 pint

Stir the egg yolks and semolina into the chopped spinach and season with a pinch of nutmeg, salt and pepper. In a frying pan, fry the onion in 30 g (1 oz) of the butter for about 5 minutes, or until transparent. Add the brain and stir gently until combined. Remove the pan from the heat, add the chopped anchovies and fold in the egg whites.

Butter a 1 litre (1¾ pint) ovenproof dish and fill it alternately with the spinach and brain mixtures. Cut the rest of the butter into pieces and dot it over the dish. Cover the dish and stand it in a baking tin filled with enough hot water to come half way up the side of the dish. Cook the pudding in a preheated 180°C (350°F or Mark 4) oven for about 30 minutes or until set. Unmould the pudding on to a warmed plate and sprinkle it with the cheese. Serve with the tomato sauce.

LILO AUREDEN
DAS SCHMECKT SO GUT

Little Mushroom Custards

Petits Pots aux Morilles

According to taste, one can add to these custards ingredients such as diced cooked sweetbreads, or diced cooked angler fish.

To serve 5

200 g	button mushrooms	7 oz
50 g	dried morels, soaked overnight in water, drained, sliced in half and rinsed thoroughly	2 oz
3	egg yolks	3
1 tsp	lemon juice	1 tsp
	sea salt	
	freshly ground pepper	
	grated nutmeg	
15 cl	*crème fraîche* or double cream	¼ pint

Put the button mushrooms, morels, egg yolks, lemon juice and a pinch each of sea salt, freshly ground pepper and grated nutmeg into the blender. Blend the mixture until a thick cream is obtained. Adjust the seasoning. Add the double cream and blend for a further 3 to 5 seconds.

Butter five individual moulds or ramekins and pour the mixture into them. Prepare a bain-marie of hot water, and put the moulds into it. Bake the custards in the bain-marie in a preheated 200°C (400°F or Mark 6) oven for about 15 minutes, or until they are set.

DANIEL BOUCHÉ
INVITATION À LA CUISINE BUISSONNIÈRE

The All-Purpose Roulade

To serve 6 to 8

About 350 g	leftover vegetables, meat or seafood, finely chopped or grated and well seasoned	About 12 oz
5	eggs, yolks separated from whites, yolks lightly beaten, whites stiffly beaten	5
	salt and pepper	
3 tbsp	flour	3 tbsp
35 cl	double cream	12 fl oz
60 g	cold unsalted butter, half of it cut into pieces	2 oz
125 g	Parmesan or Gruyère cheese, grated	4 oz
	chopped parsley or watercress	

Cover a 35 by 25 cm (14 by 10 inch) Swiss roll tin with a sheet of buttered greaseproof paper. In a large bowl, pour the beaten egg whites on to the yolks. Season with salt and pepper and sieve the flour over the mixture. Rapidly, carefully, fold the yolks and whites together, then spread the mixture evenly on to the Swiss roll tin. Bake the egg mixture in a preheated 180°C (350°F or Mark 4) oven for 7 to 8 minutes. The eggs should be firm and just beginning to turn golden.

Spread a kitchen towel on a work surface and flip the egg sheet over on to it. Peel off the paper. Scatter the leftovers over the eggs and dribble 12.5 cl (4 fl oz) of the cream over the surface. Cut half the butter into thin shavings and dot them on top. Roll up the egg sheet like a Swiss roll, beginning at one of the short ends. Use the towel to firm and guide the roll. Lightly butter a 25 cm (10 inch) gratin dish or flan tin. Carefully lift one end of the *roulade* into the dish, then slide in the whole roll so that it ends up seam downwards. Trim a small diagonal slice from both ends to neaten the *roulade*. Pour the rest of the cream over the top (the egg will act as a sponge, absorbing the cream and swelling in the baking process). Sprinkle the grated cheese down the length of the roll, dot it with the rest of the butter and bake it in a preheated 180°C (350°F or Mark 4) oven for about 30 minutes or until brown and bubbling. Garnish with parsley or watercress.

JUDITH OLNEY
COMFORTING FOOD

Asparagus Soufflé

The asparagus tips can be parboiled separately from the stalks (page 70). The stalks are then sautéed in 15 g (½ oz) of butter for 2 to 3 minutes, and the tips tossed briefly in the butter. The stalks are puréed and incorporated into the soufflé mixture. When pouring the soufflé mixture into the dish for baking, pour in half the mixture, add the asparagus tips and then pour on the rest of the mixture. To make individual soufflés, butter 6 ramekins and bake the mixture for 15 minutes only at 200°C (400°F or Mark 6).

To serve 6

175 g	asparagus, stalks peeled, cut into short lengths and parboiled for 5 minutes	6 oz
12.5 cl	thick white sauce (*page 166*) flavoured with 1 whole garlic clove, later discarded	4 fl oz
	grated nutmeg	
	salt and pepper	
3	egg yolks, beaten with 1 tbsp milk	3
4	egg whites, stiffly beaten	4

Using a food processor, purée the asparagus, then push it through a drum sieve to remove the fibres. Add it to the cooled white sauce with a pinch of nutmeg and salt and pepper. Then beat in the yolks. As soon as they are properly incorporated, fold in the egg whites, taking care that they are properly distributed. Use as light a hand as possible, stirring upwards rather than downwards. Pour the whole thing into a well-buttered 1 litre (1¾ pint) soufflé dish and bake in a preheated 190°C (375°F or Mark 5) oven for about 30 minutes. When the soufflé has risen well and is a deep golden-brown, serve without delay. Do not be afraid to open the oven door to look at it; but close the door gently. If the soufflé is insufficiently cooked in the middle when the top is brown, the oven was too hot and vice versa.

GEOFFREY BOUMPHREY
CUNNING COOKERY

Moulded Spinach Soufflé

Sformato di Spinaci

Two tablespoons of cooked ham can replace the sultanas and macaroons. Make sure as much moisture as possible is extracted from the spinach, otherwise the mixture will be too soft, and the custard will lose its shape when unmoulded.

To serve 4

600 g	spinach, trimmed, washed, parboiled for 1 minute in plenty of salted, boiling water, well drained, squeezed and chopped	1¼ lb
30 g	butter	1 oz
3	small macaroons, crushed into crumbs	3
30 g	sultanas, soaked for 30 minutes in tepid water and drained	1 oz
¼ litre	thick white sauce (*page 166*)	8 fl oz
75 g	Parmesan cheese, grated	2½ oz
2	eggs, beaten with 1 egg yolk	2
	salt and pepper	
30 cl	tomato sauce (*page 166*)	½ pint

Cook the spinach in the butter on a very low heat for about 10 minutes. Remove it from the heat, stir in the macaroon crumbs and sultanas and leave the mixture to cool.

Thoroughly butter a 20 cm (8 inch) ring mould. Mix the thick white sauce with the spinach mixture and add the grated cheese, beaten eggs and egg yolk, stirring thoroughly. Taste the mixture and add salt and pepper if necessary. Spoon the mixture into the mould and smooth it out until the top is level. Put the mould into a roasting tin half full of water and bake it in a preheated 180°C (350°F or Mark 4) oven for about 45 minutes. To test for doneness, press the custard with your finger and if it seems firm, remove it from the oven. Leave it to stand for about 5 minutes then run a knife round the inside of the mould to loosen the custard. Turn it out on to a serving dish and pour the tomato sauce into the centre before serving.

FERNANDA GOSETTI
IN CUCINA CON FERNANDA GOSETTI

Moulded Harlequin Soufflé

Sformato di Legumi Arlecchino

Any number of vegetable purées can be used to make this soufflé, as long as the proportions are always kept to 15 cl (¼ pint) purée to 6 tablespoons of white sauce and one egg. To make a white layer, use ¼ litre (8 fl oz) of white sauce, flavoured, if you like, with extra grated Parmesan cheese, plus one egg. The technique of making a layered unmoulded soufflé is shown on page 72.

To serve 6

200 g	carrots, boiled for 35 minutes, drained and sautéed in 15 g (½ oz) butter for 5 minutes	7 oz
200 g	celery, boiled for 30 minutes, drained and sautéed in 15 g (½ oz) butter for 5 minutes	7 oz
350 g	spinach, boiled for a few minutes, drained, squeezed dry and sautéed in 15 g (½ oz) butter for 5 minutes	12 oz
200 g	peas, boiled for about 10 minutes, drained and sautéed in 15 g (½ oz) butter for 5 minutes	7 oz
300 g	chicory, boiled for 30 minutes, drained, squeezed dry and sautéed in 15 g (½ oz) butter for 5 minutes	10 oz
45 cl	thick white sauce (*page 166*)	¾ pint
5	eggs, yolks separated from whites, whites stiffly beaten	5
3 tbsp	grated Parmesan cheese	3 tbsp
	salt and freshly ground pepper	
	flour	

Purée each vegetable separately by passing it through a food mill or electric blender. Measure the purée and use 15 cl (¼ pint) of it. To each purée, add 6 tablespoons of white sauce, 1 beaten egg yolk and a little Parmesan; season with salt and pepper. Fold into each purée one stiffly whipped egg white.

Butter and flour a 3 litre (5 pint) metal mould and carefully fill it with layers of the vegetable mixtures. Arrange the layers so that there is a pleasant contrast of colours. Cover the mould and put it into a bain-marie. Cook the soufflé in a preheated 180°C (350°F or Mark 4) oven for 1 hour. Remove the mould from the oven. Let it rest for a few minutes, and unmould it on to a round serving dish.

LUIGI CARNACINA
GREAT ITALIAN COOKING

Lettuce Soufflé

Soufflé de Laitues

To purée lettuce, blanch it for 5 minutes in boiling, salted water and put it through a food mill or food processor.

This soufflé can also be made with spinach, French beans, peas, courgettes, sweet potatoes and many other vegetables. For every 500 g (1 lb) of puréed vegetable used, allow 200 g (7 oz) of puréed potato.

	To serve 4	
12	round lettuces, puréed	12
5	medium-sized potatoes, baked in their jackets	5
	salt	
	grated nutmeg	
6	eggs, yolks separated from whites, whites stiffly whipped	6
200 g	butter	7 oz

Scoop out the flesh of the potatoes while they are still hot and push it through a sieve. Using a wooden spoon, beat the potato and lettuce purées together over a moderate heat for a few minutes to evaporate excess moisture. When the purée is well dried out, remove it from the heat and season it with salt and grated nutmeg. Beat in the egg yolks and butter, and fold in the egg whites. Pour the mixture into a 1 litre (1¾ pint) buttered soufflé dish or charlotte mould. Place the dish or mould in a bain-marie and bake in a preheated 180°C (350°F or Mark 4) oven for 25 minutes or until the soufflé is well risen and lightly browned. Unmould and serve immediately.

LÉON ISNARD
LA GASTRONOMIE AFRICAINE

Sorrel Soufflé

Sauerampfersoufflé

	To serve 4	
500 g	sorrel, trimmed and chopped	1 lb
60 g	butter	2 oz
100 g	white bread, crusts removed, soaked in milk and squeezed	3½ oz
4	egg yolks, 3 of them beaten	4
	salt and pepper	
3	egg whites, stiffly beaten	3
3 tbsp	top of the milk or single cream	3 tbsp

Cook the sorrel over a low heat in half the butter, stirring continuously, until it forms a purée. Mix this purée thoroughly with the soaked bread and the three beaten yolks. Melt the rest of the butter, add it to the mixture and season with salt and pepper. Fold in the beaten egg whites.

Butter and flour a 1 litre (1¾ pint) soufflé dish. Put the dish into a baking tin half filled with hot water. Bake the soufflé in a preheated 170°C (325°F or Mark 3) oven for 1 hour, or until well risen. Leave the soufflé to rest for 10 minutes out of the oven before unmoulding.

Combine the remaining egg yolk with the top of the milk or cream, and heat the mixture gently until it thickens slightly. Serve this sauce with the soufflé.

ELEK MAGYAR
KOCHBUCH FÜR FEINSCHMECKER

Courgette Soufflé

Soufflé aux Courgettes

The courgettes can be replaced by pumpkin, and the mace by coriander or saffron.

	To serve 8 to 10	
1 kg	courgettes	2 to 2½ lb
¼ litre	thick white sauce (*page 166*)	8 fl oz
50 g	Gruyère cheese, grated	2 oz
30 g	Parmesan cheese, grated	1 oz
9	eggs, yolks separated from whites, yolks beaten, whites stiffly beaten	9
	salt and pepper	
	powdered mace or grated nutmeg	
1	small onion, grated	1
	dry breadcrumbs	

Put the whole courgettes into boiling salted water and cook them, uncovered, for about 10 minutes or until tender, but do not let them disintegrate. Leave them to cool, then peel them and pass them through the fine disc of a food mill. Put the resulting purée in a large heavy-based frying pan and set it over a low heat to dry out. Stir very frequently to make sure the purée does not burn.

To the tepid thick white sauce add the cheeses, egg yolks, salt and pepper, a pinch of mace or nutmeg, the puréed courgettes and the onion. Mix well. Fold the egg whites into the courgette mixture.

Butter a 1.5 litre (2½ pint) soufflé dish and sprinkle it with breadcrumbs. Pour the mixture into the dish and bake the soufflé in a preheated 190°C (375°F or Mark 5) oven for 30 minutes, or until the soufflé is risen and golden.

NINETTE LYON
LES OEUFS

Dutch Cheese Soufflé

Kaassoufflé

To serve 4

125 g	Gouda or Edam cheese, grated	4 oz
90 g	white bread, thinly sliced, crusts removed	3 oz
2 tbsp	Dutch gin (genever)	2 tbsp
4	eggs, yolks separated from whites, yolks lightly beaten, whites stiffly beaten	4
2 tbsp	finely cut chives	2 tbsp
¼ litre	milk	8 fl oz
	ground ginger	
125 g	raw ham, finely chopped	4 oz

Butter a 1.5 litre (2½ pint) soufflé dish and line it with the slices of bread. Moisten them with the gin. Beat the egg yolks thoroughly with the cheese, chives, milk and a pinch of ground ginger. Add the ham and fold in the egg whites. Pour the mixture into the dish.

Bake the soufflé in a preheated 180°C (350°F or Mark 4) oven for about 20 to 25 minutes, or until well risen and golden. Serve straight from the oven.

LILO AUREDEN
DAS SCHMECKT SO GUT

Pancake Soufflé

Crêpes Soufflées

The method for making pancakes is shown on page 56.

To serve 4

30 cl	pancake batter (*page 164*)	½ pint
45 g	butter	1½ oz
30 g	flour	1 oz
30 cl	milk	½ pint
2 tsp	grated Parmesan cheese	2 tsp
30 g	Gruyère cheese, grated	1 oz
	salt and pepper	
3	eggs, yolks separated from whites, whites stiffly beaten	3
30 cl	tomato sauce (*page 166*)	½ pint

Make eight fairly thin 18 cm (7 inch) pancakes and keep them warm. In a small saucepan, heat the butter and the flour. As soon as the flour turns golden, gradually add the milk, blending well. When the sauce is creamy, add the cheeses and a pinch each of salt and pepper. Mix well, remove the sauce from the heat and let it cool.

Add the egg yolks to the cooled cheese sauce, then fold in the whites. Butter an 18 cm (7 inch) soufflé dish. Put the pancakes and the cheese mixture into the dish in alternate layers, beginning with a pancake. Bake the soufflé in a preheated 190°C (375°F or Mark 5) oven for 35 minutes or until the top is golden. Remove the dish from the oven. Run a knife round the inside edge of the dish to loosen the pancakes. The soufflé can be served from the dish with tomato sauce on the side or unmoulded and covered with the tomato sauce.

NINETTE LYON
LES OEUFS

Auvergne Cheese Soufflé

Soufflé au Bleu d'Auvergne

If bleu d'Auvergne cheese is not available, use another blue-veined cheese, such as Roquefort or Stilton. The technique of baking blind is shown on page 68. If the soufflé is made in a loose-bottomed cake tin, it can be unmoulded like a pie. It can also be made without the pastry case.

To serve 5 or 6

300 g	*bleu d'Auvergne* cheese, crumbled	10 oz
250 g	shortcrust dough (*page 165*)	8 oz
100 g	celery, parboiled for 5 minutes, cut into matchstick strips	3½ oz
15 g	butter	½ oz
60 cl	thick white sauce (*page 166*), cooled to tepid	1 pint
5	eggs, yolks separated from whites, whites stiffly beaten	5
	salt and pepper	
	nutmeg	

Roll out the pastry and use it to line a buttered 1 litre (1¾ pint) soufflé dish. Bake the pastry blind in a preheated 190°C (375°F or Mark 5) oven for 15 minutes or until cooked but not coloured. Sauté the celery in 15 g (½ oz) butter. To the thick white sauce, add the egg yolks, one at a time, stirring constantly, then season with salt, pepper and nutmeg. Stir in the celery and the crumbled cheese. Then fold the stiffly beaten egg whites into the mixture. Pour it into the pastry case and bake the soufflé in a preheated 170°C (325°F or Mark 3) oven for 35 to 40 minutes, or until golden-brown and well risen.

AMICALE DES CUISINIERS ET PÂTISSIERS AUVERGNATS DE PARIS
CUISINE D'AUVERGNE

Crusted Cheese Pie

To make one 23 or 25 cm (9 or 10 inch) pie

250 g	cheese, grated (mixture of Cheddar, Parmesan and Gruyère)	8 oz
10	eggs	10
$\frac{1}{4}$ litre	milk	8 fl oz
90 g	flour	3 oz
$\frac{1}{4}$ tsp each	salt and pepper	$\frac{1}{4}$ tsp each
2 tbsp	grated onion	2 tbsp
125 g	watercress	4 oz

Stir the eggs with half of the milk until smooth. Place the flour and salt in a mixing bowl, make a well in the middle and gradually whisk the rest of the milk into the flour. Then whisk in the egg mixture. Beat the batter until it is smooth. Add the pepper. Cover the bowl with a towel and let the batter stand for at least 6 hours at room temperature.

Stir the grated onion and half of the cheese into the batter. Butter or oil a 23 or 25 cm (9 or 10 inch) spring-form tin and place the tin on a baking sheet. Pour in the batter and bake in a preheated 180°C (350°F or Mark 4) oven for 20 minutes. Remove the pie from the oven and sprinkle the remaining cheese on top. Replace it in the oven for a further 25 to 30 minutes or until the top is brown and firmly crusted. The pie will expand greatly. Allow it to settle down for 10 minutes and then run a knife round the edge and open the pan at the side. Run a spatula under the pie and serve, slightly warm, surrounded with watercress.

JUDITH OLNEY
COMFORTING FOOD

Cheese Soufflés in Artichokes

To serve 6

90 g	Gruyère cheese, grated	3 oz
6	artichokes, stalks and tough outer leaves discarded	6
30 g	butter	1 oz
2 tbsp	flour	2 tbsp
20 cl	milk	7 fl oz
	salt and black pepper	
3	egg yolks, lightly beaten	3
4	egg whites, stiffly beaten	4

Bring a large pan of salted water to the boil and plunge the artichokes into it upside-down. Cook them for 20 to 40 minutes, depending on their size. Drain and cool them. When they are cool enough to handle, pull out the centre bunch of leaves from each artichoke, leaving a hollow space well enclosed with leaves. Scrape out the choke with a small sharp spoon.

To make the soufflé mixture, melt the butter in a pan, stir in the flour and cook for 2 to 3 minutes. In a separate pan, heat the milk and pour it on to the butter and flour. Blend and simmer gently for 4 to 5 minutes, stirring often, until you have a thick sauce. Stir in the grated cheese and season well with salt and pepper. Remove the pan from the heat and allow the contents to cool slightly before beating in the egg yolks. Fold in the egg whites. Spoon the mixture quickly into the artichokes. Place the artichokes on a greased baking sheet and bake them in a preheated 200°C (400°F or Mark 6) oven for 15 minutes. The mixture should be less set than the usual soufflé, resembling a thick, foamy sauce. The leaves of the artichoke are pulled off and dipped in the soufflé, then the heart is eaten with a knife and fork.

ARABELLA BOXER
ARABELLA BOXER'S GARDEN COOKBOOK

Calf's Brain Soufflés

Paszteciki w Muszlach

The preparation of brains for cooking is shown on page 33.

To serve 8

2	pairs calf's brains, soaked, cleaned, parboiled, cooled and chopped	2
1	onion, grated	1
90 g	butter, 60 g (2 oz) melted	3 oz
	salt and pepper	
4 tbsp	breadcrumbs	4 tbsp
4	egg yolks	4
1	egg white, stiffly beaten	1
4 tbsp	lemon juice	4 tbsp
2	lemons, sliced	2

Fry the grated onion in 15 g ($\frac{1}{2}$ oz) of the butter. Off the heat, mix it with the chopped brains and add pepper, salt, 2 tablespoons of the breadcrumbs and the egg yolks. Mix well and fold in the stiffly beaten egg white. Taste the mixture and add more salt if necessary.

Butter eight ramekins and fill them with the mixture. Sprinkle with the rest of the breadcrumbs and pour on 30 g (1 oz) of the melted butter. Bake the soufflés in a preheated 190°C (375°F or Mark 5) oven for 10 to 15 minutes, or until lightly browned. To serve, squeeze lemon juice over the soufflés and serve them with the slices of lemon and the remainder of the melted butter.

I. PLUCINSKA
KSIAZKA KUCHARSKA UDOSKONALONA

Herring Roe Soufflés

To serve 6

350 g	soft herring roes	12 oz
	salt and pepper	
15 cl	tepid milk	¼ pint
2	egg yolks, lightly beaten	2
30 g	butter, softened	1 oz
1½ tbsp	flour	1½ tbsp
30 g	Gruyère cheese, grated	1 oz
1	egg white, stiffly beaten	1
	paprika	

Salt and pepper the herring roes and poach them for 1 minute in the tepid milk. Drain them and divide them between six buttered ramekins.

Mix the egg yolks, butter, flour and cheese. Fold in the egg white and cover the herring roes with this mixture. Bake the soufflés in a preheated 220°C (425°F or Mark 7) oven for 5 minutes or until they are set, and put a pinch of paprika on each soufflé before serving.

RUTH LOWINSKY
MORE LOVELY FOOD

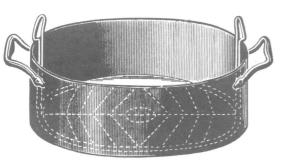

Oyster Soufflé

The technique of opening oysters is shown on page 54.

To serve 6 to 8

36	live oysters, shelled, drained, liquor reserved	36
¼ litre	milk	8 fl oz
40 g	butter	1½ oz
40 g	flour	1½ oz
4	eggs, yolks separated from whites, yolks lightly beaten, whites stiffly beaten	4
	salt and pepper	

Heat the oyster liquor and milk together. When the liquid is hot but not yet boiling, add the oysters. Simmer for about 3 minutes, or until the edges of the oysters begin to curl.

Remove the oysters from the pan and leave them to cool. Cut them into small pieces. Reserve the cooking liquid.

In a heavy saucepan, melt the butter; add the flour and blend it with the butter. Stir in ¼ litre (8 fl oz) of cooking liquid. Cook until smooth, stirring constantly. Remove the pan from the heat and slowly add the beaten egg yolks, stirring continuously. Return the pan to the heat and cook the mixture until the sauce thickens, stirring all the time. Remove the pan from the heat again.

Mix the oysters into the sauce and sprinkle it with salt and pepper. Fold in the egg whites. Pour the mixture into a well-buttered 20 cm (8 inch) casserole. Set the casserole in a shallow pan of hot water. Bake the soufflé in a preheated 180°C (350°F or Mark 4) oven for 40 minutes, or until it is risen and golden. Serve immediately.

LOUIS GARRISON
DELICIOUS SEAFOOD RECIPES

Ham Soufflé Alexandra

Soufflé de Jambon Alexandra

Note that paprika is an excellent seasoning with ham and that 45 g (1½ oz) of grated Parmesan cheese added to the ham mixture will make a very pleasant blend of flavours.

To serve 4

125 g	lean cooked ham, pounded in a mortar or very finely chopped in a food processor	4 oz
2 tbsp	cold white sauce (*page 166*)	2 tbsp
4 tbsp	hot thick white sauce, made with cream (*page 166*)	4 tbsp
2	egg yolks	2
3	egg whites, stiffly beaten	3
350 g	very small asparagus tips, parboiled for 2 to 3 minutes in salted water	12 oz
15 g	butter	½ oz

Mix the cold white sauce with the ham and put the mixture through a sieve into a saucepan. Warm it over a low heat. When it is heated through, remove it from the heat, and add the hot thick white sauce. Stir in the egg yolks one at a time, and fold in the beaten egg whites. Toss the asparagus tips rapidly in the butter, over a high heat. Preheat the oven to 200°C (400°F or Mark 6).

Butter a 1 litre (1¾ pint) soufflé dish, pour in half the soufflé mixture, add a layer of asparagus tips and then add the rest of the mixture. Reduce the oven temperature to 190°C (375°F or Mark 5) and bake the soufflé for 25 minutes or until it is risen and golden. Serve at once.

AMBROSE HEATH
GOOD SAVOURIES

Fries, Gratins and Grills

Deep-Fried Fish Rolls

Machhli ke Kofte

To serve 8 to 10

1 kg	white fish, filleted, skinned and cut into 7.5 cm (3 inch) pieces, parboiled in salted water to cover for 5 minutes, drained and cooled	2 to 2½ lb
6	medium-sized potatoes, boiled, peeled and mashed	6
2 tsp	ground coriander	2 tsp
	salt	
	cayenne pepper	
250 g	vegetable *ghee* or ¼ litre (8 fl oz) vegetable oil	8 oz
2	medium-sized onions, chopped	2
2	eggs, beaten	2
1 tsp	lemon juice	1 tsp
15 g	coriander leaves, finely chopped	½ oz
30 g	breadcrumbs or ground rice	1 oz

Skin the fish and remove any remaining bones. Mash the fish with the potatoes and add the ground coriander, salt and cayenne pepper. In a frying pan, heat 15 g (½ oz) of the *ghee* or 1 tablespoon of the oil. Add the fish and potato mixture. Cook over a medium heat, stirring constantly, until the mixture is dry, taking care not to let it burn. Remove the mixture from the frying pan and set it aside to cool.

Heat 15 g (½ oz) of *ghee* or 1 tablespoon of the oil and fry the onions until they are brown. Strain off the fat and add the onions to the fish with the beaten eggs and the lemon juice. Sprinkle with chopped coriander leaves.

Form the mixture into torpedo-shaped rolls about 7.5 cm (3 inches) long and 2 cm (¾ inch) thick. Coat the rolls lightly with breadcrumbs or ground rice and deep fry them in the rest of the *ghee* or oil until they are uniformly light brown.

KRISHNA PRASAD DAR
KASHMIRI COOKING

Fried Frogs' Legs Milanese-Style

Le Rane Dorate alla Milanese

To serve 8

48	pairs frogs' legs, soaked in equal quantities of cold water and milk for 1 hour, drained and dried	48
	flour	
2	eggs, lightly beaten	2
120 g	butter	4 oz
	salt and white pepper	
	White wine marinade	
½ litre	dry white wine	16 fl oz
4 tbsp	chopped parsley	4 tbsp
½	onion, very thinly sliced	½
	salt	
	freshly ground white pepper	

Put the prepared frogs' legs in the marinade for 1 hour, stirring occasionally. Remove them and pat them dry with a cloth. Coat them with flour and dip them in the beaten eggs.

Melt the butter in a pan and, when it is hot, sauté the frogs' legs until golden all over—about 5 minutes. Reduce the heat and continue cooking for about 15 minutes. Season with salt and white pepper and serve at once.

GIANNI BRERA AND LUIGI VERONELLI
LA PACCIADA

Deep-Fried Frogs' Legs

Grenouilles à la Vendéenne

The author recommends serving tomato sauce (recipe, page 166) flavoured with lemon juice with the frogs' legs.

To serve 4 or 5

50	pairs frogs' legs	50
2	eggs, well beaten	2
	salt and pepper	
	grated nutmeg	
4 tsp	double cream	4 tsp
60 g	fresh breadcrumbs	2 oz
	fat or oil for deep frying	

Into the beaten eggs, mix the salt, pepper, grated nutmeg and double cream, and stir well. Dip the frogs' legs in this mixture and then in the breadcrumbs. Fry them in very hot oil so that they are nice and crisp.

AMBROSE HEATH
MADAME PRUNIER'S FISH COOKERY BOOK

Frogs' Legs Provençal

Grenouilles à la Provençale

To serve 4 to 6

48	pairs small frogs' legs	48
	flour	
4 tbsp	olive oil	4 tbsp
	salt and pepper	
1	garlic clove, finely chopped	1
1 tbsp	finely chopped parsley	1 tbsp

Flour the frogs' legs. In a sauté pan, heat the olive oil until it is very hot. Sauté the frogs' legs, shaking the pan regularly and turning the frogs' legs until they are golden-brown on both sides—about 8 to 10 minutes. Just before removing them from the pan, sprinkle the frogs' legs with the salt, pepper, chopped garlic and parsley.

BENOÎT MASCARELLI
LA TABLE EN PROVENCE SUR LA CÔTE D'AZUR

Fried Elvers

Piballes de l'Estanquet

Elvers—baby eels—are found in the River Severn, and can be bought locally when in season. A few elver farms have recently been started in Britain, although at present most of their produce is exported to Italy. Elvers are very rich and 100 g (3½ oz) is a reasonable hors-d'oeuvre portion for one person.

To serve 10 to 12

1 kg	live elvers	2 to 2½ lb
About 125 g	coarse salt	About 4 oz
3 to 4 tbsp	olive oil	3 to 4 tbsp
3	chili peppers, seeded and chopped	3
	salt and freshly ground pepper	
3	garlic cloves, chopped	3
4 tbsp	chopped parsley	4 tbsp

To kill the elvers, put them in a bowl, mix them with a handful of coarse salt and leave them for 2 hours. Remove the elvers and wash them thoroughly in several changes of water until the water is clear and the elvers have lost all their sliminess. Drain thoroughly, then spread the elvers out on a cloth to dry.

Heat the oil in a heavy-based frying pan. Add the chili peppers and, when the oil is hot, the elvers. Season with salt and pepper, add the garlic and stir gently until the elvers turn opaque. The cooking time should be about 10 minutes.

Transfer the fried elvers to a warmed serving dish and sprinkle with chopped parsley.

LA REYNIÈRE
200 RECETTES DES MEILLEURES CUISINIÈRES DE FRANCE

Dieppe Shellfish Croquettes

Croquettes à la Dieppoise

To prepare mussels for cooking, soak them in cold water for at least 3 hours, changing the water several times until it is clear. Then pull off the beards. Cep is a variety of wild mushroom; dried ceps can be bought at French and Italian grocers, but must be soaked in warm water for at least 30 minutes before use. Fish velouté (recipe, page 167) is a good accompaniment.

Ordinary mushrooms may be used; but the flavour will not, of course, be quite the same.

To serve 4 to 6

24	small mussels, opened in white wine (*page 31*)	24
250 g	peeled, cooked prawns	8 oz
250 g	fresh ceps, finely chopped	8 oz
4 tbsp	oil	4 tbsp
¼ litre	thick white sauce (*page 166*)	8 fl oz
2 tsp	paprika	2 tsp
1	egg, beaten	1
60 g	dry breadcrumbs	2 oz
	oil for deep frying	

Fry the ceps in 4 tablespoons of oil for 3 minutes. Remove them from the pan and mix them with the mussels and prawns. Flavour the thick white sauce with paprika, and mix it with the shellfish and ceps. Shape the mixture into croquettes, roll them in beaten egg, then in breadcrumbs.

Heat the frying oil until it is smoking, and deep fry the croquettes until they are golden. Drain them on kitchen paper before you serve them.

AMBROSE HEATH
MADAME PRUNIER'S FISH COOKERY BOOK

Chinese Fish Cakes

Yu Bang

If pike is not available, freshwater fish such as carp or trout can be substituted, or a white fish such as hake or whiting.

To make 12 fish cakes

250 g	cooked shrimps, shelled and finely chopped	8 oz
500 g	pike fillet, washed and finely chopped	1 lb
125 g	almonds or peanuts, chopped	4 oz
125 g	lean bacon, diced	4 oz
5 tbsp	peanut oil	5 tbsp
1 tsp	salt	1 tsp
1 tbsp	flour	1 tbsp
1 tbsp	soy sauce	1 tbsp

Combine the chopped shrimps, pike, almonds or peanuts and bacon. Blend together 1 tablespoon of the peanut oil, the salt, flour and soy sauce. Add them to the fish mixture and mix well. Form into 12 small patties and fry in the rest of the hot oil until they are golden-brown on both sides.

ALICE MILLER MITCHELL (EDITOR)
ORIENTAL COOKBOOK

Bean Curd Fritters with Shrimps

Perkedel Tahu

Bean curd or tofu *can be bought from Oriental grocers.*

To serve 6

500 g	bean curd, chopped	1 lb
125 g	cooked, peeled shrimps, chopped	4 oz
1 tbsp	chopped onion	1 tbsp
1 tbsp	chopped garlic	1 tbsp
1 tbsp	chopped celery	1 tbsp
1 tbsp	flour	1 tbsp
2	eggs, beaten	2
	salt and pepper	
¾ litre	vegetable oil	1¼ pints

Mix together the bean curd, shrimps and all of the other ingredients except the oil. Heat the oil until it is very hot and drop the bean curd mixture into it, 1 tablespoon at a time. Fry the fritters until golden-brown. Remove the fritters with a slotted spoon and drain them on absorbent paper.

SEK-HIANG LIE
INDONESIAN COOKERY

Fried Shrimp Balls

Cha Hsia Ch'iu Erh

To serve 6

1 kg	fresh shrimps, shelled and minced	2 lb
125 g	fat pork, minced	4 oz
2	eggs, well beaten	2
	salt and pepper	
	lard for deep frying	

Mix the shrimps, pork and eggs together. Season lightly with salt and pepper. Roll the mixture into balls the size of walnuts and deep fry them in lard until they are an even golden-brown, about 6 to 8 minutes.

CORRINNE LAMB
THE CHINESE FESTIVE BOARD

Baked Sardines and Spinach

Les Sardines aux Épinards

To serve 4

1 kg	fresh sardines (about 20 fish), cleaned, washed and carefully dried	2 to 2½ lb
1 kg	spinach, trimmed, washed and well drained	2 to 2½ lb
200 g	coarse salt	7 oz
1 tsp	salt	1 tsp
4 tbsp	olive oil	4 tbsp

Spread half the coarse salt over the bottom of a large gratin dish. Arrange the sardines side by side in the dish and cover them with the rest of the coarse salt. Refrigerate for 1 hour.

Put the spinach into a large bowl and sprinkle with the teaspoon of salt. Mix well with both hands. Preheat the oven to 230°C (450°F or Mark 8) and put a baking sheet into it.

Remove the sardines from the gratin dish and wipe off the salt. Cut a piece of aluminium foil into eight 30 cm (12 inch) squares, and divide the spinach equally between four of them. It will be about three fingers high but will flatten during the cooking. Place five sardines side by side on each bed of spinach and sprinkle them with the oil. Cover them with the remaining sheets of foil, folding the edges over carefully to make four hermetically sealed packets.

Remove the baking sheet from the oven, lay the packets on it, and return them to the preheated oven. Cook the packets for 8 minutes. During the cooking, the packets will swell up. Each diner should be allowed to perforate his own packet in order to receive the full benefit of the delicious aroma of the sardines steaming on their bed of green, juicy spinach.

MICHEL OLIVER
MES RECETTES

Anchovy or Smoked Baltic Herring Hash

Ansjovisfräs och Böcklingfräs

So-called Swedish anchovies are in fact sprats preserved in spiced brine. They are much milder in flavour than other preserved anchovies.

	To serve 4	
5	Swedish anchovies, sprats or smoked Baltic herring, filleted and finely chopped	5
1	large yellow onion, finely chopped or 1 to 2 leeks, white parts only, finely chopped	1
30 g	butter	1 oz
4	eggs, hard boiled and coarsely chopped	4
	black pepper	

Sauté the onion or leeks in the butter until they are lightly browned. Add the anchovies and eggs. While stirring, fry the hash quickly at a high temperature for about 2 minutes or until heated through. Season with black pepper and serve.

TORE WRETMAN
SWEDISH SMÖRGÅSBORD

Spinach Catalan-Style

Espinacas a la Catalana

	To serve 6	
2 kg	spinach, trimmed, parboiled for 1 minute, drained, squeezed and chopped	4 lb
3 tbsp	olive oil	3 tbsp
1	garlic clove, chopped	1
2	salt anchovies, soaked, filleted, rinsed and chopped	2
30 g	pine-nuts	1 oz
50 g	raisins, halved	2 oz
	salt and pepper	

In a frying pan, heat the oil and add the garlic and anchovies. Next, add the chopped spinach, pine-nuts and raisins. Season with salt and pepper, toss everything together, and cook slowly for 15 to 20 minutes, stirring occasionally.

ANA MARIA CALERA
COCINA CATALANA

Chicken and Almond Fritters

Frictelle d'Amandole

This recipe is by Maestro Martino, who lived in the mid-15th century, and was the first Renaissance cook to publish his recipes. To make this almond milk, pound 100 g (3½ oz) of blanched almonds in a mortar or purée them in a food processor and add 20 cl (7 fl oz) of milk, and 1 teaspoon of rose-water. Then strain the mixture and squeeze it through a cloth. The residue left in the cloth can be reserved and used to mix with dough for an almond-flavoured pastry.

	To serve 4 to 6	
1	roast chicken breast, skinned, boned, chopped and pounded to a purée	1
15 cl	almond milk	¼ pint
2 or 3	egg whites	2 or 3
1 tsp	sugar	1 tsp
	salt and pepper	
About 60 g	flour	About 2 oz
175 g	lard or butter	6 oz

Mix the puréed chicken breast, almond milk, egg whites and sugar together. Season with salt and pepper and add enough flour to bring the batter to a firm consistency.

Heat the fat and drop spoonfuls of the mixture into it. Sauté the fritters, taking care not to overcook them, until they are golden-brown, about 3 minutes on each side.

EMILIO FACCIOLI (EDITOR)
ARTE DELLA CUCINA

Brain Cakes

The preparation of brains for cooking is shown on page 33.

	To serve 4	
500 g	brains, soaked, cleaned, parboiled and chopped	1 lb
125 g	dry breadcrumbs	4 oz
	salt and pepper	
2 tbsp	*fines herbes*	2 tbsp
3	egg yolks, beaten	3
90 g	butter	3 oz

Season the breadcrumbs with salt and pepper and mix them with the chopped brains. Add the *fines herbes* and egg yolks to the mixture. Shape the mixture into small cakes and sauté them in the butter until they are golden-brown, about 3 minutes on each side. Serve very hot.

MYRA (EDITOR)
MYRA'S COOKERY BOOK

Deep-Fried Skewered Sweetbreads with Morels

Brochettes du Puy aux Morilles

The technique of preparing sweetbreads for cooking is shown on page 32 and the technique of deep frying skewered morsels on page 84. Either fresh or dried morels—wild mushrooms—can be used: if dried, soak for 30 minutes in warm water and then drain and dry them.

	To serve 6	
2	veal sweetbreads	2
200 g	fresh morels, trimmed and washed	7 oz
175 g	butter	6 oz
250 g	York ham	8 oz
	salt and pepper	
60 g	flour	2 oz
½ litre	milk	16 fl oz
	grated nutmeg	
100 g	cheese, grated	3½ oz
2	eggs, yolks separated from whites, yolks beaten	2
	breadcrumbs	
	oil for deep frying	
	tomato sauce (*page 166*)	

In a saucepan, melt 60 g (2 oz) of the butter and add the prepared sweetbreads. Brown them lightly on a low heat for about 10 minutes. Remove them and cut them into short strips 2 by 1 cm (1 by ½ inch) and 1 cm (½ inch) thick. Slice the ham in the same way.

Put the morels in a dry saucepan and heat them very gently, so that they exude their juices. Season them, add 60 g (2 oz) of the butter and cook over a low heat for 20 minutes.

Take six small skewers and fill them alternately with the sweetbreads, ham and morels; the skewers should not be filled more than three-quarters of their length.

To prepare the coating, melt the rest of the butter, add the flour and cook over a gentle heat, stirring constantly, so that the flour browns very lightly while mixing into the butter. Pour in the milk and reduce the sauce over a medium heat,

stirring constantly. Add salt, pepper and a pinch of grated nutmeg, then the grated cheese, and continue cooking until the cheese has melted. Pour the coating into a shallow bowl, and add the egg yolks. Roll each brochette in the coating, making sure that all surfaces are coated. Lay the brochettes side by side in an oiled dish, and leave them in a cool place until the following day. The coating will form a thick layer on all the surfaces.

Beat the egg whites until stiff. Put them and the breadcrumbs into two plates. Heat the oil in a vessel large enough to hold the brochettes. Roll each brochette in the egg white, then in the breadcrumbs and deep fry it until golden-brown. Drain the brochettes on absorbent paper. Serve with tomato sauce.

LA CUISINE AUVERGNATE
L'ENCYCLOPÉDIE DE LA CUISINE RÉGIONALE

Fried Liver in Paprika

Ciğer Tavasi

The preparation of liver for cooking is shown on page 32.

	To serve 3 or 4	
250 g	lamb's liver, cut into small pieces	8 oz
1 tbsp	paprika	1 tbsp
	salt and pepper	
2 tbsp	flour	2 tbsp
2 tbsp	olive oil	2 tbsp
	coarse salt	
1	medium-sized onion, sliced	1
3	sprigs parsley, coarsely chopped	3

Roll the pieces of liver in the paprika. Salt and pepper the flour. Dip the liver into the seasoned flour. Then sauté the liver in very hot oil for about 1 minute on each side, tossing the pieces frequently, and taking care not to overcook as this will spoil the flavour. Arrange the liver on a dish and garnish it with a pinch of coarse salt, slices of raw onion and parsley.

VENICE LAMB
THE HOME BOOK OF TURKISH COOKERY

Cep and Potato Gratin

Cèpes à la Limousine

The potatoes accompanying the ceps are sometimes halved and stuffed. If you stuff the potatoes, stuff the cep caps too. Make the stuffing from the same ingredients that are used in the recipe to sprinkle on the ceps and potatoes. If the tubes under the caps of the ceps are greenish, they should be removed, for there is a strong possibility that the tubes may be wormy. Do not reduce the proportion of butter, for it serves to provide a sauce for the dish, combined with the juices of the ceps, and makes it moist.

To serve 8

800 g	ceps, caps wiped and separated from stalks, stalks chopped	1¾ lb
400 g	potatoes, cut into 5 mm (¼ inch) slices	14 oz
125 g	butter, cut into pieces	4 oz
100 g	shoulder of veal, chopped	3½ oz
100 g	neck end of pork, chopped	3½ oz
2	garlic cloves, chopped	2
4	sprigs parsley, chopped	4
	salt and pepper	

In an earthenware casserole, put alternate layers of the cep caps and potato slices. Dot with butter. Mix the cep stalks, veal, pork, garlic and parsley and sprinkle this over the cep and potato mixture. Season with salt and pepper.

Cover the dish with greaseproof paper or foil and a tight-fitting lid and bake it in a preheated 180°C (350°F or Mark 4) oven for 45 minutes.

CÉLINE VENCE
ENCYCLOPÉDIE HACHETTE DE LA CUISINE RÉGIONALE

Mushrooms in White Wine

Champignons en Ragoût à la Diplomate

To serve 6

500 g	button mushrooms, stalks and a few of the caps chopped	1 lb
15 cl	dry white wine	¼ pint
100 g	butter	3½ oz
10 cl	stock (*page 167*)	3½ fl oz
1 tbsp	chopped parsley	1 tbsp
1 tbsp	chopped chives	1 tbsp
1 or 2	shallots, chopped	1 or 2
	salt and black pepper	
1	egg yolk, beaten	1
	cayenne pepper	
	grated nutmeg	
100 g	croûtons	3½ oz

In a saucepan, heat 15 g (½ oz) of the butter with the stock and wine. Add the chopped mushrooms, parsley, chives, shallots, salt and pepper and cook over a high heat for 2 to 3 minutes.

Remove the pan from the heat. Cut 30 g (1 oz) of the butter into pieces and whisk it with the egg yolk into the mushroom mixture. Add a pinch each of cayenne pepper and grated nutmeg. Keep the mixture warm.

Sauté the whole mushroom caps in the rest of the butter over a high heat for a few minutes or until well browned.

Scatter the croûtons in the bottom of a buttered gratin dish. Spread the chopped mushroom mixture over them and arrange the whole mushroom caps on top. Put the dish into a preheated 230°C (450°F or Mark 8) oven and cook for 5 to 10 minutes, or until heated through. Serve very hot.

G. PORTEVIN
CE QU'IL FAUT SAVOIR POUR MANGER LES BONS CHAMPIGNONS

Mushroom Gratin

Croustade Rideloise

The author recommends using wild mushrooms, such as chanterelles, morels, field mushrooms, blushers etc. Cultivated mushrooms can be substituted. The goat cheese used here is a soft cheese which has been left for a few days to dry out, and thus becomes hard enough to grate. The recipe comes from Le Grand Monarque restaurant at Azay-le-Rideau in France.

To serve 6

500 g	wild mushrooms, washed, trimmed and sliced	1 lb
30 g	butter	1 oz
	salt and pepper	
175 g	cooked ham, diced	6 oz
¼ litre	white sauce (*page 166*)	8 fl oz
3 tbsp	*crème fraîche* or double cream	3 tbsp
2 tsp	coarsely chopped parsley	2 tsp
6	large 1 cm (½ inch) thick slices rye or wholemeal bread, grilled or fried in walnut oil	6
1	egg	1
2 tbsp	grated Sainte-Maure goat cheese	2 tbsp

Cook the mushrooms in the butter over a low heat until they give up their juices, about 10 minutes. Salt and pepper them. Mix the mushrooms with the ham, white sauce, 2 tablespoons of the cream and the parsley. Adjust the seasoning.

Arrange the slices of bread on a buttered baking sheet and heap the mixture on to them. In a bowl, beat the egg, the rest of the cream and the grated goat cheese. Season to taste.

Pour the egg and cheese mixture over the ham and mushroom mixture. Cook the dish in a preheated 230°C (450°F or Mark 8) oven for 3 to 5 minutes to brown. Serve immediately.

PAUL-JACQUES LÉVÈQUE (EDITOR)
LES BONNES RECETTES DE LA CUISINE TOURANGELLE

Baked Mushrooms

Gebackene Pilze

To serve 4 to 6

500 g	mushrooms, sliced	1 lb
45 g	butter	1½ oz
	salt	
	pepper (optional)	
1 tsp	flour	1 tsp
¼ litre	soured cream	8 fl oz
30 g	Gruyère or Parmesan cheese, grated	1 oz

Sauté the mushrooms in 30 g (1 oz) of the butter for a few minutes, until they give up their liquid. Season with a little salt, and pepper if desired. Sprinkle the mushrooms with the flour, cook for a few more minutes, then add the soured cream. Bring to boiling point, then pour the mixture into a gratin dish. Melt the remaining butter and pour it over the top; sprinkle with the grated cheese and bake the dish in a preheated 200°C (400°F or Mark 6) oven for about 12 to 15 minutes, until the topping is bubbly and light golden.

KULINARISCHE GERICHTE: ZU GAST BEI FREUNDEN

Baked Fresh Garlic

Ail Nouveau au Four

Use only freshly picked garlic: the season is mid-June. The garlic should be served on buttered toast.

To serve 6

1 kg	garlic (about 8 heads), green parts and roots cut off	2 to 2½ lb
40 g	butter, cut into 8 pieces	1½ oz
About 5 tsp	salt	About 5 tsp
20 cl	water	7 fl oz

Generously butter a gratin dish and sprinkle it with 1 teaspoon of salt. Put the garlic into the dish. Into the top of the garlic head, where the stems have been cut away, put 3 pinches of salt and a knob of butter. Pour the water into the dish and bake it in an oven preheated to 200°C (400°F or Mark 6) for 50 minutes or until tender, basting the garlic every 10 minutes with the cooking juices. If necessary, add a little more water during the cooking.

MICHEL OLIVER
MES RECETTES

Stuffed Celery

To serve 4

8	sticks celery, cut into 2.5 cm (1 inch) pieces, parboiled in salted water for 5 minutes and drained	8
30 g	butter	1 oz
125 g	mushrooms, finely chopped	4 oz
30 g	flour	1 oz
20 cl	milk	7 fl oz
	salt and pepper	
60 g	Cheddar cheese, grated	2 oz

In a saucepan, melt the butter and stew the mushrooms on a low heat until they are soft. Sprinkle them with the flour, stir in the milk and season with salt and pepper. Cook, stirring continuously, until the sauce thickens.

Arrange the celery in a buttered gratin dish. Pour the mushroom sauce over the celery and sprinkle with the grated cheese. Bake the dish in a preheated 220°C (425°F or Mark 7) oven for 10 minutes or until lightly browned.

RUTH LOWINSKY
LOVELY FOOD

Baked Leeks

Überbackener Lauch

To serve 4

8	leeks, trimmed, dark-green parts removed	8
12.5 cl	water	4 fl oz
½ tsp	salt	½ tsp
30 g	butter, melted	1 oz
2 tbsp	breadcrumbs	2 tbsp
45 g	cheese, grated	1½ oz
½ tsp	paprika	½ tsp

Slice the leeks in half lengthwise, wash them thoroughly, then cut them crosswise into 2.5 cm (1 inch) slices. Bring the water to the boil with the salt, add the leeks, cover, and simmer for 10 minutes. Transfer the leeks with their cooking liquid to a shallow ovenproof dish, pour on the melted butter and sprinkle with the breadcrumbs. Mix the cheese and paprika together and sprinkle it over the leeks. Put the dish under a hot grill for 5 minutes to brown on top.

ARNE KRÜGER AND ANNETTE WOLTER
KOCHEN HEUTE

Scalloped Salsify

To serve 6

750 g	salsify, washed and trimmed	1½ lb
100 g	butter, cut into pieces	3½ oz
60 g	fresh breadcrumbs	2 oz
	salt	
	freshly ground black pepper	
10 cl	double cream	3½ fl oz

Boil the salsify in salted water for 15 to 20 minutes or until tender when pierced with the tip of a knife. Drain, scrape and slice the salsify into 2.5 cm (1 inch) pieces. Pack the salsify, in layers, into a buttered baking dish alternately with 75 g (2½ oz) of the pieces of butter and a layer of fresh breadcrumbs, well seasoned. The top layer of salsify should be covered with breadcrumbs, with the remaining butter melted and spooned over them. Pour the cream over the mixture and cover the dish closely. Bake in a preheated 190°C (375°F or Mark 5) oven for 30 minutes. Then put the dish under a hot grill for a few minutes until the top is delicately browned.

MARION HARLAND
MARION HARLAND'S COMPLETE COOK BOOK

Vegetable Loaf

Pain Parmentier

To serve 6 to 8

500 g	potatoes, peeled	1 lb
250 g	courgettes, peeled and finely chopped	8 oz
250 g	aubergines, peeled and finely chopped	8 oz
1	onion, finely chopped	1 oz
1	head celery, trimmed and finely chopped	1
1	lemon, juice strained	1
	salt and pepper	
30 g	flour	1 oz
60 g	pine-nuts	2 oz
4 tbsp	single cream	4 tbsp

Grate the potatoes into a bowl, sprinkling them from time to time with the lemon juice to prevent them blackening, and adding salt and pepper. Stir in the flour and pine-nuts, then the chopped vegetables and knead roughly. Add enough water to obtain a fairly soft paste that will drop from a spoon.

Pour the mixture into an oiled 25 cm (10 inch) pie dish and spread it out evenly with a knife. Pour on the cream and bake it in a preheated 190°C (375°F or Mark 5) oven for about 1 hour or until the top is nicely golden.

LA CUISINE LYONNAISE

Vegetable Gratin

Le Gratin Provençal

This dish will be even more succulent if extra Parmesan cheese is sprinkled between the vegetable layers. One may also intersperse a couple of layers of small sweet peppers, seeded and cut into thin strips.

To serve 6 to 8

500 g	onions, sliced	1 lb
500 g	courgettes, peeled, sliced and parboiled for 1 minute and drained	1 lb
3 or 4	tomatoes, skinned, seeded and cut into quarters or thick rounds	3 or 4
500 g	aubergines, peeled, sliced and parboiled for 2 to 3 minutes, and drained	1 lb
20 cl	olive oil	7 fl oz
	salt and pepper	
60 g	dry breadcrumbs	2 oz
60 g	Parmesan cheese, grated	2 oz

Sauté the onions in half the oil, until they are transparent. Spread a layer of the onions in a large gratin dish. Spread a layer of the courgettes on top, then a layer of tomatoes, and a layer of aubergines. Sprinkle with olive oil and a pinch each of salt and pepper. Repeat the layers until all the vegetables have been used up. Sprinkle with the breadcrumbs and grated cheese and the rest of the oil. Bake in a preheated 170°C (325°F or Mark 3) oven for about 1 hour or until browned.

JEAN-NOEL ESCUDIER
LA VÉRITABLE CUISINE PROVENÇALE ET NIÇOISE

Spinach and Cheese Balls

Storzapreti à la Bastiaise

If brocciu *cheese is not available,* ricotta *may be substituted.*

To serve 6

750 g	spinach, trimmed and chopped or Swiss chard, ribs removed and chopped	1½ lb
400 g	*brocciu* cheese, mashed with a fork	14 oz
100 g	Parmesan cheese, grated	3½ oz
2	eggs, beaten	2
	salt and pepper	
	grated nutmeg	
4 tbsp	flour	4 tbsp
30 cl	meat roasting juices, or juices from a beef or kid stew	½ pint

Mix the spinach or Swiss chard with the *brocciu* cheese, eggs, salt, pepper, a pinch of grated nutmeg and about half of the grated cheese. Mix well and fashion into little 5 cm (2 inch) balls in the palm of your hand.

Put a large pan of salted water on a high heat and bring to the boil. Coat the cheese balls lightly with the flour and drop them into the boiling water. As each ball rises to the surface, remove it with a skimmer and transfer it to a buttered gratin dish. Pour the meat juices over the balls, sprinkle with the rest of the grated cheese and cook in a preheated 180°C (350°F or Mark 4) oven for 15 minutes or until the cheese melts.

CHRISTIANE SCHAPIRA
LA CUISINE CORSE

Cheese and Bacon Slices

Croque Lorraine

To serve 8

150 g	Gruyère cheese, grated	5 oz
150 g	smoked bacon, diced	5 oz
8	slices sandwich bread	8
40 g	butter	1½ oz
2	onions, coarsely chopped	2
4	eggs, beaten	4
10 cl	double cream	3½ fl oz
	salt and pepper	

With a biscuit cutter or the rim of a glass, cut the bread into eight rounds. In a frying pan, fry the rounds in the butter until they are golden. Drain them and lay them in a buttered gratin

dish. Fry the onions and bacon in the same frying pan, until golden-brown. Then drain them and put them in a bowl with the eggs, cream, cheese, salt and pepper. Mix them well and spoon the mixture evenly over the rounds of bread. Bake them in a preheated 220°C (425°F or Mark 7) oven for 10 minutes, or until the mixture is set and lightly browned.

NINETTE LYON
LES OEUFS

Baked Aubergines with Cheese

Parmigiana di Melanzane

The dish can be made *in bianco,* that is, without tomato sauce.

To serve 4

750 g	aubergines, sliced lengthwise into pieces about 5 mm (¼ inch) thick	1½ lb
60 g	Parmesan cheese, grated	2 oz
250 g	*mozzarella* cheese, thinly sliced	8 oz
About 1 tbsp	salt	About 1 tbsp
8 cl	oil	3 fl oz
8	fresh basil leaves, chopped	8
30 cl	tomato sauce (*page 166*)	½ pint
20 g	butter, cut into pieces	¾ oz

Spread the aubergine slices out in a large dish or in a sieve, sprinkle them generously with salt and leave to drain for 30 minutes. Then rinse them and pat them dry with absorbent paper. Fry the aubergine slices in the hot oil until they are brown, turning them frequently, and taking care they do not overcook. Drain the aubergines and lay them on kitchen paper to absorb the excess oil.

Mix the chopped basil leaves with the grated cheese. Butter a deep 20 cm (8 inch) cake tin and cover the bottom with a layer of aubergines. Pour on a little tomato sauce, then sprinkle with the grated cheese and basil mixture, and place a few slices of *mozzarella* cheese here and there. Cover with a second layer of aubergines, then some tomato sauce, grated cheese and basil and a few slices of *mozzarella,* and continue filling the tin with the layers until the ingredients are all used up, finishing with a layer of sauce and *mozzarella* cheese. Dot the top with the pieces of butter, and bake the dish in a preheated 190°C (375°F or Mark 5) oven for about 20 minutes. Serve in the tin.

FERNANDA GOSETTI
IN CUCINA CON FERNANDA GOSETTI

Glazed Oysters

Huîtres Glacées

The technique of opening oysters is shown on page 54.

	To serve 4	
24	live oysters, opened , on the half shell	24
4 tbsp	chopped parsley	4 tbsp
6	spring onions, finely chopped	6
	freshly ground black pepper	
60 g	Parmesan cheese, grated	2 oz

Drain the oysters of excess liquid. Butter an ovenproof serving dish and arrange the oysters in it. Season them with the parsley, spring onions and pepper and sprinkle them with the grated cheese. Bake them in a preheated 200°C (400°F or Mark 6) oven for 10 minutes to glaze them.

LE MANUEL DE LA FRIANDISE

Roasted Oysters on the Half Shell

The technique of opening oysters is shown on page 54.

	To serve 4	
24	shelled oysters, in the deep half of their shells	24
1½	lemons, juice strained	1½
2 tsp	paprika	2 tsp
60 g	dry breadcrumbs	2 oz
30 g	butter, melted	1 oz

Sprinkle the oysters with the lemon juice and a little paprika. Toss the breadcrumbs in the butter and sprinkle a teaspoon of the mixture over each oyster. Bake the oysters in a preheated 180°C (350°F or Mark 4) oven just until the oysters begin to curl, about 5 minutes. Cook and serve them in relays, as they must be eaten while they are hot.

JESSIE CONRAD
HOME COOKERY

Baked Fish

Farce d'Anguille

	To serve 8 to 10	
500 g	eel, skinned and boned	1 lb
500 g	carp, skinned and boned	1 lb
60 g	stale white bread, crusts removed, soaked in milk and squeezed almost dry	2 oz
4 tbsp	*fines herbes*	4 tbsp
90 g	mushrooms, finely chopped	3 oz
	salt and pepper	
12.5 cl	double cream	4 fl oz

Mince together finely the flesh of the eel and the carp; mix with it the bread soaked in milk, the *fines herbes*, chopped mushrooms, salt, pepper and the cream. See that the mixture is quite smooth. Place it in a buttered ovenproof terrine or dish and cook uncovered in a 170°C (325°F or Mark 3) oven for 40 minutes or until it is firm in the centre.

X. M. BOULESTIN AND A. H. ADAIR
SAVOURIES AND HORS-D'OEUVRE

Smoked Herring and Eggs

This is a traditional smörgåsbord *dish from Gästrikland, a small Swedish province on the Baltic coast.*

	To serve 6	
6	smoked herrings, filleted and skinned	6
3	eggs	3
	salt and pepper	
1 tbsp each	dill and chives, finely cut	1 tbsp each
17.5 to 25 cl	milk, or half milk and half cream	6 to 8 fl oz

Butter an ovenproof casserole and cover the bottom with the fish fillets. Salt and pepper them sparingly and sprinkle them with the dill and chives. Beat the eggs and milk (or milk and cream) together, season with salt and pepper and pour over the fish. Bake the dish in a preheated 200°C (400°F or Mark 6) oven for 15 to 20 minutes. The egg and milk mixture should be set and lightly browned.

OSKAR JAKOBSSON (EDITOR)
GOOD FOOD IN SWEDEN

Herring Savoury

	To serve 2	
2	salt herrings, soaked overnight in water, drained, skinned and filleted	2
30 g	dry breadcrumbs	1 oz
30 g	butter, cut into pieces	1 oz
4 tbsp	double cream	4 tbsp
2 tsp	chopped chervil	2 tsp

Coat the fillets thoroughly with the breadcrumbs, arrange them in a buttered gratin dish and dot them with the butter. Bake the fillets in a preheated 190°C (375°F or Mark 5) oven for 5 to 10 minutes. Then pour the cream over the herrings and bake them for a further 10 minutes or until the herrings are soft. Sprinkle them with the chopped chervil.

INGA NORBERG (EDITOR)
GOOD FOOD FROM SWEDEN

Sardines Stuffed with Spinach

Sardines Farcies aux Épinards

The technique of boning and stuffing is shown on page 78.

	To serve 12	
24	fresh sardines, heads removed, tails left on, cleaned and boned	24
1 kg	spinach, trimmed, rapidly parboiled for 1 minute, drained, squeezed and chopped	2 to 2½ lb
10 cl	olive oil	3½ fl oz
1	medium-sized onion, chopped	1
	salt and pepper	
	grated nutmeg	
4 tbsp	breadcrumbs	4 tbsp

Lay the cleaned sardines open side upwards on a cloth. Heat 4 tablespoons of the oil in a pan, and cook the chopped onion until it is transparent. Add the spinach, season with salt and pepper and a pinch of grated nutmeg. Cook over a high heat for a few minutes, stirring several times.

Remove the pan from the heat. Put a tablespoon of spinach mixture on each sardine and roll the fish round the stuffing, starting at the head end and leaving the tail free. Use the rest of the spinach mixture to line the bottom of a gratin dish large enough to just hold the rolled-up sardines securely. Arrange the sardines in the dish, half-sunk in the spinach mixture lining the dish, with their tails in the air. Sprinkle them with the breadcrumbs, then with the remaining olive oil, and bake in a preheated 220°C (425°F or Mark 7) oven for about 15 minutes. Serve in the baking dish.

JEAN-NOEL ESCUDIER
LA VÉRITABLE CUISINE PROVENÇALE ET NIÇOISE

Jansson's Temptation

Janssons Frestelse

So-called Swedish anchovies are in fact sprats preserved in spiced brine. They can be obtained at grocers specializing in Swedish products. If they are not obtainable, the nearest substitutes are herring or sprats similarly preserved. For this traditional Swedish dish, the onion and anchovies are often layered between the potatoes. Double cream can be substituted for the double cream and milk.

	To serve 6 to 8	
6	Swedish anchovies, filleted	6
3 tbsp	anchovy brine	3 tbsp
2 to 3	large yellow onions, sliced	2 to 3
60 g	butter	2 oz
6	medium-sized potatoes, peeled, cut into matchstick strips and dried on a kitchen towel	6
1 tbsp	toasted breadcrumbs	1 tbsp
	salt and white pepper	
17.5 cl	double cream	6 fl oz
17.5 cl	milk	6 fl oz

Sauté the onions in half of the butter until they are soft and golden, about 12 minutes. Spread them in the bottom of a buttered baking dish. Distribute the anchovies evenly over the onions. Cover them with the potato strips. Mix the breadcrumbs with a pinch each of salt and pepper and sprinkle them on top of the potatoes. Dot with the remaining butter. Bake the dish in a preheated 220°C (425°F or Mark 7) oven for 15 to 20 minutes. Pour first the brine from the anchovies, then the cream and the milk over the dish and bake it for another 20 to 25 minutes, or until the top is golden, the potatoes are soft and almost all the liquid has been absorbed.

TORE WRETMAN
SWEDISH SMÖRGÅSBORD

Baked Herrings Estonian-Style

Harengs à l'Esthonienne

To serve 6

3	large salt herrings, filleted, soaked in milk for 30 minutes and drained	3
About 175 g	dry breadcrumbs	About 6 oz
2½ tbsp	double cream	2½ tbsp

Pound the herring fillets and pass them through a sieve. Weigh them and mix them well with an equal weight of dry breadcrumbs and the cream. Butter six individual gratin dishes and pour the mixture into them. Bake the herring mixture in a preheated 170°C (325°F or Mark 3) oven for 10 to 15 minutes, or until heated through.

A. PETIT
LA GASTRONOMIE EN RUSSIE

Anchovies with Oranges

Alici all'Arancia

To serve 4 to 6

1 kg	fresh anchovies, heads removed, cleaned and filleted	2 to 2½ lb
3	oranges, juice squeezed from 2, 1 thinly sliced	3
1	lemon, very thinly sliced	1
200 g	green olives, stoned and finely chopped	7 oz
60 g	pine-nuts, finely chopped	2 oz
2 tbsp	finely chopped parsley	2 tbsp
1	small green chili pepper, seeded and chopped	1
	salt	
3 tbsp	olive oil	3 tbsp
20 cl	dry white wine	7 fl oz
8 tbsp	dry breadcrumbs, lightly browned under a grill	8 tbsp

Arrange the anchovies in a shallow earthenware dish, interspersed with slices of lemon. Sprinkle with the chopped olives, pine-nuts, parsley and green chili pepper. Season with salt, then pour on the olive oil and the white wine. Sprinkle the dish with the breadcrumbs.

Bake the anchovies in a preheated 180°C (350°F or Mark 4) oven for 15 minutes. Then pour the orange juice over the dish. Return to the oven and bake for another 15 minutes. Garnish with orange slices before serving.

PINO CORRENTI
IL LIBRO D'ORO DELLA CUCINA E DEI VINI DI SICILIA

Baked Anchovy Fillets

Filets d'Anchois à l'Exquise

The coulis *called for in this recipe originally meant the juices from roasting meat. At the time this recipe was published—in 1796—a* coulis *was a concentrated meat essence obtained from simmering a mixture of chopped lean veal and ham in repeated additions of white wine. The* coulis *can be replaced by a velouté sauce (recipe, page 167) or by veal stock (recipe, page 167), reduced to a thick, syrupy consistency.*

To serve 4

16	salt anchovies, filleted, soaked for 30 minutes, rinsed, drained and well dried	16
4	slices of bread, crusts removed	4
60 g	butter	2 oz
15 cl	coulis	¼ pint
2	shallots, chopped	2
2 tbsp	chopped parsley	2 tbsp
2	spring onions, chopped	2
40 g	Parmesan cheese, grated	1½ oz
30 g	dry breadcrumbs	1 oz
1	lemon, juice squeezed	1

Slice the bread into fingers and fry it gently in the butter until golden, about 5 to 7 minutes on each side. Pour half the *coulis* into an ovenproof dish and add the shallots, parsley, spring onions and half the grated cheese. Arrange the fingers of bread on top and cover them with the anchovy fillets, arranged in a lattice-work pattern. Pour on the rest of the *coulis*. Sprinkle with the rest of the cheese and the breadcrumbs.

Bake the dish in a preheated 200°C (400°F or Mark 6) oven for 10 to 12 minutes or until browned on top, or brown it under a hot grill. Serve it hot, sprinkled with the lemon juice.

LE MANUEL DE LA FRIANDISE

Calf's Brain with Anchovies

Kalbshirn mit Sardellen

The preparation of brains for cooking is shown on page 33.

To serve 4

1	calf's brain, soaked, membrane removed, parboiled, cooled and finely chopped	1
5	salt anchovies, soaked for 15 minutes, filleted, drained and chopped	5
3 tbsp	white wine	3 tbsp
12.5 cl	double cream	4 fl oz
1	egg yolk	1
1 to 2 tsp	capers, drained and rinsed	1 to 2 tsp
5	almonds, blanched and slivered	5
30 g	dry breadcrumbs	1 oz
30 g	butter, cut into pieces	1 oz

Mix the brain thoroughly with the anchovy fillets, white wine, cream, egg yolk, capers and almonds. Butter four ramekins and fill them with the brain mixture. Sprinkle them with breadcrumbs and dot with the butter. Bake the brain mixture in a preheated 200°C (400°F or Mark 6) oven for 12 to 15 minutes, or until browned.

LILO AUREDEN
WAS MÄNNERN SO GUT SCHMECKT

Aberdeen Ramekins

To serve 4

275 g	smoked haddock	9 oz
¼ litre	milk	8 fl oz
30 g	butter	1 oz
30 g	flour	1 oz
90 g	Cheddar cheese, grated	3 oz
8 cl	double cream	3 fl oz
	salt and pepper	
2	tomatoes, thinly sliced	2

Place the haddock in a saucepan and pour in the milk. Bring the milk to the boil, remove the pan from the heat, cover it and allow it to stand for 10 minutes. Remove the fish from the pan, reserving the liquid. Flake the haddock, taking care to remove all the skin and bones. In another saucepan, melt the butter and stir in the flour. Cook for a few minutes stirring constantly, then strain in the reserved cooking liquid and whisk over a gentle heat until the sauce is smooth. Add 60 g (2 oz) of the grated cheese, with the cream, salt and pepper. Continue to stir over a gentle heat until the sauce thickens.

Butter four ramekins and arrange the thinly sliced tomatoes in them. Add the fish, pour the sauce over it and sprinkle the tops with the remaining cheese. Place the ramekins under a grill until golden-brown—8 to 10 minutes.

KENNETH MITCHELL (EDITOR)
THE FLAVOUR OF BRITAIN

Baked Fish Ragout

Fischragout Überbacken

To steam cod, cook it in a steamer over rapidly boiling salted water for 20 minutes, or until cooked through. For a more elaborate version of this dish, replace the cod and capers with parboiled asparagus tips, cooked flaked crab and lightly sautéed mushrooms.

To serve 6

500 g	cod, filleted, steamed and flaked	1 lb
1 tbsp	capers	1 tbsp
	salt and pepper	
1 tbsp	lemon juice	1 tbsp
2 tbsp	chopped parsley	2 tbsp
2	eggs	2
3 tbsp	double cream	3 tbsp
2 tbsp	grated Parmesan cheese	2 tbsp
1 tbsp	dry breadcrumbs	1 tbsp
15 g	butter, cut into small pieces	½ oz
3	lemons, quartered	3

Butter six individual ovenproof dishes or scallop shells. Mix the fish with the capers and divide the mixture between the dishes. Season with salt, pepper and a few drops of lemon juice; sprinkle with the parsley. Beat the eggs with the cream and pour them over the mixture. Sprinkle with the grated cheese and breadcrumbs and dot with the butter. Bake in a preheated 220°C (425°F or Mark 7) oven for 10 minutes, or until lightly browned. Serve with lemon wedges.

HEDWIG MARIA STUBER
ICH HELF DIR KOCHEN

Poached Eggs Celestine

Oeufs Pochés à la Celestine

To fry bread, heat just enough butter or oil to almost cover the slices. When the fat is hot, put in the slices and fry gently for about 5 minutes on each side until the surface is lightly coloured; the colour will deepen when the bread is removed from the pan. Drain the slices on absorbent paper.

	To serve 6	
6	eggs, poached	6
175 g	cooked, peeled shrimps, coarsely chopped	6 oz
45 cl	fish velouté (*page 167*)	¾ pint
6	slices bread, fried	6

Stir the shrimps into the fish velouté. Lay the fried bread on a lightly buttered gratin dish, cover each slice with the shrimp sauce and put a poached egg on top. Put the dish into a preheated 200°C (400°F or Mark 6) oven for 2 to 3 minutes, and serve as hot as possible.

A. KENNEY-HERBERT ("WYVERN")
FIFTY LUNCHES

Mussels in White Sauce

Moules au Gratin

The technique of cleaning and cooking mussels in white wine to open them is shown on page 31.

	To serve 3	
1 litre	live mussels, cleaned and opened in white wine	1¾ pints
150 g	butter	5 oz
1 tbsp	flour	1 tbsp
2	egg yolks, beaten	2
½	lemon, juice strained	½
3 tbsp	dry breadcrumbs	3 tbsp
60 g	cheese, grated	2 oz
2 tbsp	chopped parsley	2 tbsp

Reserve the mussel cooking liquid. Shell the mussels and arrange them in a buttered, shallow, ovenproof dish.
Melt 80 g (2½ oz) of the butter in a pan and mix in the flour. Add the mussel cooking liquid and bring to the boil. Remove the pan from the heat. Beat the sauce into the egg yolks. Stir the mixture and put it in a pan with 30 g (1 oz) of the butter and the lemon juice. Continue stirring until the butter has melted. Remove the pan from the heat and strain the sauce through a very fine sieve. Pour the sauce over the mussels and sprinkle them with the breadcrumbs and grated cheese. Dot them with the remaining butter and brown them in a preheated 200°F (400°C or Mark 6) oven for about 10 minutes. Sprinkle them with the chopped parsley just before serving.

M. ÉDOUARD NIGNON (EDITOR)
LE LIVRE DE CUISINE DE L'OUEST-ÉCLAIR

Belgian Shrimp Gratin

Belgischer Garnelenauflauf

	To serve 4	
250 g	cooked, peeled shrimps	8 oz
6	hard-boiled eggs, sliced	6
1 tbsp	flour	1 tbsp
1 tsp	mustard powder	1 tsp
1 tsp	salt	1 tsp
¼ litre	double cream	8 fl oz
1 tbsp	finely chopped parsley	1 tbsp
2 tbsp	grated Emmenthal cheese	2 tbsp

Butter a shallow ovenproof dish and fill it with alternate layers of shrimps and egg. Stir the flour, mustard powder, salt and cream together and bring to the boil, stirring continuously. Remove the mixture from the heat, add the parsley and cheese, and pour the mixture over the shrimps and eggs. Bake it in a preheated 220°C (425°F or Mark 7) oven for about 15 minutes, or until the top is golden and bubbling.

THEODOR BÖTTIGER AND ILSE FROIDL
DAS NEUE FISCHKOCHBUCH

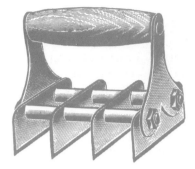

Rappie Pie with Clams

Rapure

To open the clams, put 1 cm (½ inch) of water in a large shallow pan. Bring the water to the boil and place in it as many clams as will fit in one layer. Cover the pan and cook for 2 to 3 minutes until the shells open.

The secret of the dish is to extract all the liquid from potatoes and replace it by another liquid. Rappie pies can be made with meat or chicken, but there are grounds for thinking that the version with clams may be the earliest.

	To serve 6	
18 to 24	soft-shell clams, steamed open, meat minced, juice reserved	18 to 24
250 g	salt pork, finely diced	8 oz
1.5 kg	potatoes	3 lb
	pepper	

Place the pork in a 30 by 20 cm (10 by 8 inch) baking tin. Leave the pan over a low heat until the bottom is coated with melted fat. Then remove the pieces of pork and reserve them.
Peel and grate 150 g (5 oz) of potatoes at a time and place them in a cheesecloth, which must then be twisted so as to wring out as much liquid as possible. Collect the potato liquid in a bowl, so that you can measure it.

Add to the clam juices enough water to bring the volume up to that of the liquid extracted from the potatoes. Bring this mixture to the boil, then add the wrung-out potatoes, little by little. The potato will swell up as it absorbs the new liquid. When this operation is completed, place a layer of the potatoes in the bottom of the baking tin, cover this with the minced clams, then another layer of potatoes and so on—the pie can have three layers or five. Season with pepper to taste and sprinkle the little bits of pork over the top.

Bake the pie in a preheated 200°C (400°F or Mark 6) oven for 20 minutes, then reduce the heat to 180°C (350°F or Mark 4) and continue to bake for another hour or so, when the top of the pie will be brown and crusty.

ALAN DAVIDSON
NORTH ATLANTIC SEAFOOD

Frogs' Legs Gratin

Cuisses de Grenouilles à la Façon de Jacques les Omelettes

	To serve 4	
48	pairs small frogs' legs	48
2	shallots, finely chopped	2
1	garlic clove, peeled and chopped	1
2	sprigs parsley, chopped	2
300 g	breadcrumbs, sieved	10 oz
	salt and pepper	
400 g	butter, melted and cooled	14 oz

Mix the shallots, garlic and parsley with the breadcrumbs. Season the frogs' legs with salt and pepper, and dip them in the cooled melted butter. Coat the frogs' legs thoroughly with the breadcrumb mixture.

Take a fairly deep gratin dish and butter it generously. Lay the frogs' legs in it, fill the spaces between them with the breadcrumb mixture, and pour on the rest of the melted butter. Bake in an oven preheated to 200°C (400°F or Mark 6) for 15 to 20 minutes or until the top is lightly browned.

AMICALE DES CUISINIERS ET PÂTISSIERS AUVERGNATS DE PARIS
CUISINE D'AUVERGNE

Scotch Woodcock

To make anchovy butter, soak two filleted salt anchovies in cold water for up to 30 minutes. Drain them well on kitchen paper and pound them in a mortar with pepper, half a clove of garlic and 30 g (1 oz) softened butter. Mix thoroughly and chill the butter until needed.

	To serve 4	
6	eggs, well beaten	6
60 g	butter	2 oz
4	slices hot toast	4
30 g	anchovy butter	1 oz
4	salt anchovies, filleted, soaked and drained	4
60 g	Cheddar cheese, grated	2 oz

Melt the butter and scramble the eggs in it until they have a creamy consistency. Spread the hot toast with the anchovy butter and cover it with a layer of scrambled eggs. Put two anchovy fillets over the eggs on each slice of toast, sprinkle with grated cheese and glaze quickly under a hot grill, so that the cheese just melts.

X. M. BOULESTIN AND A. H. ADAIR
SAVOURIES AND HORS-D'OEUVRE

Peruvian Kebabs

Anticucho

These snacks, which have become Peru's national dish, are sold on wooden skewers by street vendors, or eaten at home before the main course, often with young, fresh sweetcorn. They are served rare, with a chili dip.

To make the chili dip, seed and chop five to six dried hot red chilis, and pour 30 cl (½ pint) of boiling water over them. Leave them to soak for 2 hours, then drain them thoroughly and purée them in a blender with 5 tablespoons of olive oil, 1 finely chopped garlic clove, a pinch of salt and 2 to 3 tablespoons of hot stock or water.

Take care not to overcook the kebabs, as the meat can easily become dry and hard.

	To serve 4	
1	calf's heart, soaked in water for 1 hour, tubes and tendons removed, cut into equal-sized cubes	1
30 cl	wine vinegar	½ pint
30 cl	water	½ pint
1	onion, grated	1
1	garlic clove, crushed	1
½ to 1 tsp	cayenne pepper or 2 to 3 chili peppers, finely chopped	½ to 1 tsp
1	bay leaf	1
3	allspice berries, crushed	3
3	peppercorns, crushed	3
	salt	
	sugar	
2 tbsp	olive oil	2 tbsp

Prepare a marinade with the vinegar, water, onion, garlic, cayenne pepper or chili peppers, bay leaf, crushed allspice and peppercorns, salt and a pinch of sugar. Put the meat into the marinade—it should be well covered—toss it gently, and leave it overnight.

On the following day, remove the meat from the marinade, arrange it on short skewers, and brush it with the olive oil. Grill the meat over hot coals or under a high heat for about 6 minutes, turning the skewers once during the cooking.

GRETE WILLINSKY
KULINARISCHE WELTREISE

Chicken Liver Brochettes

Spiedini di Fegatini

	To serve 4	
8	chicken livers, trimmed and halved	8
250 g	spicy garlic frying sausage, cut into 16 chunks	8 oz
12 to 16	sage leaves	12 to 16
	oil	
	salt	

Thread the livers and sausage on to skewers alternately with the sage leaves. Brush the brochettes with oil and grill them for 15 to 20 minutes, turning them frequently. Season the brochettes with salt before serving them.

STELLA DONATI
PIATTOFORTE

Skewered Liver

Spiedini di Fegato

The author recommends using home-made bread. Rye or French bread can also be used.

	To serve 4	
300 g	pig's or calf's liver, cut into small dice	10 oz
1	pork caul, cut into sixteen 5 cm (2 inch) squares	1
20	bay leaves, halved	20
2	sweet red or green peppers, seeded and cut into large dice	2
200 g	spiced garlic sausage, cut into large dice	7 oz
125 g	bread, cut into large dice	4 oz
4 tbsp	oil	4 tbsp
	salt and pepper	

Divide the liver into 16 equal portions. Wrap each portion of liver in a piece of pork caul. Thread a skewer with a piece of bay leaf, then with a small "bag" of liver, a second piece of bay leaf, a piece of pepper, a piece of sausage and a piece of bread.

Fill another three skewers in the same way. Brush the brochettes with the oil and season them with pepper. Grill them on a moderate heat, turning frequently, for about 20 minutes or until well browned. Season with salt and serve.

STELLA DONATI
PIATTOFORTE

Devilled Bones

Roast goose or turkey bones and necks can be treated similarly.

To serve 4

250 to 300 g	meaty bones from a joint of roast rib of beef	8 to 10 oz
½ tsp	cayenne pepper	½ tsp
2 tsp	Dijon mustard	2 tsp

Sprinkle the bones with a mixture of the cayenne pepper and mustard and grill them; serve them immediately. No forks and knives required.

X. M. BOULESTIN AND A. H. ADAIR
SAVOURIES AND HORS-D'OEUVRE

Skewered Sweetbreads

Des Hâtelets de Ris de Veau

The blanching and cleaning of sweetbreads is shown on page 32. This recipe was first published in 1787.

To serve 4 to 6

1	pair calf's sweetbreads, blanched, cleaned and cut into small pieces	1
1 tbsp	flour	1 tbsp
60 g	butter	2 oz
3 tbsp	finely chopped parsley	3 tbsp
3 to 4	spring onions, finely chopped	3 to 4
250 g	calf's or chicken liver, cut into small pieces	8 oz
125 g	streaky bacon, cut into lardons and blanched for 2 minutes in boiling water	4 oz
	salt and pepper	
	breadcrumbs	

Cook the flour in the butter over a low heat until the flour is lightly coloured. Stir in the parsley and spring onions, then the sweetbreads, liver and bacon. Season with salt and pepper. Remove the pan from the heat when the liver has become slightly firm. Thread the pieces of meat on to wooden skewers, coat with the remaining pan juices, and roll the skewers in breadcrumbs. Lay the skewers on racks and chill them in the refrigerator for at least 30 minutes.

Grill or pan fry the skewers, turning them two or three times during cooking, for 8 to 10 minutes.

PIERRE JOSEPH BUC'HOZ
L'ART DE PRÉPARER LES ALIMENTS

Skewered Mussels

Brochettes de Moules

Green bacon can be used if preferred. To ensure that the bacon is cooked through when the mussels are ready, first parboil, then sauté the bacon for a few minutes before threading it on to the skewers; the cooking time can then be reduced. Melted butter can be used to coat the skewers instead of beaten eggs. The method for cleaning mussels and cooking them in white wine is shown on page 30.

To serve 4

48	large mussels, cleaned, opened in white wine and shelled	48
150 g	rashers smoked bacon, cut into small strips	5 oz
60 g	dry breadcrumbs	2 oz
1	egg, beaten in a shallow bowl with salt and pepper	1
3 tbsp	oil	3 tbsp

Thread four skewers with two mussels and one or two strips of bacon alternately. Put the breadcrumbs in a shallow bowl. Roll the skewers first in the beaten egg, then in the breadcrumbs, and sprinkle them lightly with oil. Preheat the grill and grill the skewers for up to 15 minutes or until browned, sprinkling them frequently with oil and turning them often.

LÉONE BÉRARD
POISSONS ET FRUITS DE MER

North Vietnamese Recipe for Fish Brochettes

Cha Ca Nuong

Nuoc mam, Vietnamese fish sauce, is obtainable from Oriental grocers, but if it is not available, Chinese oyster sauce or fish gravy can be substituted. Shrimp paste, imported from Malaysia, is available in Chinese grocers, as is rice spirit.

Any sea fish with firm flesh, such as mackerel or grouper, may be used in this recipe.

To serve 6

750 g	fish, filleted, skinned and cut into 3 cm (1¼ inch) cubes	1½ lb
175 g	streaky bacon, cut into 3 cm (1¼ inch) pieces	6 oz
3 tbsp	oil	3 tbsp
4	spring onions, chopped	4
60 g	peanuts, dry roasted and pounded	2 oz

	Fish marinade	
3 tbsp	oil	3 tbsp
3 tbsp	nuoc mam	3 tbsp
2 tbsp	rice spirit	2 tbsp
	ground turmeric	
15 g	ginger root, finely chopped	½ oz
2 tsp	shrimp paste	2 tsp

Mix the marinade ingredients together and marinate the fish cubes for 2 to 3 hours. Thread 12 skewers with alternating pieces of fish and streaky bacon.

Heat the oil and add the spring onions. Grill the brochettes, basting the fish with the oil and spring onion mixture. Sprinkle the pounded peanuts over the brochettes before serving.

ALAN DAVIDSON
SEAFOOD OF SOUTH-EAST ASIA

Seafood Kebabs

Spiedini alla Marinara

If porgy is not available, use sea bream, which comes from the same family, or other firm-fleshed salt-water fish.

	To serve 4	
250 g	fresh Dublin Bay prawns, shelled	8 oz
250 g	squid, eyes, skin, viscera, beak and bone discarded	8 oz
250 g	cuttlefish, viscera, cuttlebone and beak discarded	8 oz
250 g	porgy, cleaned, filleted and skinned	8 oz
4 tbsp	olive oil	4 tbsp
1	garlic clove, crushed	1
4 tbsp	chopped parsley	4 tbsp

Cut the shellfish, cephalopods and fish into pieces roughly the same size that are large enough to be threaded on to skewers. Put the pieces on the skewers.

Warm the olive oil with the garlic and parsley. Grill the skewered seafoods on an open grill brushing them as they cook with the olive oil mixture. Turn the skewers frequently. Cooking takes only a few minutes—time enough to catch the smoky taste of the fire without losing the tang of the sea.

SOPHIA LOREN
EAT WITH ME

Standard Preparations

Fish or Chicken Mousseline

This recipe is for a rich mousseline, suitable for use as a stuffing. For a more delicate mousseline, you can increase the quantity of cream to 35 cl (12 fl oz).

For a firmer mousseline that can be formed into dumplings and poached (*recipe, page 112*), use two small egg whites and 15 cl (¼ pint) of cream, and do not whip the cream.

If desired, a pinch each of cayenne pepper and grated nutmeg, or ¼ teaspoon of powdered saffron dissolved in 1 teaspoon of boiling water, can be added while pounding the flesh. For texture and flavour, any of the following can be mixed into a purée after the cream has been incorporated: chopped pistachio nuts; cooked, chopped prawns, shrimps or mussels; a mushroom and onion *duxelles (page 8)*; sautéed chopped mushrooms; chopped truffles.

	To make about 60 cl (1 pint) mousseline	
250 g	white or pink fish fillets, skinned, or chicken breast, skinned, sinews removed	8 oz
	salt and pepper	
1	large egg white	1
¼ litre	double cream	8 fl oz

In a mortar, pound the fish or chicken to a smooth purée with a pestle. Season with salt and pepper and add the egg white a little at a time, pounding after each addition until it is completely incorporated. Alternatively reduce the flesh to a purée in a food processor, add the seasoning and egg white and process the mixture again. A little at a time, rub the purée through a fine meshed sieve, using a plastic dough scraper for a drum sieve or a wooden pestle for any other sieve. Pack the purée into a glass or metal bowl and press plastic film against the surface. Place the bowl in a larger bowl containing crushed ice and refrigerate for at least 1 hour.

Remove the bowls from the refrigerator. Pour off the water from the large bowl and add more crushed ice. Using a wooden spoon, work a little double cream into the mixture. Return the bowls to the refrigerator for 15 minutes. Continue beating in small quantities of cream, refrigerating for 15 minutes between each addition and replacing the crushed ice as necessary. Beat the mixture vigorously as soon as it becomes soft enough to do so. When about half the cream has been incorporated, refrigerate the mixture for a few minutes. Lightly whip the remaining cream and incorporate it into the purée. Refrigerate until ready for use.

Pancakes

To make 8 to 10 pancakes

60 g	flour	2 oz
1 tsp	salt	1 tsp
3	eggs	3
¼ litre	milk or water	8 fl oz
2 tbsp	brandy (optional)	2 tbsp
1 tbsp	*fines herbes* (optional)	1 tbsp
40 g	unsalted butter, melted	1½ oz

Pour the flour and salt into a bowl, make a well in the centre and break in the eggs. Pour the milk or water into the well. Working from the centre, gradually whisk the eggs and milk or water into the flour. If you like, add the brandy or the *fines herbes*. Stir in the melted butter as soon as the batter is smooth and has the consistency of single cream. Do not whisk the mixture beyond this stage.

To cook the pancakes, heat a crêpe pan or small frying pan over a medium heat. Grease it lightly with a little extra butter for the first pancake only. Pour in just enough of the batter to lightly coat the pan. The batter should sizzle as it touches the hot metal. As you pour, tilt and roll the pan to spread the batter as evenly and as thinly as possible. Excess batter that does not set at once should be poured back into the bowl.

Cook the pancake until the edges begin to curl and the underside is evenly coloured, about 30 seconds. Then loosen the edges with a palette knife and flip the pancake over, either with your fingers or with the palette knife. Cook the underside of the pancake until it is lightly coloured and dry—about 20 seconds should be sufficient.

Before making a fresh pancake, stir the batter in case it has separated. Remove the pan from the heat for a few seconds to prevent it overheating. As the pancakes are made, stack them in a pile to keep them warm.

A Wine or Vinegar Court-Bouillon

This court-bouillon is a general-purpose poaching liquid for most fish and shellfish. A couple of fennel stalks and a clove of garlic may also be included if desired.

To make about 2 litres (3½ pints) court-bouillon

½ litre	white or red wine or 20 cl (7 fl oz) wine vinegar	16 fl oz
1 each	large onion and carrot, sliced	1 each
2	garlic cloves, crushed	2
1	stick celery, diced	1
60 g	parsley	2 oz
2	sprigs dill (optional)	2
1	bay leaf	1
1.5 litres	water	2½ pints
	salt	
5 or 6	peppercorns	5 or 6

Put the vegetables, herbs, water and vinegar, if using, into a large pan and season with a pinch of salt. Bring to the boil, then reduce the heat, cover, and simmer for 15 minutes. Pour in the wine, if using, and simmer for a further 15 minutes, adding the peppercorns 10 minutes before the end of cooking.

Beurre Blanc

To make 30 to 45 cl (½ to ¾ pint) sauce

6 tbsp	dry white wine	6 tbsp
6 tbsp	white wine vinegar	6 tbsp
3	shallots, very finely chopped	3
	salt	
	pepper	
250 to 400 g	cold unsalted butter, cut into small pieces	8 to 14 oz

In a heavy stainless steel or enamelled saucepan, boil the wine and vinegar with the shallots and a pinch of salt until only enough liquid remains to moisten the shallots. Remove the pan from the heat and allow it to cool for a few minutes. Season the mixture with pepper. Place the pan on a fireproof mat over a very low heat and whisk in the butter, a handful at a time, until the mixture has a creamy consistency. Remove from the heat as soon as all the butter has been incorporated.

Olive Oil Dough

This dough is intended for a baked pie or tart crust. To make a dough suitable for deep frying, halve the quantity of olive oil. The technique of making the dough is shown on page 22.

To make about 350 g (12 oz) dough		
250 g	flour	8 oz
	salt	
1	egg	1
10 cl	olive oil	3½ fl oz
About 4 tbsp	tepid water	About 4 tbsp

In a large bowl, mix the flour and salt. Break in the egg and add the olive oil and tepid water. With a fork, stir the ingredients until they cohere in a mass. Gather the dough with both hands and squeeze it into a ball. Knead it with your knuckles and fingertips until it is smooth and comes away cleanly from the sides of the bowl. Wrap it in plastic film and leave it to rest for at least 1 hour at room temperature before rolling it out thinly as for shortcrust dough.

Olive oil puff dough. The technique of making this dough is shown on page 24. Reserve 1 tablespoon of the oil and use the rest to make a dough, moistening it with 2 or 3 tablespoons of water. Leave it to rest for 1 hour at room temperature.

Flour the work surface and roll out the dough into one long strip. Using a pastry brush, lightly paint two-thirds of the strip with some of the reserved olive oil. Do not use too much oil, lest it be squeezed out when the dough is folded and make the work surface too greasy for rolling out the dough. Lift the unpainted end of the strip and fold it over the central third of the dough. Fold the remaining third of the dough on top. Give the dough a quarter turn so that the open edges face you, roll it out again and paint and fold it as before.

Leave the dough to rest for 1 hour before turning the dough and painting, rolling and folding it again. Leave it to rest for 1 hour and repeat the process before rolling it out.

Shortcrust and Rough-Puff Dough

One simple formula produces dough for both plain shortcrust and for rough-puff dough, though the proportions differ. Shortcrust dough is made with about half the weight of fat to flour; rough-puff dough uses a little more fat. The rough-puff here may be used in any recipe calling for puff dough. The quantity of dough given here will line a 20 cm (8 inch) flan tin or six small flan tins. To make a 30 cm (12 inch) tart shell, increase the quantities by half. If you like, half the butter can be replaced by lard.

To make 250 g (8 oz) dough		
125 g	flour	4 oz
¼ tsp	salt	¼ tsp
60 to 125 g	cold unsalted butter, cut into small pieces	2 to 4 oz
3 to 4 tbsp	cold water	3 to 4 tbsp

Mix the flour and salt in a mixing bowl. Add the butter and cut it into the flour rapidly, using two table knives, until the butter is in tiny pieces. Do not work for more than a few minutes. Add half the water and, with a fork, quickly blend it into the flour and butter mixture. Add just enough of the rest of the water to allow you to gather the dough together with your hands into a firm ball. Wrap the dough in plastic film or waxed paper and refrigerate it for at least 1 hour, or, alternatively, put it in the freezer for about 20 minutes until the surface is slightly frozen.

To roll out shortcrust dough. Remove the ball of dough from the refrigerator or freezer and put it on a cool floured surface (a marble slab is ideal). Press the dough out partially with your hand, then give it a few gentle smacks with the rolling pin to flatten and render it more supple. For a tart shell, roll out the dough from the centre, until the dough forms a circle about 1 cm (½ inch) thick. Turn the dough over so that both sides are floured and continue rolling until the circle is about 3 mm (⅛ inch) thick. Roll the dough on to the pin, lift up the pin and unroll the dough over the flan tin. Trim the dough to within 1 cm (½ inch) of the rim of the tin, turn the edges under, press the double thickness of dough to the rim firmly with thumb and forefingers and crimp the edges.

To roll out rough-puff dough. Place the dough on a cool floured surface and smack it flat with the rolling pin. Turn the dough over to make sure that both sides are well floured, and roll out the dough rapidly into a rectangle about 30 cm (1 foot) long and 12 to 15 cm (5 to 6 inches) wide. Fold the two short ends to meet each other in the centre, then fold again to align the folded edges with each other. Following the direction of the fold lines, roll the dough into a rectangle again, fold again in the same way, wrap in plastic film and refrigerate for 1 to 2 hours or for 15 to 20 minutes in the freezer. Repeat this process two or three more times before using the dough. Always let the dough rest in the refrigerator or freezer in between the times it is rolled out.

Spicy Tomato Sauce

To make about 30 cl (½ pint) sauce

3	large tomatoes, skinned, seeded and chopped	3
2	garlic cloves, unpeeled, lightly crushed	2
4 or 5	coriander seeds, lightly crushed	4 or 5
2 tbsp	finely chopped parsley	2 tbsp
1 tbsp	finely cut chives	1 tbsp
1 tbsp	finely chopped chervil	1 tbsp
1 tsp	finely chopped tarragon	1 tsp
4 tbsp	olive oil	4 tbsp

Put all the ingredients into a saucepan. Stand the saucepan on a trivet in a large pan. Fill the pan with enough warm water to reach just above the level of the contents of the saucepan. Put the pan on a low heat and warm the sauce, stirring occasionally, for at least 30 minutes or until the flavours are well mingled. Do not let it boil. Remove the garlic cloves before serving.

Tomato Sauce

When fresh ripe tomatoes are not available, use canned Italian plum tomatoes. The sauce can be flavoured with herbs other than those given below; parsley, basil, oregano and marjoram are all suitable substitutes.

To make about 30 cl (½ pint) sauce

750 g	very ripe tomatoes, chopped	1½ lb
1	onion, finely chopped	1
1 tbsp	olive oil	1 tbsp
2	garlic cloves, chopped	2
1 tsp	thyme	1 tsp
1	bay leaf, chopped	1
1 to 2 tsp	sugar (optional)	1 to 2 tsp
	salt and freshly ground pepper	

In a large enamelled or stainless steel saucepan, gently fry the onion in the oil until soft but not brown. Add the other ingredients and simmer for 20 to 30 minutes or until the tomatoes have been reduced to a thick pulp. Sieve the mixture using a wooden pestle or spoon.

Return the sauce to the heat, to warm through. If a thicker consistency is required, simmer the sauce, uncovered, for 20 to 30 minutes, stirring frequently to prevent sticking. Season the sauce to taste just before serving.

Hollandaise Sauce

To make about 30 cl (½ pint) sauce

3	egg yolks	3
1 tbsp	cold water	1 tbsp
250 g	cold unsalted butter, cut into small pieces	8 oz
	white pepper, cayenne pepper, and salt	
1 tsp	strained lemon juice	1 tsp

In a bain-marie, heat some water until it simmers, then reduce the heat to low. Place a saucepan in the bain-marie, put the egg yolks and the cold water in the saucepan and beat them until the yolks are smooth. Whisk a handful of the butter into the yolks and, when the butter has been absorbed, continue adding the diced butter in this way until all of it has been used. Beat until the sauce becomes thick and creamy. Season the sauce with white pepper, cayenne pepper and salt to taste and add the lemon juice.

White Sauce

This recipe can be used whenever béchamel sauce is required.

To make about 40 cl (¾ pint) sauce

30 g	butter	1 oz
2 tbsp	flour	2 tbsp
60 cl	milk	1 pint
	salt	
	pepper	
	freshly grated nutmeg (optional)	
	double cream (optional)	

Melt the butter in a heavy saucepan. Stir in the flour and cook, stirring, over a low heat for 2 to 5 minutes. Pour in all the milk, whisking constantly to blend the mixture smoothly. Increase the heat and continue whisking while the sauce comes to the boil. Season with a very little salt. Reduce the heat and simmer for about 40 minutes, stirring every so often to prevent the sauce from sticking to the bottom of the pan. Add pepper and a pinch of nutmeg if desired; taste for seasoning. Whisk again until the sauce is perfectly smooth and add cream if you prefer a richer, whiter sauce.

Thick white sauce for stuffings and soufflé base: make the sauce as above, but double amounts of butter and flour. Cook the sauce until it is almost too thick to pour—about 10 minutes—stirring constantly to keep it from sticking.

Very thick white sauce for deep frying: melt 125 g (4 oz) of butter and stir in 60 g (2 oz) of flour. Cook the mixture, stirring constantly, for 2 minutes. Pour in ½ litre (16 fl oz) of milk and whisk for 5 minutes. Remove the pan from the heat.

Velouté Sauce

The technique of making a velouté sauce is shown on page 10.

To make about 30 cl (½ pint) sauce

60 cl	fish or veal stock (*below and right*)	1 pint
30 g	butter	1 oz
2 tbsp	flour	2 tbsp

Melt the butter in a heavy saucepan over a low heat. Stir in the flour to make a roux and cook, stirring, for 2 to 3 minutes. Pour the stock into the pan, whisking constantly. Raise the heat and continue to whisk until the sauce comes to the boil. Reduce the heat to low, and move the saucepan half off the heat so the liquid on only one side of the pan simmers. A skin of impurities will form on the still side. Remove the skin periodically with a spoon. Cook the sauce for about 40 minutes to reduce it and to eliminate the taste of flour.

Fish Stock

To make about 2 litres (3½ pints) stock

1 kg	fish trimmings (bones, heads, skin), rinsed and cut into pieces	2 to 2½ lb
About 2 litres	water	About 3½ pints
1 each	carrot and onion, sliced	1 each
2	sticks celery, sliced	2
2	garlic cloves, crushed	2
30 g	parsley stalks	1 oz
1	large sprig thyme	1
3 or 4	wild fennel branches	3 or 4
1	bay leaf	1
	salt	
½ litre	dry white wine	16 fl oz
4	peppercorns (optional)	4

Put the fish trimmings into a large pan. Add the water to cover. Bring to a simmer over a low heat. With a large, shallow spoon, skim off the scum that rises to the surface. Skim until no more scum rises, then add the vegetables, herbs and salt. Partially cover the pan and simmer the contents for 15 minutes. Add the wine, return the liquid to the boil and simmer for 10 to 15 more minutes. If you like, add the peppercorns 10 minutes before the end of cooking. Strain through a colander lined with two layers of damp muslin.

Veal Stock

Beef stock can be prepared in the same way, but 2 kg (4 lb) of beef cuts—tail, shank or chuck—should be substituted for the meaty veal trimmings, and the cooking time should be at least 1 hour longer. The veal knuckle bone can be omitted for a less gelatinous stock. For a mixed stock, use about 3 kg (6 to 7 lb) of meaty bones and trimmings of veal, beef and/or chicken.

To make 2 to 3 litres (3½ to 5 pints) stock

1	veal shank and knuckle bone, sawn into 5 cm (2 inch) pieces	1
2 kg	meaty veal trimmings and/or chicken trimmings	4 lb
3 to 5 litres	water	5 to 8 pints
4	carrots, scraped and topped	4
2	large onions, 1 stuck with 2 or 3 cloves	2
1	whole garlic head, unpeeled	1
1	stick celery	1
1	large bouquet garni, including leek	1
	salt	

Put a metal trivet into a heavy stock-pot. Put the pieces of bone into the stock-pot and place the meat on top of them. Add cold water to cover by 5 cm (2 inches). Bring to a simmer over a low heat, starting to skim as impurities rise to the surface. Keep skimming, occasionally adding a glass of cold water, until no more scum rises. Do not stir, lest you cloud the stock.

Add the vegetables, bouquet garni and a little salt to the pot, pushing them down into the liquid so that everything is submerged. Continue skimming until the liquid boils. Reduce the heat to very low and cook, partially covered, at a bare simmer for 5 hours, skimming off the surface fat 3 or 4 times.

Strain the stock by pouring it through a colander into a large bowl or clean pot. Discard the bones, meat trimmings, vegetables and bouquet garni. Cool the strained stock, then leave it overnight in the refrigerator. Skim off the fat and reheat the stock to liquefy it before making a velouté.

Recipe Index

English recipe titles are listed by categories such as
"Artichokes", "Cheese", "Flan", "Sauce" and
"Stuffed Vegetables" and within those categories
alphabetically. Foreign recipe titles are listed
alphabetically without regard to category.

General Index/Glossary

Included in this index are definitions of many of the culinary terms used in this book: definitions are in italics. The recipes in the Anthology are listed in the Recipe Index on page 168.

Allspice: *the dried berry—used whole or ground—of a member of the myrtle family. Called allspice because it has something of the aroma of clove, cinnamon and nutmeg combined.*
Almonds, 58
Aluminium foil, 9, 12, 66, 73
Anchovies, 17; in garlic butter on vegetable tart, 21
Angler fish, 30
Apple corer, 50
Aromatic vegetables, 10
Aromatics: *all substances—such as vegetables, herbs and spices—that add aroma and flavour to food when used in cooking.*
Artichokes, fritters, 82-83; in little stews, 28, 38; marinating, 82; preparation, 28; sautéed, 77; stuffed, 43, 46-47
Asparagus, in little stews, 27, 28, 40; preparation, 29
Assembling, little stews, 36-37
Aubergines, 20; stuffed, 50-51
Bacon, 18, 27, 68; in little stews, 32, 33, 40; removing salt, 33; on skewers, 88
Bain-marie: *a large pot or vessel in which water is heated so that a smaller pot can be placed inside and its contents cooked or heated. Used for custards, creams and other preparations that cannot tolerate direct heat or boiling; see also Water bath*
Baking, 77; bread cases, 35; clams, 55; custard dishes, 65, 67; frogs' legs, 81; gratins, 37; oysters, 55; pies, 19, 25; quiches, 69; soufflés, 71, 73, 75; stuffed vegetables, 49, 51; tarts, 21; vol-au-vents, 35; see also Baking blind, Pre-baking
Baking blind, 68-69; see also Pre-baking
Basil, 15, 20
Batter, for deep frying, 77, 82; pancake, 56, 86
Bay leaves, 10, 11, 14, 31
Beans, 6; see also Broad beans, Flageolet beans, French beans
Beef, 9; boiled, in pie filling, 24; casings, 58, 60; chopped, in stuffings, 50; leftover stew as stuffing, 57; marrow, 32, 40, 64
Beetroot, 50
Beurre blanc, 14, 15, 27, 36; with little stews, 38; with mousseline, 61
Blanch: *to plunge food into boiling water for a short period. Done for a number of reasons: to remove strong flavours; to soften food, such as vegetables, before further cooking; to facilitate the removal of skins or shells.*

Another meaning is to whiten.
Blanched almonds: *almonds that have been peeled by blanching (q.v.).*
Blender, 7, 13
Boiling, onions, 48; rice, 6; spinach, 8
Bone marrow, in little stews, 32, 40; in savoury custard, 64
Boning, sardines, 19, 78
Boudins blancs, 58-59
Bouquet garni: *bunch of mixed herbs—the classic three being parsley, thyme and bay leaf—used for flavouring sauces and stews;* 58
Brains, 12; fritters, 82-83; in little stews, 32, 33, 36-37; marinating,82; sautéed, 77; in stuffings, 43, 46, 50, 51
Brandy, 28, 43
Bread, cases for little stews, 27, 34, 35, 38, 40; soaking, 7; in stuffings, 6, 7, 50, 58-59
Breadcrumbs, 6, 77; coating before cooking, 58, 77, 80-81, 84-85; gratin tops, 27, 36, 37, 41, 46, 47, 55, 78, 79; making, 7; in stuffings, 49, 54, 57
Broad beans, 46
Brocciu: *a soft, unripened sheep's milk cheese. Brocciu or broccio is its Corsican name—in France it is called brousse.*
Brochettes, 84-85, 88
Butter, 35; beurre blanc, 15, 27, 36, 38; in coatings, 80-81, 88; in doughs, 17; garlic, 6, 7, 55; in pancake batter, 56; in puff dough, 20; in quiches, 61; in sauces, 10, 11, 12, 36, 37, 39, 40, 41; for sautéing, 33, 80, 88; in shortcrust dough, 18; in stuffings, 6, 7, 24-25, 49
Cabbage, leaves, stuffed, 44; lining for savoury custard, 66-67; in pie filling, 24
Carrots, in court-bouillon, 30; in fish stock, 10; puréed, in soufflé, 73; in red wine sauce, 11
Casings, 5, 43; bread, 27, 34, 35, 38, 40; pastry, 17, 27, 34, 35, 39, 40; rice, 27, 34, 41; see also Pancakes, Pies, Satchels, Sausage casings, Tarts, Turnovers
Caul: *web-like fatty membrane that protects a pig's intestines. Used to wrap food, such as sausages or vegetables, during cooking. Also known as lace-fat;* 77
Cauliflower, 82
Cayenne pepper, 7
Celery, in court-bouillon, 30; in fish stock, 10; in stuffings, 54
Chard, in layered pudding, 63, 66-67; leaves, stuffed, 44
Cheddar, gratin finishes, 49
Cheese, 64, 84; gratin tops, 27, 36, 48, 57, 78; in quiches, 63, 68; in soufflés, 72-73; in stuffings, 6, 7, 48, 56; see also Cheddar, Cottage cheese, Gruyère, Parmesan, Ricotta
Chervil, 15, 82
Chicken, 12, 60; in boudins blancs, 59; in little stews, 27, 39; in stuffings, 43, 57
Chicken livers, fritters, 82-83; in little stews, 32, 36, 40; marinating, 82; in savoury custard, 63, 64

Chili peppers: *numerous varieties of small, finger-shaped hot peppers, native to tropical America and the West Indies.*
Chives, 15, 67, 82
Chopping, meat, 9; truffles, 29
Clams, 30; baked in shell, 54-55
Clarified butter: *butter from which the water, milk solids and salt have been removed.*
Cloves, 58
Coatings, butter and breadcrumbs, 80-81, 88; flour and beaten egg, 80, 82; white sauce, egg and breadcrumbs, 84-85
Colander, 9
Colouring, sauces, 10, 12, 13, 39, 41; soufflés, 72-73
Coriander, 15, 58
Cottage cheese, 7, 86
Courgettes, 20; fritters, 82-83; marinating, 82; stuffed, 43, 50-51
Court-bouillon, for brains, 32, 33; seafood, 30, 38, 39, 41; snails, 53
Crayfish, 30, 60
Cream, 48, 49, 72; almond-flavoured, 59; in mousseline, 60-61; in quiches, 68, 69; in stuffings, 43, 59; in tomato sauce, 15; in velouté, 10, 36, 38, 39, 40, 41, 72, 74; in white sauce, 12, 57
Crème fraîche: *slightly ripened, sharp-tasting double cream widely available in France. The nearest equivalent is fresh double cream which can be substituted in most recipes where crème fraîche is required.*
Crimping, to seal pastry, 22
Croûtons: *small cubes of bread fried in butter and used as garnish.*
Cucumber, extracting moisture, 29; for little stews, 28, 29; in vol-au-vents, 39
Curd cheese, 7
Currants, in stuffings, 44
Custards, 63; layered pudding, 66-67; moulded, 64-67; quiches, 63, 68-69; savoury, 64-65
Deep frying, brochettes, 84-85; fritters, 82-83; oil for, 82; ravioli, 86-87; stuffed pancakes, 86-87; temperature, 82
Dough, 17; for deep frying, 77; olive oil, 22, 86; olive oil puff, 24-25, 34; rough-puff, 20-21, 34, 69; shortcrust, 18-19, 68; see also Pastry
Duxelles, 6, 8, 29; with brains and tomato gratin, 36-37; in stargazey pie, 18-19; in stuffings, 46, 57
Egg whites, 25; coating before cooking, 84; in custards, 64; in mousseline, 60; in soufflés, 63, 70, 72, 74; in stuffings, 43
Egg yolks, in boudins blancs, 59; in coatings, 84; in custards, 64; glazes, 20, 25, 35; in soufflés, 70, 72, 74; in velouté, 10, 11, 36, 38, 45
Eggs, 77; beaten, on stuffed aubergines, 51; coating before cooking, 77, 80, 82, 84, 88; in custards, 63; in doughs, 17, 22,